The Right of *Actio Popularis* before International Courts and Tribunals

Queen Mary Studies in International Law

Edited by

Malgosia Fitzmaurice
Sarah Singer

VOLUME 31

The titles published in this series are listed at *brill.com/qmil*

The Right of *Actio Popularis* before International Courts and Tribunals

By

Farid Ahmadov

BRILL
NIJHOFF

LEIDEN | BOSTON

Library of Congress Cataloging-in-Publication Data

Names: Ahmadov, Farid Turab, 1979- author.
Title: The right of actio popularis before international courts and tribunals / by Farid Ahmadov.
Description: Leiden ; Boston : Brill Nijhoff, 2018. | Series: Queen Mary studies in international law ; VOLUME 31 | Includes bibliographical references and index.
Identifiers: LCCN 2018030858 (print) | LCCN 2018031352 (ebook) | ISBN 9789004380981 (ebook) | ISBN 9789004366978 (hardback : alk. paper)
Subjects: LCSH: Civil procedure (International law) | Locus standi. | Popular actions.
Classification: LCC KZ6250 (ebook) | LCC KZ6250 .A365 2018 (print) | DDC 341.5/5--dc23
LC record available at https://lccn.loc.gov/2018030858

Typeface for the Latin, Greek, and Cyrillic scripts: "Brill". See and download: brill.com/brill-typeface.

ISSN 1877-4822
ISBN 978-90-04-36697-8 (hardback)
ISBN 978-90-04-38098-1 (e-book)

This book is printed on acid-free paper and produced in a sustainable manner.

Contents

Acknowledgments

This book started as a DPhil Thesis which I wrote in Oxford University under supervision of professors Vaughan Lowe and Catherine Redgwell. I owe a debt of gratitude to both for their continuous support and guidance. Both had been a great source of inspiration and outstanding academic and personal mentors.

I also would like to thank Professor Stefan Talmon who was my College Advisor at St. Anne's and was always ready to assist me well beyond his formal duties.

I would like to gratefully acknowledge editors and reviewers at Brill for their most valuable comments.

Many thanks to my friends and colleagues Professor Antonios Tzanakopoulos, Dr. Asif Hameed, Aytakin Mustafayeva, Dr. Markos Karavias, Dr. Mehmet Karli, Dr. Miles Jackson and all participants of the weekly research seminars at Oxford University for their most helpful intellectual contributions.

My special thanks go to Patricia Jimenez. She is a true friend and had been irreplaceable in making most incisive comments on the draft of the book.

I also owe special thanks to my wife Nurlana and four children for their patience, care and continuous support.

Lastly, I would like to express my deepest gratitude to my parents. Nothing would have been possible without their selfless love.

Table of Cases

ICJ/PCIJ

ECtHR

ITLOS

CJEU

WTO DSB/AB

ICTY/ICTR

Other Cases

List of Abbreviations

ACHR	(Inter-)American Convention on Human Rights
AJIL	American Journal of International Law
ASR	Articles on State Responsibility (International Law Commission)
BYIL	British Yearbook of International Law
CCPR	(International) Covenant on Civil and Political Rights
CJEU	Court of Justice of the European Union
CTS	Consolidated Treaty Series
CMLR	Common Market Law Review
Diss. Op	Dissenting Opinion
Doc.	Document
EC	European Community
ECHR	European Convention of Human Rights and Fundamental Freedoms
EJIL	European Journal of International Law
ELR	European Law Review
EPIL	Encyclopedia of Public International Law
Eur. Comm'n HR	European Commission on Human Rights
ECtHR	European Court of Human Rights
GA	(United Nations) General Assembly
GATT	General Agreement on Tariffs and Trade
GYIL	German Yearbook of International Law
HJIL	Harvard Journal of International Law
HRLJ	Human Rights Law Journal
HRQ	Human Rights Quarterly
ICJ	International Court of Justice
ICLQ	International and Comparative Law Quarterly
ICTY	International Criminal Tribunal for the Former Yugoslavia
ILC	International Law Commission
ILM	International Legal Materials
ILO	International Labour Organisation
ILR	International Law Reports
ITLOS	International Tribunal for the Law of the Sea
LJIL	Leiden Journal of International Law
LNTS	League of Nations Treaty Series
NILR	Netherlands International Law Review
Nordic JIL	Nordic Journal of International Law
NYIL	Netherlands Yearbook of International Law

PCIJ	Permanent Court of International Justice
RdC	Recueil des Cours
Res.	Resolution
RIAA	Reports of International Arbitral Awards
SAYIL	South African Yearbook of International Law
SC	(United Nations) Security Council
Sep.	Op. Separate Opinion
Ser.	Series
SWA	South West Africa cases
TFEUEC	Treaty on the Functioning of the European Union
UN	United Nations
UNC	United Nations Charter
UNCLOS	United Nations Law of the Sea Convention
UNTS	United Nations Treaty Series
UNYB	United Nations Yearbook
US	United States
VCLT	Vienna Convention on the Law of Treaties
Virginia JIL	Virginia Journal of International Law
WTO	World Trade Organization
Yb.	Yearbook
YbILC	Yearbook of the International Law Commission
YbECHR	Yearbook of the European Convention of Human

Introduction

Actio popularis has long been the subject of a heated academic debate.[1] International legal scholarship can be divided into ardent supporters of the concept,[2] profound sceptics,[3] and those who hold a middle ground, believing that the

1 C. Gray, 'The 2014 Judicial Activity of the International Court of Justice' (2015) 109 *AJIL* 583; F. Voeffray, *L'actio popularis, ou la défense de l'intérêt collectif devant les juridictions internationales,* (Institut universitaire de hautes études internationales, 2004); E. Schwelb, 'The *Actio Popularis* and International Law' (1972) 2 *Israel Yearbook on Human Rights*; A. Rubin, '*Actio popularis, Jus Cogens* and *Offences Erga Omnes?*' (2001) 35 *New England Law Review*; P. Bekker, 'Reflections on the ICJ's Oil Platform Decision: Protecting International Shipping Channels During Hostilities and the Oil Platforms Case: *Actio Popularis* Revisited?' (2004) 29 *The Yale Journal of International Law*; W. Aceves, 'Actio Popularis? The Class Action in International Law', (2003) *The University of Chicago Legal Forum*; B Naumovič, 'Reflexions sur l'actio popularis en droit international, dans le cadre de la responsabilité internationale', in: *Responsibility of States. Thesaurus Acroasium* Vol. XX (1993); I Seidl-Hohenveldern, 'Actio Popularis im Völkerrecht?', 14 Communicazione e Studi (1975); C. Schall, 'Public Interest Litigation Concerning Environmental Matters before Human Rights Courts: A Promising Future Concept', (2008) 20 *Journal of Environmental Law*, pp. 417–453; D. French, 'From the Depths: Rich Pickings of Principles of Sustainable Development and General International Law on the Ocean Floor – the Seabed Disputes Chamber's 2011 Advisory Opinion', (2011) 26 *The International Journal of Marine and Coastal Law*, pp. 525–546; C. Tams, *Enforcing Obligations Erga Omnes in International Law,* (CUP, Cambridge, 2005); R. Wolfrum, 'The Outer Continental Shelf: Some Considerations Concerning Applications and the Potential Role of the International Tribunal for the Law of the Sea', Statement by the President of ITLOS (2008) 73rd Biennial Conference of the International Law Association, Rio de Janeiro, Brazil; T. Gazzini, "The Legal Nature of WTO Obligations and The Consequences of Their Violation', (2006) 17(4) *EJIL*; p. 726; M. Ragazzi, *The Concept of International Obligations Erga Omnes,* (Oxford, Clarendon Press 1997).

2 T. Elias, 'Introduction to the Debate', in J. Weiler, A. Cassese, M. Spinedi (eds.), *International Crime of States: A Critical Analysis of the ILC's Draft Article 19 on State Responsibility,* (Walter De Gruyter, Berlin, 1989), p. 193. Elias fiercely advocated (in the context of draft Article 19) for extending the right of action for breaches which affect collective/public/general interests of the international community to States other than those 'immediately concerned'. G. Gaja, "*Jus Cogens* Beyond the Vienna Convention," 172 RDC ADI 1981-III, p. 280; C. Jenks, 'The General Welfare as a Legal Interest', in G. Wilner (eds.), *Jus et Societas,* Essays in Tribute to Wolfgang Friedman, (Martinus Nijhoff Publishers, The Hague, 1979), pp. 154–158; E. Root, The Outlook for International Law,' (1916) *AJIL* 10(1), pp. 7–9; P. Jessup, *A Modern Law of Nations: An Introduction* (New York, Macmillan, 1948), p. 11.

3 P. van Dijk, *Judicial Review of Governmental Action and the Requirement of an Interest to Sue* (Alphen aan den Rijn, Netherlands, 1980), pp. 473–474 and 520; K. Marek rejects the possibility of *actio popularis* in absence of centralized judicial (or legal) system and argues that *Barcelona Traction* case and developments in the ILC allowing for non-injured States to invoke responsibility would "invite mob-justice". 'Criminalizing State Responsibility', (1978–1979) *Revue Belge de droit international*, XIV, p. 481; Bruno Simma also expressed scepticism regarding

DOI:10.1163/9789004380981_002

concept belongs to a *de lege ferenda.*[4] Notwithstanding this diversity of views, *actio popularis* has been used in a variety of contexts. Frequent references to *actio popularis* have been seen in the context of claims brought before international courts and tribunals. However, outside the context of judicial claims, *actio popularis* has been relied upon to broadly invoke state responsibility to protect collective interests,[5] as grounding for the operation of universal jurisdiction,[6] or institutionalized acts taken to protect collective interests.[7]

future of *actio popularis* and noted: "But let us be realistic: the idea that a significant part of United Nations Member States would be prepared to involve the Court in the issues listed in Article 19 is simply utopian". B. Simma, 'Bilateralism and Community Interest in the Law of State Responsibility', in Y. Dinstein (eds.), *International Law at the Time of Perplexity, Essays in Honour of Shabtai Rosenne* (Martinus Nijhoff Publishers, Dordrecht, 1989) p. 838. Simma did not change his view even more than fifteen years after his first statement on this issue due to the continued unwillingness on the part of States to embrace the concept of *erga omnes.* B. Simma, 'Universality of International Law from a Perspective of a Practitioner' (2009) *EJIL* 20(2) p. 275. Judge Manfred Lachs also expressed his scepticism concerning the right of *actio popularis* in international law. With reference to the famous *dicta* of the ICJ in the *Barcelona Traction* case he noted that 'there is a long way from the dictum of the Court to *actio popularis*', 'The Development and General Trends of International Law in Our Times' (1980) 169, *Recueil des Cours de l'Académie de Droit International.* p. 341.

4 T. Kamminga, *Inter-State Accountability for Violations of Human Rights*, (University of Pennsylvania Press, Philadelphia, 1992), pp. 176–185; H. Thirlway, 'The Law and Procedure of the International Court of Justice 1960–1988', (1989) 1 *BYIL* 102. O. Schacter, *International Law in Theory and Practice,* (Martinus Nijhoff, Hague, 1991), p. 345; G. Danilenko and W. Czaplinski stated with respect to the future of *actio popularis* that "Notwithstanding certain passages of the judgment in the *Barcelona Traction* case, contemporary international law seems not to have accepted any *actio popularis* in the case of violations of peremptory norms, although one cannot exclude its acceptance in the future – in our opinion, the notion of the 'injured State' as formulated in Article 5 of the Sixth Report on State responsibility by W. Riphagen can be interpreted in this sense". 'Conflict of Norms in International Law', (1990) 21 *Netherlands Yearbook of International Law*, pp. 10–11. C. Gray, *Judicial Remedies in International Law,* (Clarendon Press, Oxford, 1990), pp. 214–215.

5 See p. 293, para. 2 of the Commentary to Chapter 1, Part III of Articles on State Responsibility, ILC Report on the Work of its Fifty-Third Session (23 April-1 June and 2 July-10 August 2001), UN Doc. A/56/10; Responsibility to protect collective interests can be invoked by third party countermeasures. See respectively, C. Hillbruger, 'The Right of Third States to Take Countermeasures', in C. Tomuschat & J M Thouvenin (eds.), *The Fundamental Rules of the International Legal Order,* (Martinus Nijhoff Publishers, Leiden, 2006), p. 269.

6 For instance, Cheriff Bassiouni states in this regard: "In the exercise of universal jurisdiction, a State acts on behalf of the international community in a manner equivalent to the Roman concept of *actio popularis*". "Universal Jurisdiction for International Crimes: Historical Perspectives and Contemporary Practice" (2001) 42 *Vanderbilt Journal of International Law,* p. 88.

7 Institutional acts to protect collective interests are exemplified in Article 35 of the UN Charter which entitles "any member of the United Nations to bring any dispute or any situation to the attention of the General Assembly or the Security Council". See T. Schweisfurth, 'Commentary on Article 35 of the UN Charter', in B. Simma (eds.), *The Charter of the United Nations: A Commentary,* Vol. I, (2nd ed, OUP, Oxford, 2002), pp. 609–610. For the same view see also

The scope of this book however is confined to examination of *actio popularis* solely as a judicial concept, i.e. the right to bring a claim before international courts and tribunals. While the existing literature only briefly considers *actio popularis* as a judicial concept,[8] the works by Voefrey and Christian Tams can be named amongst the most serious of contributions.[9] However, Professor Tam's treatment of *actio popularis* is limited in scope because it examines the concept solely as a claim brought before the International Court of Justice.[10] Conversely, Voefrey's comprehensive study of the concept proposes the *actio popularis* in a variety of international courts and tribunals. His study however lacks an analytical framework and fails to highlight the judicial policy concerns, which underpin approaches adopted by international courts and tribunals to the question of standing in general and the right to *actio popularis* in particular. The present book aims to fill these gaps.

The debates concerning *actio popularis* as a judicial concept commenced with the *South West Africa* cases where the ICJ very simply defined the concept as a "right resident in any member of a community to take legal action in vindication of a public interest".[11] Whilst the ICJ acknowledged the concept under domestic law, it stated that *actio popularis* was alien to international law as it stood at the time of the decision.[12]

The Court's definition of *actio popularis* underlines two main aspects. The first aspect requires the existence of a 'community' and of 'public' interests. Such interests exist in various areas of international law and they are identified and extensively examined in Chapter 3 of the book.

From a methodological viewpoint identifying public interests in international law is central to analysis of *actio popularis*. It serves the purpose of illustrating the link between the change in the normative structure of international law, which is manifested in the transition from bilateralizable obligations to obligations established to protect collective interests, and the way in which such a transition affects the nature of international litigation. Hence, any meaningful conceptualization of *actio popularis* will be based on the

---

H. Neuhold, 'The United Nations System for the Peaceful Settlement of Disputes', in F. Cede & L Sucharipa-Behrmann, (eds.), *The United Nations Law and Practice*, (Kluwer Law International, The Hague, 1999), p. 65. For the view that *actio popularis* can take the form of references of disputes or situations to the United Nations General Assembly and the Security Council, see B. Ernest, *The State Immunity Controversy in International Law*, (Springer, 2005), p. 299.

8 (n1).

9 Voeffray (2004); Tams (2005).

10 Tams (2005), pp. 48–96.

11 Ethiopia v South Africa; Liberia v South Africa, (Second Phase),1966 ICJ Rep., 6, para. 88, p. 47.

12 Ibid.

conception of obligations owed to the international community as a whole (*erga omnes*) or a group of states, which share collective interests (obligations *erga omnes partes*).

The second aspect of the statement in the *South West Africa* case concerning *actio popularis* relates to the ICJ's decision on the status (legality) of *actio popularis* in international law in general and, on the face of it, be interpreted as the ICJ's rejection of *actio popularis* under customary international law or general principles of law. Therefore, the statement raises a fundamental question regarding the competence of a single international court or a tribunal to pronounce on the status of *actio popularis* in international law in general. This question sets the overall framework for the treatment of *actio popularis* in the book and compels addressing the following central questions.

First, whether the proliferation of international courts and tribunals requires treatment of the question of the legality of *actio popularis* solely as a right before each international court or tribunal and therefore precludes an argument in favour of the existence of *actio popularis* as a rule of customary international law or a general law principle. Second, whether the right of *actio popularis* is a question of judicial policy which informs decisions of international courts and tribunals to allow or dismiss *actio popularis* through hermeneutics of procedural rules (rules of standing) in light of the community character of substantive norms.

A third question is whether States which take action in vindication of public interest do so in the capacity of *parens patria*,[13] i.e. as an "all-purpose representative" of the international community or act *erga singulum,* i.e. in their own interest which they derive as members of the international community.[14]

---

13 Literally "parent of the country". As a rule it refers to the role of a State as a sovereign and guardian of persons under legal disability. *Parens patriae* originates from English common law where the King had a royal prerogative to act as a guardian to persons with legal disabilities such as infants, idiots, and lunatics. In the United States, the *parens patriae* function belongs to the states. Black's Law Dictionary 1114 (6th ed. 1990). On the meaning of *parens patriae* as a right of a sovereign to represent the interests of its nationals see S. Murphy, *The United States Practice in International Law: Volume 1,* (CUP, Cambridge, 1999–2001), p. 186. In the context of the right of States to act in protection of collective interests James Crawford noted that "... in a decentralized system, there is no all-purpose representative, no *parens patriae* who can act securely on the collective behalf". J. Crawford, 'Responsibility to the International Community as a Whole', (2001), *Journal of Global Legal Studies,* 8(2), p. 315.

14 For the view that obligations *erga omnes* are split into *erga singulum* with each State protecting its individual interests see Separate Opinion of Judge Weeremantry, *East Timor* case, (Portugal v Australia) (Merits), 1995 ICJ Rep., 90, p. 172.

Another issue pertaining to *actio popularis* is that the academic literature traditionally links *actio popularis* to the concept of rights and obligations *erga omnes* by making violation of *erga omnes* a condition precedent to instituting *actio popularis* claims.[15] The much relied upon *obiter* of the ICJ in the *Barcelona Traction* case[16] which spurred the academic debate about the nature of *erga omnes* obligations and the consequences of their violation is often interpreted to have vested the right in all members of the international community to invoke responsibility of States for breaches of *erga omnes* obligations.[17]

The book argues that reliance on the *erga omnes* concept to validate the bases of *actio popularis* is not invariably necessary.[18] Jennings and Watts were right to say that "although the notion of *actio popularis* is in some respects associated with that of rights and obligations *erga omnes*, the two are distinct and, to the extent that they are accepted, each may exist independently of the

15 K. Zemanek, 'New Trends in the Enforcement of *Erga Omnes* Obligations', (2000) 4 *Max Planck Yearbook of International Law*, p. 11. See also a Resolution of the Institut de Droit International which states that a right of *actio popularis* arises from the breach of obligations *erga omnes*. IDI Resolution, Institut de Droit International, *Resolution: Obligations Erga Omnes in International Law* art. 1, Aug. 27, 2005, *available at* http://www.idi-iil.org/idiE/navig_chon2003.html, art. 3. T. Meron was amongst the most ardent advocates of the view that violation of obligations *erga omnes* vests in all States the right to bring claims before international tribunals. *The Humanization of International Law*, (Martinus Nijhoff Publishers, 2006), p. 249. However, see Coffman who argues that *East Timor* case was a major attack on the enforceability of *erga omnes* obligations before the International Court of Justice. P Coffman, 'Obligations *Erga Omnes* and Absent Third-Party States', (1996) 38 *German Yearbook of International Law*, p. 286.

16 Belgium v Spain, (Merits), 1970 ICJ Rep., 3, p. 32, para. 33.

17 M. Byers, 'Conceptualizing the Relationship between *Jus Cogens* and *Erga Omnes* Rules' (1997) 66(2–3) *Nordic Journal of International Law*, pp. 212–213. However, other commentators argue that ICJ's *obiter* does not introduce *actio popularis* because paragraph 91 of the same judgment states that such a right of protection at a universal level is limited to the state of nationality. R. Lefeber, 'The Exercise of Jurisdiction in the Antarctic Region and the Changing Structure of International Law: The International Community and Common Interest' (1990) 21 *Netherlands Yearbook of International Law*, p. 97; P. Okowa, 'Issues of Admissibility and The Law on International Responsibility', in M. Evans (eds.), *International Law*, (3rd ed. Oxford, OUP), pp. 492–494.

18 Chinkin notes in this regard quoting the famous *dicta* from the *Barcelona Traction case:* "However, the Court in *Barcelona Traction* was not discussing procedural rights, and the actual decision in that case does nothing to promote the notion of protection of third party interests through development of judicial procedures" (Chinkin on p. 217 of the same article defines *actio popularis* as a "third party claim made on behalf of the international community"). C. Chinkin, 'Symposium: The East Timor Case before the International Court of Justice', 1993(4) *EJIL*, p. 218.

other".[19] However, the identification of community obligations which are established to protect collective/community interests (obligations *erga omnes* or *erga omnes partes*) is a point of departure. These obligations, as Costelloe puts it "exist for the purposes of furthering a collective interest of all States, and the breach of which gives rise to an admissible claim by any State...".[20] Hence, the study adopts a more functional approach and identifies various community (collective) interests (obligations) in international law that may serve as a basis to institute *actio popularis*.[21] However, this premise is without prejudice

---

19 R. Jennings & A. Watts, *Oppenheim's International Law,* Vol I, (9th ed. Longman, London, 1996), p. 5; The term *'erga omnes'* has been defined in a number of different ways. Its literal translation from Latin as 'against all' is unhelpful. Given the confusion connected with the use of the term the special rapporteur Crawford and subsequently the ILC decided to drop the term in the text of Articles on State Responsibility. Fourth Report on State Responsibility, ILC, Report of the International Law Commission on the Work of its 53rd Session (23 April-1 June, 2 July-10 August 2001) A/CN.4/517, para. 49. On the various meanings of the term *erga omnes* see also Ragazzi (1997), pp. 1–5, Tams (2005), pp. 97–115. P. Van Dijk also rejected a link between obligations *erga omnes* and *actio popularis*. Van Dijk (1980), p. 474. See also J. Pauwelyn, who rightly argues that *actio popularis* may be brought even under bilateralizable treaties if the treaty authorizes such action. It is when the treaty is silent on the existence of such a right that the need arises to establish whether it is designed to protect collective interests. *Conflict of Norms in Public International Law: How WTO Law Relates to Other Rules of International Law,* (CUP, Cambridge, 2003), p. 55. S. Rosenne too is amongst the scholars who denies the view that *actio popularis* are the consequence of the existence of *erga omnes* obligations. *The Law and Practice of the International Court:* 1920–1966, (Martinus Nijhoff Publishers, Leiden, 1997), p. 1203. Lefeber, with reference to celebrated *obiter* in the *Barcelona Traction* case noted in this regard: "The Court did not intend the recognition of *erga omnes* obligations to be a general recognition of an *actio popularis* in international law. According to the Court, the existence of an *actio popularis* depends on the content of the obligation, or better, on the content of the corresponding right of protection. That is, even in the case of an *erga omnes* obligation, the content of the obligation may be such as to render the right to bring a claim before the Court conditional on demonstration by the applicant state of an individual substantive interest, such as the bond of nationality in the case of a denial of justice". R. Lefeber, *Transboundary Environmental Interference and the Origin of State Liability,* (Martinus Nijhoff Publishers, Leiden, 1996), p. 117.

20 D. Costelloe, *Legal Consequences of Peremptory Norms in International Law,* (CUP, Cambridge, 2017), p. 24.

21 Both the literature and the case law of various international courts and tribunals use the terms "public interests", "community interests", "general interests", "common interests", "collective interests" interchangeably as referring to one and the same concept. From a methodological point of view and for the purposes of convenience the book will refer to "collective interests" as defined in the commentary to the Articles on Responsibility of States for Internationally Wrongful Acts. Paragraph 7 of the commentary on Article 48 states that the main purpose of collective interests is "... to foster a common interest, over and above any interests of the States concerned individually". The term "general interest"

to the view that *actio popularis* does not invariably depend on existence of community obligations (owed *erga omnes* or *erga omnes partes*) and the book shall explore cases when reliance on *erga omnes* is unnecessary to bring *actio popularis* claims.[22]

This book not only provides a conceptual framework for operation of *actio popularis* in international law but also articulates practical hurdles and implications for bringing *actio popularis* claims before international courts and tribunals.

Chapter 1 of the book identifies the framework within which *actio popularis* is utilized. It starts by exploring the origins of *actio popularis* as applied in Roman law. The Chapter further examines *actio popularis* under the municipal legal systems of selected countries. However, references to *actio popularis* under domestic law by no means serve the purpose of establishing *actio popularis* as a general law principle or providing the evidence of state practice to establish it under customary international law. *Actio popularis* under domestic law is examined simply to draw comparisons and point to differences in how the concept can be applied under municipal and international law. The Chapter further highlights the different contexts in which the academic literature utilizes the concept of *actio popularis*. While acknowledging that *actio popularis* is used in the context of third party countermeasures and institutionalized third party actions[23] the Chapter defines the scope of the analysis by limiting it exclusively to the question of the legality of *actio popularis* before various international courts and tribunals. Even if customary international law allows for third party measures to protect collective interests this does not automatically resolve the question of standing before international courts and tribunals. The entitlement to invoke responsibility and access to judicial fora are two distinct issues.[24] A claim before an international court or tribunal is

---

in the book is used to refer to the overall interest of States parties to the treaty to protect the system itself under treaties which are bilateralizable in nature.

22 *Actio popularis* is usually invoked when the violation of collective interests is involved. There are, however, exceptions to this rule. For instance, Article 4 of the Agreement on Subsidies and Countervailing Measures (SCM) and obligations deriving from the Article XXIII(1) of the General Agreement on Trade in Services (GATS) exemplify treaties of a bilateralizable nature but which provide for collective enforcement. Although these treaties are not established to protect collective interests (in fact they are bilateralizable) they vest in States parties a right to take action irrespective of a personal injury. The State parties act in the general interest of protection of the system itself. See J, Pauwelyn, *Conflict of Norms* (2003), p. 55. For more extensive discussion see pp. 197–208 of the book.

23 See notes 5, 6 and 7.

24 A. Vermeer-Kunzli, 'A Matter of Interest: Diplomatic Protection and State Responsibility *Erga Omnes*,' (2007) 56 *Int'l & Comp. L.Q*, p. 571.

subject to satisfaction of standing requirements, which are not uniform in international law and vary from one international court or tribunal to another. In international law "each court has distinctive features and operates in a particular legal and political context"[25] and this feature compels examination of *actio popularis* not as a right under customary international law or as imported by general law principles but as a right before every international court and tribunal by taking into account the distinctive political and legal contexts within which each international court or tribunal operates.

Chapter 2 examines the first element of *actio popularis*, i.e. that the claim be brought to protect collective interests. The Chapter highlights the difficulties associated with developing a uniform conception of collective interests in international law because of the absence of a centralized law-making process through which such interests can be established. In order to identify the collective interests in international law the Chapter shifts to analysis of the normative structure of international law and describes the nature of obligations therein. The Chapter adopts already existing classification of obligations in international law into bilateralizable and multilateral, the latter defined as obligations established to protect collective interests, and furnishes abundant evidence of such obligations in various areas of international law. The Chapter proceeds to provide an in-depth overview of debates in the ILC on the nature of obligations in international law and demonstrates the shift in the attitudes of States towards gradual recognition of the concept of multilateral obligations. The Chapter further explores the ways in which the classification of obligations in international law into bilateralizable (established to protect individual/special interests of States) and 'multilateral' (established to protect collective interests) affects the ways in which States can institute proceedings before international courts and tribunals by way of *actio popularis*. Chapter 3 deals with enforcement of collective interests. It highlights the connection between relativization of international normativity in favour of recognition of collective interests and a corresponding right of enforcement of such interests. The Chapter examines the ILC's work on state responsibility to illustrate the debates around the right of states to enforce collective obligations and carefully analyzes a central question of whether injury and damage must be preconditions to invoke responsibility.[26] The analysis of the state comments on the

25 Y. Shany, 'Assessing the Effectiveness of International Courts: A Goal-Based Approach' (2012) 106 *AJIL*, p. 229. See also T. Ginsburg who states: "A rational court must be conscious of other actors in the political system". 'Bounded Discretion in International Judicial Law-Making', (2004–2005) 45, *Va.J. Int'l L.*, p. 657.

26 Arangio Ruiz proposed to consider all states as injured in cases of violation of *erga omnes* and *jus cogens* obligations. Fourth Report on State Responsibility, YbILC, 1992, Vol. II, Part One, paras. 92–93, p. 34.

Draft Articles on State Responsibility as well as reports of Special Rapporteurs suggests that some states regarded injury and damage as a condition precedent to invoke responsibility.[27] The Chapter argues, that this approach if adopted by the ILC, would preclude *actio popularis* because actions to protect collective interests should not require showing damage or injury. The Chapter concludes by providing a transition into Chapter 4, which concerns judicial enforcement of collective obligations.

In Chapter 4, it is argued that "bipolar" litigation, i.e. litigation, which aims to protect litigants' special interests, is inadequate to protect collective interests. Therefore, procedural mechanisms have to be introduced which are fit to judicially protect collective interests. Traditionally, any claim brought before a competent court requires an interest to sue. This is true of most international courts and tribunals and the requirement to show interest is embodied in such concepts as "dispute", "victim requirement", "direct and individual concern" etc.[28] These concepts serve the sole purpose of avoiding the flood of "bypasser" claims and to circumscribe the circle of potential claimants to those which are specially affected. However, the Chapter argues that these concepts are not set in stone and can be construed to allow for protection of collective interests.

Chapter 5 focuses on the right of *actio popularis* before the ICJ. The Chapter juxtaposes two divergent interpretations of the legal dispute adopted by the ICJ in the *Mavrommatis Palestine Concessions* and *South West Africa cases* to argue that the question of legality of *actio popularis* before the ICJ depends on the construction of the notion of "dispute/legal dispute" embodied in Article 36(2) of the ICJ Statute as well as other international treaty instruments. By referring to the open-ended definition of "dispute" in the *Mavrommatis Palestine Concessions* case[29] the Chapter argues that such a broad definition of the term opens the door for *actio popularis*. Conversely, the ICJ's definition of a dispute in the *South West Africa* cases as a disagreement between the parties about their individual (special) interests precludes *actio popularis*. These two cases illustrate how the admissibility of *actio popularis* before the ICJ may depend on the court's interpretation of its standing provisions, in this case the concept

27 Argentinian comments on Draft Article 3. Reproduced in First Report on State Responsibility of James Crawford, p. 28, paragraph. 108. Also see paragraph 1 of comments by French Government. Document A/CN.4/488 and Add. 1–3.

28 Article 36(2) of the ICJ Statute, Article 34 of the European Convention on Human Right and Fundamental Freedoms, Article 263(4) of the Treaty on Functioning of the European Union.

29 The PCIJ defined dispute as follows: "A dispute is a disagreement on a point of law or fact, a conflict of legal views or of interests between two persons". PCIJ, Series A-No. 2, August 30th, 1924, pp. 279–280.

of a "legal dispute". It is further submitted that the celebrated *obiter* in the *Barcelona Traction* case[30] should be construed as an attempt to extend the scope of the ICJ's jurisdiction and devise a new procedural tool in the form of *actio popularis* in order to enforce collective interests.

Chapter 5 raises another important question, namely, whether *actio popularis* should be treated as a matter of procedural or substantive law. This question leads to analysis of the sources of *actio popularis*. Indeed, *actio popularis* as an issue of standing before the court is traditionally treated as a question of a procedural character and as such as question to be decided by each and every international tribunal through interpretation of standing provisions. Chapter 5 further explores the link between the nature of substantive norms and the interpretation of the standing rules. It argues that in cases when *actio popularis* is not expressly stipulated in the treaty instruments such a right may be inferred by construction of the standing rules as well as the hermeneutics of primary norms (substantive obligations) with due regard to State practice. Chapter 5 addresses the link between the hermeneutics of the optional clause declarations and the obligations owed to the international community. It is argued that claims brought before the ICJ under optional clause declarations to protect community interests were based on the belief that the ICJ should interpret such declarations permissively to infer the right of *actio popularis* in light of the state practice which supports the right to invoke responsibility for violations of obligations owed to the international community as a whole. The analysis is based on the ICJ's decisions in the *Genocide,*[31] *South West Africa, Northern Cameroons,*[32] *Nuclear Tests,*[33] *Questions Concerning Extradition,*[34] and *Whaling in Antarctica*[35] cases. The Chapter will argue that the *Extradition Proceedings* case marks a shift towards recognition of *actio popularis* before the ICJ and exemplifies a case in which *actio popularis* was a direct consequence of the

30 *The Case Concerning Barcelona Traction, Light and Power Company Limited,* (Belgium v Spain), (2nd phase), [1970] ICJ Rep. p. 3, para. 33.

31 *Case Concerning Application of the Convention on the Prevention and Punishment of the Crime of Genocide* (Bosnia and Herzegovina and Serbia v Montenegro) (Merits) [2007] ICJ Rep. p. 43; *Case Concerning Application of the Convention on the Prevention and Punishment of the Crime of Genocide* (Bosnia and Herzegovina v Yugoslavia), (Preliminary Objections), [1996], p. 595.

32 *Northern Cameroons case* (Cameroon v United Kingdom) (Preliminary Objections), 1963, ICJ Rep., p. 15.

33 *Nuclear Tests Cases* (Australia v France) (Merits), [1974], ICJ Rep., p. 253.

34 *Questions Relating to the Obligation to Prosecute or Extradite* (Belgium v Senegal), (Merits), 2012 ICJ Rep., p. 422.

35 *Whaling in the Antarctic* (Australia v Japan: New Zealand intervening), (Merits), 2013 ICJ Rep., p. 18.

ICJ's hermeneutics of the substantive obligations under the Torture Convention as established to protect collective interests. The Chapter also addresses cases of *actio popularis* expressly authorized by treaty instruments. It provides in depth analysis of these instruments (jurisdictional clauses) and identifies the differences in the wording of the jurisdictional clauses which as the book claims explicitly provide for *actio popularis*. This part of the Chapter focuses on analysis of the *Polish Upper Silesia,*[36] *Interpretation of the Statute of the Memel Territory,*[37] and *Wimbledon*[38] cases to illustrate the difference in the ICJ/PCIJ's approach to the question of standing to protect collective interests informed by the wording of jurisdictional clauses. The Chapter further clarifies the ICJ's misleading statement in the 1966 *South West Africa* decision that *actio popularis* was "not known to international law" by arguing that the ICJ did not intend to make a pronouncement regarding status of *actio popularis* under customary international law. It is submitted that the ICJ's restrictive construction of the jurisdictional clause of the Mandate Agreement may have been informed by lack of state practice regarding enforcement of collective interests under general international law. The Chapter further argues that the famous *obiter* in the *Barcelona Traction* case may be construed as an attempt by the ICJ to revisit the *South West Africa* cases and extend the Court's jurisdiction to adjudicate claims brought under optional clause declarations to protect collective interests that arise from obligations owed to the international community as whole. Finally, Chapter 5 tackles the issue of a procedural bar to enforcement of collective interests before the ICJ. It considers how an indispensable third-party rule precludes enforcement of collective interests before the ICJ.

Chapter 6 addresses the question of *actio popularis* before other international courts and tribunals. This Chapter consists of four sections analysing *actio popularis* before ITLOS, the CJEU, the ECtHR, and the WTO DSB respectively. The first Section seeks to identify the causes of action to protect collective interests before ITLOS. It determines the obligations, which are established to protect collective interests under UNCLOS to assess the possibility of enforcing such interests before ITLOS. Because UNCLOS does not explicitly vest in States the right to bring *actio popularis* claims this section will explore whether such a right can be introduced by permissively interpreting the standing

36 *German Interests in Polish Upper Silesia* (Germany v Poland), 1925 P.C.I.J. (ser. A) No. 6 (Aug. 25).

37 *Interpretation of Statute of Memel Territory* (UK v Lithuania), 1932 P.C.I.J. (ser. A/B) No. 49 (Aug. 11).

38 *S.S. Wimbledon* (UK v Japan), 1923 P.C.I.J. (ser. A) No. 1 (Aug. 17).

rules under UNCLOS. The same methodology will be applied in the course of examination of the possibility of bringing *actio popularis* claims in the context of the WTO DSB, the CJEU and the ECtHR. The Chapter will explore the standing provisions of each of the mentioned international courts and tribunals to answer the following two questions. First, whether the substantive norms (or primary norms) are established to protect collective or general interests. Second, whether the relevant court or tribunal is willing to interpret the rules of standing so permissively as to allow for *actio popularis* to enforce collective or general interests under treaty instruments which establish these judicial bodies.

The book concludes by considering a correlation between judicial policy concerns and *actio popularis*. The final chapter highlights the judicial policy concerns of international courts and tribunals which inform interpretation of standing provisions. Although most international courts and tribunals face similar policy concerns, some judicial policy concerns are unique to the environment (institutional or otherwise) within which each international court or tribunal operates. More specifically, the Chapter examines the policies of judicial deference and judicial activism to illustrate the ways in which the courts' interpretative powers in the light of judicial policy concerns may have an effect on the admissibility of *actio popularis* claims.

CHAPTER 1

Identifying the Elements and Operational Framework of *actio popularis*

This Chapter provides an overview of *actio popularis* as understood in Roman law and applied in modern legal systems. It seeks to identify the elements of *actio popularis* in domestic law with a view of assessing the possibility of applying those elements in international law. The Chapter defines the context for operation of *actio popularis* in international law as being confined solely to the right to bring claims to protect public interests before international courts and tribunals.

1 Elements of *actio popularis* in Roman Law and Municipal Legal Systems

The origins of the concept of *actio popularis* can be traced back to Roman law as a right of any member of community to bring action for facts which affect public interest, yet the concept is also well known to modern municipal legal systems.[1]

Roman Law recognized various types of injuries (injuria).[2] Under Roman law injury was generally defined as a willful violation of a right *in rem* that one has in respect of one's own person.[3] All types, with the exception of one, had an actual victim of injuria. The exception referred to situations when no person was actually harmed but there was a possibility of harm which stemmed from some potentially hazardous activity or object. Thus, the example noted by Justinian was "if at a spot where men commonly pass anything is kept so placed or hung that it might, if it fell, do harm to someone.[4] For this there is

1 W. Buckland, *Roman Law,* (Cambridge University Press, 1932), p. 694.

2 Iniuria (D.9.2.27.14) – The term has multiple meanings. Undisputable meaning of the term is 'contrary to law', i.e. a wrongful act, unlawfulness "all that has been done non iure i.e., against the law (contra ius). W. Buckland, *A Manual of Roman Private Law*, second edition, (Cambridge University Press, Cambridge, 1953) 326; See also E. Polay, *Injuria Types in Roman Law*, (Akadémiai Kiadó, Budapest, 1986), p. 7.

3 Gaius Institutions, see Book I. (Rights in rem in respect of one's own person) in W. Hunter, *A Systematic and Historical Exposition of Roman Law*, (2nd ed., London, William Maxwell & Son, 1885), p. 145.

4 D.9.3.1. in G. Samuel, *Law of Obligations and Legal Remedies,* Cavendish (Publishing Limited, 2001, Second ed. London), p. 97.

 | DOI:10.1163/9789004380981_003

a fixed penalty of ten aurei".[5] The person in breach is penalized despite that no harm is caused to any particular person.[6] Such a measure aimed at ensuring the safety of streets and public.[7] "This injury is called a quasi-delict (*quasi ex maleficio*). This means nothing, however, except that it is a late addition to the roll of delicts, made not by any statute, but by the judicial authority of the Praetor".[8] Despite treating the above instance as one of the forms of the iniuria any member of the public could 'recover the penalty' from the occupier in an *actio popularis.*[9] Similarly, anyone could claim a penalty (which amounted to fifty aurei) for murder of a free man, although the next of kin or any other interested person had a preferential right of suit[10] action taken by anyone not relative or not interested in the case was treated as *popularis.*[11] Therefore, such actions (which were named *'actiones populares'*) were regarded as taken in the 'public interest by any member of the public'.[12]

W.W. Buckland, in distinguishing between *actiones populares* and *privata* in Roman law, notes that the former recognizes the right of any member of community to bring action for facts which affect public interests.[13] Such public interests which warranted *actiones populares* under Roman law included *sepulchri violati,*[14] *res delictae,*[15] *res suspensiae,*[16] and

5 Justinian, 4, 5, 1 in W. Hunter, (1885), p. 150. See also, T. Sandars, *The Institutes of Justinian,* (The Lawbook Exchange Ltd., New Jersey, 2007), p. 469.

6 D. 9, 3, 5, 11, in W. Hunter, (1885), p. 150.

7 D. 9, 3, 1 in Ibid.

8 Ibid.

9 Justinian's Digest, Dig. 9. 3. 5. 13. quoted in R. Lee, *The Elements of Roman Law,* (4th ed., London, Sweet & Maxwell Ltd., 1956), p. 402.

10 Dig. 9. 3. 5, 5. in Ibid.

11 Dig. 9. 3. 1, 5. in Ibid.

12 The idea behind introducing *actiones populares* was to fill the possible lacunae in the criminal legislation. Ibid.

13 W. Buckland, Roman Law, (1932), p. 694.

14 For an *actio popularis,* see, e.g., the action against the violation of a tomb, Digest 47, 12, 3 pr.: Violation, desecration, of a grave. The wrongdoer could be sued for damages by the person who had the *ius sepulchri* over the grave under the *actio sepulchri violati.* This was an *actio popularis* so that if the person interested in the first place did not accuse the culprit, any Roman citizen could do so. Berger *Encyclopedic Dictionary of Roman Law* (The American Philosophic Society, Philadelphia, 1953), p. 767.

15 *Actio de deiectis vel effusis* – A praetorian action against a householder for throwing things or pouring liquids from his dwelling, so as to harm people on the street. The householder is responsible also if his slave, guest, or child did so. Justinian listed such cases among obligations which arise "as if from a delict". Similar responsibility arose when things were located or suspended on the outside of a house or in a window in such a way as to endanger passers-by. The pertinent action was *actio de positis ac suspensis.* A. Berger, (1953), p. 342.

16 This was a quasi-delict and referred to responsibility which arose when things were located or suspended on the outside of a house or in a window in such a way as to endanger

albi corruptio.[17] The right to sue in these cases did not belong to one particular person, save in cases of *sepulchri violati* and *res delictae* where the rights of action were competing and only when the person specially affected was unable or unwilling to take action the right would transfer to the members of general public.[18]

Actio popularis was thus distinguishable from other types of *actio* in Roman law by the following features. Firstly, the *iniuria* (i.e. of a wrongful act) was not specific to one person, as there was no actual victim of the *iniuria*. The likelihood of a potential damage did not affect the popular character of claims. Secondly, the right to demand remedy, including payment of penalty (compensation), belonged to any person subject to preferential rights of demand of the relatives or other interested persons in cases of *sepulchri violati*. In this case the right of any member of the public to bring *actio popularis* was secondary to the right of action by the victim of the *iniuria* and was possible only if the person affected was unwilling to take the action. Thirdly, *actiones populares* were aimed at protection of public interests in general rather than individual interests. All other actions in Roman law could only be brought if the claimant was personally affected. Like other legal concepts in Roman law *actio popularis* too has made its way to modern municipal legal systems.

Domestic laws of various countries have enacted *actio popularis* into their legislation. In Europe an attempt to introduce *actio popularis* in domestic law for environmental issues was made via adoption of the Aarhus Convention.[19] Article 9(3) of the Convention imposes an obligation on each State party to the Convention to "ensure ... that members of the public have access to administrative or judicial procedures to challenge acts and omissions by private persons and public authorities which contravene provisions of its national law relating to the environment".[20] Amongst the European countries which have

---

passers-by. However, Buckland maintains that action for *res suspensis is actio popularis* rather than *actio de positis ac suspensis*. (1932) 695.

17 W. Buckland, (1932), p. 695. Action for spoiling, damaging or falsifying the praetorian edict promulgated on the Album. The action is penal, in factum, and popular. A. Berger (1953), p. 342.

18 W. Buckland (1932), p. 695.

19 Convention on Access to Information, Public Participation in Decision-making and Access to Justice in Environmental Matters, 25 June 1998.

20 Thus States parties to Aarhus Convention, which legislate *actio popularis* act in compliance with obligations under Article 9(3). P. Černý, *Practical application of Article 9 of the Aarhus Convention,* in 10 EU Countries – Comparative Remarks, in Report on Access to Justice in Environmental Matters, 2010, 10. See also M Fitzmaurice, 'Environmental Degradation', in D. Moeckli, S. Shah, S. Sivakumaran (eds.), *International Human Rights Law,* (OUP, Oxford, 2010), pp. 605–606.

legislatively prescribed the right to bring *actio popularis* claims are Spain,[21] Estonia, Slovenia, the Netherlands,[22] Lithuania, and Italy[23] The laws of these countries vest the right of action in public interest either in any member of the public or in a particular group of persons or entities, mostly NGOs, which act on behalf of the public as a whole. The areas where *actio popularis* claims are most utilized include 'land use, town and country planning, use of national parks, coastal waters, criminal law, environmental law,[24] protection of historical heritage'.[25] By bringing action before relevant courts those vested with the right of action seek to protect collective or diffuse interests[26] rather than individual interests of their own.[27] Under domestic laws of other countries

21 For instance, popular actions in Spain are envisaged under Article 125 of the Spanish Constitution. *Actio popularis* has been upheld by Spanish Constitutional Court as a "fundamental right". Tribunal Constitucional, Judgment of 11.7.1983 – S TC 62/1983, legal ground 2 quoted in Rosa Ana Alija Fernández, The 2014 Reform of Universal Jurisdiction in Spain: From All to Nothing, *Zeitschrift für Internationale Strafrechtsdogmatik*, 13/2014, p. 724.

22 Anyone who participated in the consultation process with public authority in the Netherlands and objected against the decision is entitled to challenge that decision via judicial review proceedings. In addition, courts in the Netherlands extended the right to bring civil suits to NGOs in environmental protection cases. The Courts' case law on standing was subsequently incorporated into Civil Code and Environmental Protection Act. J. Bonine, 'The Public's Right to Enforce Environmental Law', in Stephen Stec (eds.), *Handbook on Access to Justice under the Aarhus Convention*, (ProTertia, 2003), p. 32.

23 E. Pozo Vera, An inventory of EU Member States' measures on access to justice on environmental matters. The Aarhus Convention: how are its access to justice provisions being implemented? (Belgium 2 June 2008), 5. Available at http://ec.europa.eu/environment/aarhus/pdf/conf/milieu.pdf.

24 This, under Article 18(1) of the Spanish Law 29/1998 of July 13 on Administrative Jurisdiction, includes 'protection of water, protection against noise pollution, protection of soil, air pollution, rural and urban planning and land use, nature conservation and biodiversity, woodlands and forest management, waste management, chemical products, including biocides and pesticides, biotechnology, other emissions, discharges and releases of substances into the environment, environmental impact assessment'. Under Spanish law *actio popularis* claims are allowed 'whenever a public authority acts or fails to act in breach of environmental legislation'. P Hidalgo, Group Litigation in Spain, National Report, p. 6 (available at http://globalclassactions.stanford.edu/sites/default/files/documents/spain_national_report.pdf.

25 Pozo Vera, (2008), p. 5.

26 For instance, Spanish legislation distinguishes between the two notions. Under Article 11 of the Spanish Civil Procedure Act 'collective interests' refer to 'interests of identifiable group of persons', but 'diffuse interests' are interests which belong to "indefinite or hardly determinable plurality of consumers and users".

27 Pozo Vera, (2008), p. 5.

actio popularis claims are also brought to prevent the potential damage to unspecified persons.[28] Except for being legislatively prescribed the *actio popularis* can also be introduced via judicial interpretation. In India, for instance, the rules of standing were liberalized by courts to 'innovate new methods and devise new strategies for the purpose of providing access to justice to large masses of people who are denied their basic human rights…'.[29]

The overview of Roman law and of modern domestic legal systems allows to identify the following features of the *actio popularis* claims in municipal law: (a) action is brought to protect public/diffuse interest rather than individual or special interest of the claimant (this means that the claimant brings action before the court without having suffered any injury or material damage);[30] (b) action is brought to preclude potential damage/ injury; (c) action is brought either by a person as a member of the community or by a specially appointed representative which represents the interests of the community;[31] (d) under municipal law *actio popularis* claims are either enacted by law or introduced via judicial interpretation of the rules of standing. Another distinct, yet not always a requisite feature of *actio popularis* claims, is that it can be brought to

28 For instance, *actio popularis* are available under Colombian Civil Code in two forms and both act as the representatives of the public and can claim compensation from the wrongdoer: (1) "popular action in benefit of goods used by the public" and (2) "popular actions for contingent injury". The former is envisaged in Article 1005 of the Colombian Civil Code and allows for claims to vindicate the damage done to the public goods, like roads, public squares etc. and is taken either by relevant state organ or any person member of the public. The latter cause of action is envisaged in Article 2359 of the Civil Code and is aimed at preventing potential damage "… as a result of any imprudent act or negligence on the part of some person" which "constitutes a threat to *unspecified* persons; but if the damage threatens specific persons, only one of these may file the action". See S. German, *Popular Actions and the Defense of the Environment in Colombia,* Third International Conference on Environmental Enforcement, President, Fundepublico, Calle 71-No. 5-83, Santafé de Bogotá, Colombia, pp. 262–263.

29 *SP Gupta v Union of India* (1981) Supp SCC 87 (Indian Supreme Court) in S. Freedman, *Human Rights Transformed: Positive Rights and Positive Duties,* (OUP, Oxford, 2008), p. 126.

30 Such claims seek to protect the interests shared by and of importance to a defined group/ collectivity or a general community rather than an individual. By bringing a claim to protect collective interests the individual claimant, in a way, 'usurps the right of representing the public interest'. See Stockport District Waterworks C. v Manchester Corporation (1862) 9 Jur.N.S. 266. Opinion of Lord Westbury L.C., p. 267.

31 The latter may, depending on the nature of the wrongful conduct, i.e. whether the conduct is criminal or civil in nature, be either a NGO or other person or a State organ.

rectify the future damage.[32] This feature is not shared by simple *actio* which is ordinarily advanced to remedy the damage which has already been inflicted.[33] Claims brought to preserve the environment for future generations exemplify this feature of *actio popularis* claims.[34]

2 Defining the Operational Context for *actio popularis* in International Law

In international law the focus of the debate about the concept has been whether *actio popularis* constitutes a permissible means of invoking responsibility of states for certain internationally wrongful acts. Study of the literature reveals that the concept has been utilized in a variety of contexts. Therefore, the answer to the question concerning the legality of *actio popularis* requires first and foremost identifying the contexts in which the concept is used. In the literature and in the case law of international courts and tribunals the concept has been understood both in the judicial sense, i.e. as a right to bring a claim before an international court or tribunal, and in a non-judicial sense, i.e., as a right to invoke responsibility to protect collective interests by other than judicial means. Divergent approaches to the meaning/definition of *actio popularis* derive from the *dicta* of the ICJ's decision in the *Barcelona Traction* case. The Court stated in this case:

> When a State admits into its territory foreign investments or foreign nationals, whether natural or juristic persons, it is bound to extend to them the protection of the law and assumes obligations concerning the

32 B. Tamanaha, *Law as a Means to an End: Threat to the Rule of Law*, (CUP, Cambridge, 2006), p. 161.

33 Ibid.

34 It has been argued that climate change concerns all and hence all states regardless of whether they are specially affected have 'standing to make representations to any other concerning the latter's climate-affecting policies or activities'. F. Kirgis, 'Standing to Challenge Human Endeavours that Could Change the Climate', (1990) 84(2), *AJIL*, p. 527. See also L. Teclaff, 'International Law and the Protection of the Oceans from Pollution', (1971–1972), 40 *Fordham L. Rev.*, p. 543. P. Lawrence, 'Justice for Future Generations: Environment, Discourses, International Law and Climate Change' in B. Jessup and K. Rubenstein (eds.), *Environmental Discourse in Public and International Law*, (CUP, Cambridge, 2012), p. 35. S. Abed, *Chapter 9, Paraguay* in L Kotzé, S. Alexander, R. Paterson (eds.), *The Role of Judiciary in Environmental Governance: Comparative Perspectives*, (Kluwer Law International, 2009), p. 314. M. Fitzmaurice, *Contemporary Issues in International Environmental Law*, (Edward Elgar, Cheltenham, 2009), p. 148.

> treatment to be afforded them. These obligations, however, are neither absolute nor unqualified. In particular, an essential distinction should be drawn between the obligations of a State towards the international community as a whole, and those arising vis-à-vis another State in the field of diplomatic protection. By their very nature the former are the concern of all States. In view of the importance of the rights involved, all States can be held to have a legal interest in their protection; they are obligations *erga omnes*.[35]

The final sentence of this paragraph can arguably be construed both as a recognition of the legal interest to bring an action before international courts and tribunals but also as a right to invoke responsibility by other available means, e.g. countermeasures.[36]

References to *actio popularis* beyond the judicial context are not infrequent and include both institutionalized[37] and decentralized reactions by States against the violations of obligations established to protect the interests of the international community as a whole.[38] The latter can take the form of countermeasures by States other than injured States in protection of collective interests.[39] Examples of institutionalized actions include forcible measures to which the UN Security Council can resort under Chapter 7 of the UN Charter.[40]

35 *Barcelona Traction* (Merits) (1970).

36 Christian Tams argues that paragraph 33 of the *Barcelona Traction* case does not preclude an interpretation in favour of right of action by way of countermeasures in cases of violation of *erga omnes* obligations. (2005), p. 162.

37 On the view that collective action should be institutionalized see V. Gowlland-Debbas, *Collective Responses to Illegal Acts in International Law: United Nations Action in the Question of Southern Rhodesia,* (Martinus Nijhoff Publishers, Leiden, 1990), p. 270.

38 C. Eagleton, *The Responsibility of States in International Law* (New York University Press, New York, 1928), pp. 224–226. However, Eagleton himself firmly believed in the idea that collective responses could only be centralized.

39 H. Gould, *The Legacy of Punishment in International Law,* (Palgrave Macmillan, 2010), pp. 77–78. See Arangio-Ruiz's Fifth Report on the State practice as regards the reactions of States other than as he puts it, the "principal victim" (otherwise for Ruiz all States are injured as a result of international crimes) States against violations of *erga omnes* (or crimes as Ruiz puts it). Fifth Report of Arangio Ruiz, YbILC, 1993, Vol. II(1), pp. 44–45, paras. 184–185. Also see para. 202 of the same report for practice of the UN Security Council on applying sanctions for particularly serious breaches of international law. p. 47.

40 P. Dupuy, 'A General Stocktaking of the Connections between the Multilateral Dimension of Obligations and Codification of the Law of Responsibility', (2002), 13(5), *EJIL*, pp. 1066–1067. See also A. Gattini, 'A Return Ticket to "Communitarisme", Please', (2002), 13(5), *EJIL*, p. 1182. Bruno Simma views the Covenant of the League of Nations and the UN Charter as first attempts to secure collective interests. B. Simma, (1989), p. 823.

Klein argues that Security Council Resolution 687 (1991), which imposed obligations on Iraq to compensate Kuwait for the environmental and other damage caused to Kuwait as a result of its occupation, represents an example of collective/institutionalized enforcement of obligations, which affected the interests of the international community as a whole.[41] Action taken under Article 35 of the UN Charter can also be viewed as an *actio popularis* of a non-judicial character. Under this article "any member of the United Nations may bring any dispute, or any situation of the nature referred to in Article 34, to the attention of the Security Council or of the General Assembly". This Article lays the ground for action by the UN member with respect to the dispute or situation involving any member or non-member State of the United Nations.[42] The State exercising its power of initiative under Article 35(1) need not show any special interest of its own to justify bringing a case before the Security Council.[43]

The foregoing analysis demonstrates that the concept of *actio popularis* is not confined to actions brought before international courts or tribunals. However, as has been pointed out, the non-judicial conception of *actio popularis* in international law falls outside the scope of the present book. The centrepiece of this book is to conceptualize *actio popularis* as a judicial phenomenon.

3 *Actio popularis* as a Judicial Concept: Proliferation of International Courts and Tribunals – a Bar to a Unified Conception of *actio popularis* in International Law

The starting point of inquiry in most research done on *actio popularis* as a judicial concept is whether bringing such claims is lawful under international law. This question is most likely provoked by the famous passage in the *South West Africa* cases where the ICJ stated unequivocally that although *actio popularis* is known to domestic legal systems, such claim remains unknown to international law.[44] The ICJ stated as follows:

---

41 K. Pierre, 'Responsibility for Breaches of Obligations Deriving from Peremptory Norms of International Law', (2002), 13 *EJIL*, p. 1242.

42 See T. Schweisfurth, (2002), pp. 609–610. For the same view see also H. Neuhold, 'The United Nations System for the Peaceful Settlement of Disputes', in F. Cede and L. Sucharipa-Behrmann (eds.), *The United Nations Law and Practice*, (Kluwer Law International, The Hague, 1999), p. 65.

43 T. Schweisfurth, (2002), pp. 609–610.

44 It must be noted that at the time the ICJ decided on *South West Africa* cases some international treaty instruments had stipulated for the right of action to protect collective interests. For instance: Inter-state proceedings by way of *actio popularis* were and are still

> For these reasons the Court, bearing in mind that the rights of the Applicants must be determined by reference to the character of the system said to give rise to them, considers that the "necessity" argument falls to the ground for lack of verisimilitude in the context of the economy and philosophy of that system. Looked at in another way moreover, the argument amounts to a plea that the Court should allow the equivalent of an *'actio popularis',* or right resident in any member of a community to take legal action in vindication of a public interest. But although a right of this kind may be known to certain municipal systems of law, it is not known to international law as it stands at present: nor is the Court able to regard it as imported by the "general principles of law" referred to in Article 38, paragraph 1 (c), of its Statute.[45]

On the face of it, ICJ's statement, especially the words "*actio popularis* is unknown to international law" may, be construed as a pronouncement on the legality of *actio popularis* under general (customary) international law. However, such a reading of the statement is implausible. The ICJ's decision in the *South West Africa* cases could be explained by the Court's unwillingness to permissively construe the jurisdictional clauses of the Mandate Agreement because at the time of the decision there was very little, if any, evidence of state practice to support the actions (whether judicial or non-judicial) aimed at protection of collective interests. To the contrary, there was significant opposition to the very notion of community (public interests). The ICJ's statement should be understood in the context of juxtaposition of the procedural norms (the ICJ's rules of standing) with substantive norms (norms established to protect collective interests). In the absence of a belief on the part of the Court that such substantive norms existed in international law and that general international

---

permissible under the European Convention on Human Rights. The same is true of ILO. Article 26(1) of the ILO Constitution states: "Any of the Members shall have the right to file a complaint with the International Labour Office if it is not satisfied that any other Member is securing the effective observance of any Convention which both have ratified in accordance with the foregoing articles". So far eleven complaints have been filed. Complaint (article 26) – 2003 – Belarus – C087, C098; Complaint (article 26) – 1975 – Chile – C001, C111; Complaint (article 26) – 1983 – Dominican Republic and Haiti – C029, C087, C095, C098, C105; Complaint (article 26) – 1985 – Federal Republic of Germany – C111; Complaint (article 26) – 1968 – Greece – C087, C098; Complaint (article 26) – 1963 – Liberia – C029; Complaint (article 26) – 1996 – Myanmar – C029; Complaint (article 26) – 1987 – Nicaragua – C087, C098, C144; Complaint (article 26) – 1982 – Poland – C087, C098; Complaint (article 26) Portugal – 1962, C105; Complaint (article 26) – 1989 – Romania – C111; Complaint (article 26) – 2010 – Zimbabwe – C087, C098.

45 *South West Africa* cases (1966) 47, para. 88.

law allowed enforcement of such norms the Court's refusal to relax its standing rules (procedural rules) was very logical.

Indeed, both in international and domestic law *actio popularis* can be introduced either via authoritative judicial interpretation of the rules of standing or via norms which explicitly prescribe *actio popularis*. In international law States may introduce *actio popularis* either by concluding international treaties which will expressly allow for *actio popularis* before the relevant international tribunal established under the same treaty instrument or, in the absence of express treaty provisions, the relevant international tribunal, may introduce *actio popularis* through interpretation of dispute settlement clauses of the treaty. However, regardless of the means devised to introduce *actio popularis* the scope of application of *actio popularis* in international law will be limited only to States parties to the relevant international treaty instrument. Conversely, under municipal law the *actio popularis* becomes part and parcel of the legal order with its binding effect on every person within the jurisdiction of the state.[46] This difference prompts a conclusion that in the absence of a centralized law-making process, centralized judiciary and a hierarchy of courts a unified approach to the question of standing and particularly *actio popularis* in international law is impracticable.[47] The difference also defines the divergent purposes for which *actio popularis* claims can be utilized under domestic and international law. For instance, whereas the primary objective of *actio popularis* under domestic law is to curb the public authorities and to ensure that they refrain from acting in breach of law, for *actio popularis* in international

---

46 Unlike domestic law (criminal law or torts in particular) where the law (norms) applies to the organized community as a whole, international law is prevailingly bilateralist (fragmented) in nature. Comments by Riphagen, YbILC 1985, Volume I, 1890th meeting, paragraphs 10–11, p. 87.

47 E. Posner and J. Yoo, 'Judicial Independence in International Tribunals', (2005) 93, *California Law Review*, pp. 3, 11. Vaughan Lowe rightly notes that if ECJ's and ECtHR's roles extend beyond merely settling the disputes between parties but 'more generally to elucidate and develop the rules instituted by the Convention' (1978 Eur. Court HR, Ser.A, vol. 25, p. 62) on issues of wider community interest, "the ICJ, and, even more, arbitral tribunals, do not see themselves as having the same crucial role in the promotion of a legal system: they consider their function to be essentially confined to the settlement of existing disputes". Advisory proceedings constitute exceptions. V. Lowe, *The Settlement of Disputes in International Law*, (OUP, Oxford, 1999), p. 14. Proposals have been made to pursue protection of public interests through advisory proceedings. As far as protection of environment is concerned ECOSOC, IMO, WHO, IAEA, and possibly even UNEP could use the right to request advisory opinion on issues which fall within their competence (Article 96(2) of the UN Charter). P. Birnie, A. Boyle, C. Redgwell, *International Law and the Environment*, (OUP, Oxford, 3rd ed., 2009), pp. 253–254.

law this objective can hardly be set.[48] The reasons for this are twofold. The first reason is that the concept of 'public authorities' is alien to international law. The second reason lies in the structural differences between international and domestic law. The structural difference (rather deficiency) of international law, manifested in the absence of a centralized judiciary or legislature makes it difficult for *actio popularis* claims to be brought before international tribunals in order to achieve the stated objectives.[49] Decentralized character of 'international judiciary' where each international tribunal has its own distinct objectives defined by the thematic context precludes even a possibility of setting a unified objective which all international tribunals aspire to achieve.[50] International tribunal, which operates as an organ of an international organization or as part of an institution will strive to achieve the institutional objectives defined by its constitutive instruments. Needless to say that these objectives will very often differ from one international tribunal to another.

As has been noted, the structural difference of international law, i.e. absence of the organized 'international community' and a judiciary able to give interpretations of law, with binding force for all international courts and tribunals, precludes developing a uniform criteria for admissibility of *actio popularis* applicable across all courts.[51] Such criteria could have been developed provided

---

48 S. Thio, *Locus Standi and Judicial Review,* (Singapore University Press, Singapore, 1971), pp. 2–3. Even within EU law, for instance, Article 263(1) of the Treaty on the Functioning of the European Union the Member States, the Commission, the Council and the European Parliament are vested with the power to challenge acts of the EU Institutions with the aim of protection of the public interest. In carrying out this function Member States represent "individual national interests, the Council represents 'collective national interests', the European Parliament a pan-European democratic voice and the Commission a pan-European non-governmental public interest". This category of applicants is referred as privileged. See D. Chalmers, G. Davies & G. Monti, *European Union Law: Cases and Materials*, (CUP, Cambridge, 2nd ed., 2010), pp. 413–414.

49 Charney states two main reasons against the hierarchy of international tribunals with the ICJ as a "Supreme Court of International Law". First, unwillingness of States to accept the ICJ's jurisdiction and second, the straightjacket which the ICJ, as a "Supreme Court", may impose on the dispute settlement alternatives which States normally resort to in a non-hierarchical system of international courts and tribunals. J. Charney, 'The Impact on the International Legal System of the Growth of the International Courts and Tribunals' (1998–1999), 31 *N.Y.U.J. Int'l L. & Pol.,* pp. 697, 698.

50 Ibid.

51 The ICTY noted in this regard: "In international law, every tribunal is a self-contained system (unless otherwise provided)". *Prosecutor v Tadić, Decision on the Defense Motion for Interlocutory Appeal on Jurisdiction,* Case No. IT-94-1-AR72, para. 11 (Int'l Crim. Trib. Former Yugo., App. Chamber, Oct 2, 1995), reprinted in 35 I.L.M. 32 (1996).

that international community had its 'supreme court' with decisions binding on all other international courts and tribunals.[52] However, as it stands at present, the idea of a supreme court of the international community seems to be utopian. In fact, there is a reverse trend manifested in increasing proliferation of the international courts and tribunals.[53] The latter has led to fragmentation of both substantive[54] and procedural international law.[55] As a result, international courts and tribunals independently develop their own interpretations of the rules of standing with due regard to the institutional objectives and political contexts within which they operate. Although it is true that the law of international adjudication, i.e. procedural law, has elements which are "common" to all international courts and tribunals,[56] stark differences exist amongst international courts and tribunals on the questions concerning *jus standi* and acceptance of the jurisdiction of courts.[57] The question of admissibility of *actio popularis*, as a question of standing before the court, is not an

52 R. Jennings, 'The United Nations at Fifty: The International Court of Justice After Fifty Years', (1995), 89 *AJIL*, p. 504.

53 B. Kingsbury, 'Foreword: Is Proliferation of International Courts and Tribunals A Systemic Problem?', (1999) 31 *New York University Journal of International Law and Politics*, p. 684; P. Dupuy, 'The Dangers of Fragmentation or Unification of the International Legal System and the International Court of Justice', (1999) 31 *New York University Journal of International Law and Politics*, p. 792. T. Buergenthal, Proliferation of International Courts and Tribunals: Is It Good or Bad?, *Leiden Journal of International Law*, (2001) 14(2), pp. 267–275. M. Koskenniemi, Fragmentation of International Law: Postmodern Anxieties, *Leiden Journal of International Law*, (2002) 15(3), pp. 553–579.

54 Examples include interpretation of effective control principle by ICTY, Appeals Chamber, *Prosecutor v Tadić*, 15 July 1999, (Case no. IT-94-1-A), paras. 98–145 and ICJ (*Military and Paramilitary Activities in and against Nicaragua case* (Nicaragua v USA), [1986], ICJ Rep. 14. Also, divergent approaches to the requirement to show legal interest in order to bring a claim before courts by the ICJ (*South West Africa* cases) and WTO DSB in the *EC Banana* cases. Panel Report, *European Communities – Regime for the Importation, Sale and Distribution of Bananas*, 22 May 1997, WT/DS27/R/ECU).

55 Professor Thirlway rightly pointed out that "there is no fully developed general theory of international procedural law, defining its sources, for example". H. Thirlway, 'Procedural Law and the International Court of Justice' in V. Lowe and M. Fitzmaurice (eds.), *Fifty Years of the International Court of Justice* (CUP, Cambridge, 1996), p. 389.

56 For analysis of fragmentation and commonality of procedural law see B. Chester, *A Common Law of International Adjudication*, (OUP, Oxford, 2007), p. 7.

57 See Jenning's analysis of the divergent approaches to the effects of reservations to the jurisdiction of the ECHR and ICJ by these two tribunals. Jenning's analysis is based on the ECHR's decision in *Loizidou v Turkey* case (Series A., No. 310 23 April, 1995). R. Jennings, 'The Judiciary, International and National, and the Development of International Law', (1996) 45 *Int'l & Comp.L.Q*, p. 5.

exception. The reasons for these differences are twofold. The first reason is explicitly normative, i.e. depends on the explicit provisions of the international treaty, which either explicitly prohibit or allow for claims of *actio popularis* nature. For instance, often, constitutive instruments of international tribunals spell out different conditions for admissibility of a claim. Some instruments contain express provisions (norms), which envision *actio popularis*, others explicitly prohibit such claims. It is even possible that a single instrument both allows and prohibits claims of an *actio popularis* nature. The European Convention on Human Rights[58] exemplifies the point. By making a victim requirement as a condition of admissibility of a claim in individual complaints the ECHR intends to reject *actio popularis*.[59] However, in cases of inter-state applications the ECHR contains an express entitlement for any state party to the Convention to bring applications against another State party without evidence of the injury.[60] The second reason lies in the different judicial policies, which guide international tribunals in their interpretation of the rules of standing for the purposes of their jurisdiction.[61] Such interpretations are made possible in cases when the rules of standing are not clear enough and leave the judicial bodies a room for either permissive or restrictive interpretation of standing rules in order to exclude or open the door for *actio popularis*. It has to be noted that most rules of standing are inherently unclear. Concepts such as a dispute, legal interest, victim requirement, individual concern, impairment of the benefit are not precisely defined in the constitutive instruments of the courts and tribunals. Their meanings are clarified and determined through judicial interpretation. Differences in normative stipulation and judicial construction of rules concerning *jus standi* before international courts and tribunals serve as a major obstacle or even make it impossible to develop uniform criteria of admissibility of *actio popularis* which would be suitable for all international courts and tribunals.

The above notwithstanding, *actio popularis* claims, regardless of the international tribunal involved, do share common features. Claims of this nature are invariably brought to protect interests extending beyond special (particular, individual) interests of the claimant State. They aim to protect collective/

58 Adopted in Rome 4 November 1950. For a detailed discussion on the right of *actio popularis* before the ECtHR see pages 161–172 of the book.

59 Article 34 of the ECHR.

60 Ibid, Article 33.

61 M. Pinto, 'Fragmentation or Unification Among International Institutions: Human Rights Tribunals' (1998–1999), 31 *N.Y.U.J. Int'l L.&Pol.*, p. 834.

community obligations whether established to protect interests within a given region or area or the international community as a whole. The following chapter attempts to identify collective/community obligations in international law and will illustrate the ways in which *actio popularis* claims can be utilized to protect the interests established by such obligations.

CHAPTER 2

Understanding the Elements of *actio popularis*

The elements of *actio popularis*, which have been outlined in Chapter 1 above require a more detailed analysis. The first of these elements requires that *actio popularis* be brought to protect collective/community interests as opposed to individual/special interests of the claimant.[1] *Actio popularis* is used as a means of enforcing obligations owed *erga omnes* (owed to the international community as whole) or owed *erga omnes partes* (established to protect collective interests of group of states[2] and, in a very specific context, the general interests of States parties to the international legal instrument. However, linking *actio popularis* to obligations owed to the international community requires bringing clarity to the latter concept. Indeed, the discourse about community interests has spurred debates regarding means of their enforcement. Despite the rhetoric favouring international community interests States have been reluctant to devise centralized mechanisms to enforce such interests. On the other hand, States have been cautioned by the high risk of decentralized enforcement turning into disguised protection of individual interests of powerful States against the weak. The reason partly lies in the international community being less integrated with its members having profoundly divergent interests and antagonist values.[3] Unlike national community, where vital community interests serve as unifying (integrating) factors, States at international level have more profound differences to unite for greater good and devise mechanisms of securing the common good.[4] Simma and Paulus note in this regard: "A 'community' does not only possess an inside aspect but also presupposes an

1 Whereas the concept of collective interests will be used in conjunction with the concept of special/individual interests the concept of individual/special interests will be analysed in conjunction with interrelated notions such as injury, damage, rights, legal interest, nullification and impairment of advantages, individual concern, victim requirement etc.

2 See commentary on Articles 42 and 48 of the Articles on State Responsibility, YbILC, *2001*, vol. II, Part 2, pp. 117 and 126.

3 E. Luard, *International Society* (New York, 1990), pp. 6–10.

4 C de Visscher, *Théories et réalités en droit international public*, 4th edn. (Paris, 1970), pp. 111–114. One of such unifying factors is external threat. Higgins states in this regard: "What may be an appropriate and sensitive interpretation for the Western European democracies is not necessarily so for a global system embracing highly diverse political and economic systems. This is often strongly held by the Western members [of the Committee] themselves". R. Higgins, *'The United Nations: Still a Force for Peace',* (1989) 1(8) *Mod.L.Rev.*, p. 8.

 | DOI:10.1163/9789004380981_004

outside, an environment against which it defines and delineates its identity. In the case of an all-embracing community like the international one, it is unclear who or what constitutes this 'outside'".[5]

Indeed, traditional international law was designed to secure States' individual interests without mechanisms to protect community interests.[6] States lacked sense of community, which would have been welded together by common values and interests and all international legal instruments of states (unilateral acts, bilateral and multilateral agreements etc.) were reflections of States' individual interests.[7] Hence, enforcement mechanisms conceived by States were fit to secure individual interests only.[8]

Modern international law has moved away from exclusively State centric and interest driven legal order towards gradual recognition of community values.[9] *Actio popularis* had been perceived as one of the tools to enforce such values (interests). However, the main challenge to using *actio popularis* as a means of enforcement of community interests in international law comes from the very vagueness of the notion of "international community". For many the concept lacks clarity and is conceptually flawed.[10] Nevertheless,

---

5 B. Simma and A. Paulus, "The 'International Community': Facing the Challenge of Globalization," (1998) 2, *EJIL* 9 (2), p. 268. See also C. Ford, 'Judicial Discretion in International Jurisprudence: Article 38(1)(C) and "General Principles of Law". (1994–1995), 5 *Duke J. Comp. & Int'l L.*, p. 80.

6 A. Paulus, "Reciprocity Revisited", in U. Fastenrath/R. Geiger/ D.E. Khan/ A. Paulus/ S. von Schorlemer/C. Vedder (eds.), *From Bilateralism to Community Interest: Essays in Honour of Judge Bruno Simma*, 2011, p. 123.

7 The central question was whether the international community was something more than organization of States with aggregate individual interests but whether it has values extending beyond such individual interests. D. Kritsiotis, 'Imagining the International Community', *EJIL* (2002), Vol. 13, No. 4, p. 967. See also R. Kolb, *Theory of International Law,* (Hart Publishing, Oxford, 2016), p. 91. For instance, France and the United Kingdom in their comments on para. 2 of Draft Article 19 expressed scepticism about the concept of "obligation essential for the protection of fundamental interests of the international community". Both raised questions as to the meaning of the words "fundamental", "essential", "international community" but more importantly as to the who will determine the meaning of these terms. See para. 1 of Comments by France and paras. 1 and 2 of Comments by UK. Document A/CN.4/488 and Add. 1–3. See also similar comments by the United States, para. 2 of Draft Article 19. Document A/CN.4/488 and Add. 1–3. YbILC, 1998, Volume II, Part 1, pp. 121–122. See S. Villalpando, 'The Legal Dimension of the International Community: How Community Interests Are Protected in International Law' (2010) 21 *EJIL* 2, p. 388.

8 R. Kolb, (2016), p. 71.

9 Ibid, p. 73.

10 See for example Dis. Op. of Judge Fitzmaurice, *Legal Consequences for States of the Continued Presence of South Africa in Namibia Notwithstanding Security Council Resolution,* Ad. Op., ICJ Rep. 1971, p. 16, at pp. 240–241. Diss. Op. of Judge Xue, *Questions Relating to the Obligation to Prosecute or Extradite* (Belgium v Senegal), ICJ Rep. 2012, p. 422, at pp.

extensive references to the international community (or international community of States)[11] in variety of contexts can be found in case law,[12] the

574–575. Declaration of Judge Donoghue, *Questions Relating to the Obligation to Prosecute or Extradite* (Belgium v Senegal), ICJ Rep. 2012, p. 422, at pp. 588–589. In his Diss. Op. F. De Castro noted: "The Applicant has no legal title authorizing it to act as spokesman for the international community and ask the Court to condemn France's conduct. The Court cannot go beyond its judicial functions and determine in a general way what France's duties are with regard to the freedoms of the sea". *Nuclear Tests* case (Australia v France), ICJ Rep. 1974, p. 253, at p. 390.

11 Bruno Simma notes that international community is not confined to States and includes human beings, "From Bilateralism to Community Interest in International Law", *RdC* 250 (1994), p. 234. On the meaning of international community not confined to states see also McCorquodale, International Community and State Sovereignty: An Uneasy Symbiotic Relationship, in C. Warbrick and S. Tierney (eds.), Towards an 'International Legal Community'? The Sovereignty of States and the Sovereignty of International Law (British Institute of International and Comparative Law, 2006), p. 261. For narrow (limited to States) and wider (including other subjects of international law) meanings of international community see H. Mosler, 'International Legal Community' in R. Bindschedler et al. (eds.), Encyclopaedia of Public International Law, (Max Planck Institute), (North-Holland, Amsterdam, 1995), Vol. 2, pp. 1251–1254, at p. 1252. Cançado Trindade noted in this regard: "the legal order binds everyone (the ones ruled as well as the rulers); the *droit des gens* regulates an international community constituted of human beings socially organized in States and co-extensive with humankind". Sep. Opinion, *Accordance with International Law of the Unilateral Declaration of Independence in Respect of Kosovo,* Ad. Op., ICJ Rep. 2010, p. 403, at p. 552. For the choice between the terms "international community of States" or "international community as a whole" see paragraph 18, of the Commentary to Article 25 of the Articles on State Responsibility.

12 Multiple references to international community (obligations *erga omnes* or *erga omnes partes*) were made in the *Case Concerning United States Diplomatic and Consular Staff in Tehran* (USA v Iran), ICJ Rep. 1980, p. 3, at p.19, para. 36 with reference to the SC Resolution No. 457(1979), paras. 91, p. 42 and 92, p. 43; *Legality of the Threat or Use of Nuclear Weapons,* Ad. Op., ICJ Rep. 1996, p. 226, at p. 258, paras. 82, 83 and p. 265 para. 103 in which the Court notes that nuclear non-proliferation "remains without any doubt an objective of vital importance to the whole of the international community today". *Barcelona Traction* (n.29), p. 3, at p. 32; *Questions Relating to the Obligation to Prosecute or Extradite* (Belgium v Senegal), ICJ Rep. 2012, p. 422, at p. 458, para. 103; *Jurisdictional Immunities of the State* (Germany v Italy, Greece Intervening), ICJ Rep. 2012, p. 99, at p. 141, para. 94; *Case Concerning Armed Activities on the Territory of Congo* (Democratic Republic of Congo v Rwanda) (Jurisdiction and Admissibility), ICJ Rep. 2006, p. 6, at pp. 23 and 30, paras. 34 and 58; *Case Concerning East Timor* (Portugal v Australia), ICJ Rep. 1995, p. 90, at pp. 94, 95; *Nuclear Tests* cases (New Zealand v France), ICJ Rep. 1974, p. 457, at p. 474, para. 53; *Legal Consequences of the Construction of a Wall in the Occupied Palestinian Territory,* Ad. Op., ICJ Rep. 2004, p. 136, at pp. 171, para. 88, 199, paras. 155, 156, 157; *Legal Consequences for States of the Continued Presence of South Africa in Namibia Notwithstanding Security Council Resolution,* Ad. Op., ICJ Rep. 1971, p. 16, at p. 56, para. 126. Also, International Tribunal for Rwanda stated in J. Kambanda case that both the crime of genocide and crimes against humanity affect not only the persons directly involved, but humanity as a whole. Judgment of 04.09.1998, paras. 15–16.

literature,[13] opinions of judges,[14] and international legal instruments.[15] Although neither ICJ's case law nor VCLT defines these terms, the literature and case law usually links the concepts to the existence of common higher values

13 See for instance, G. Hernandez, A. Reluctant Guardian: The International Court of Justice and The Concept of "International Community", *BYIL*, 2013, p. 3. U. Fastenrath/R. Geiger/D.E. Khan/A. Paulus/S. von Schorlemer/C. Vedder (eds.), From Bilateralism to Community Interest: Essays in Honour of Judge Bruno Simma, (OUP, Oxford, 2011); S. Rosenne, "Bilateralism and Community Interest in the Codified Law of Treaties", in Transnational Law in a Changing Society – Essays in Honour of P. Jessup (eds.), W. Friedmann, L. Henkin, and O. Lissitzyn, (Columbia University Press, N.Y./London, 1972); B. Simma, "Universality of International Law from the Perspective of a Practitioner", *EJIL* 20 (2009), p. 265; R. Ago, 'Pluralism and the Origins of the International Community' 3 *Italian Yearbook of International Law* (1977), p. 30; G. Shaffer, International Law and Global Public Goods in Pluralist World, *EJIL* (2012), Vol. 23 No. 3, pp. 669–693. E. Morgera, Bilateralism at the Service of Community Interests? Non-judicial Enforcement of Global Public Goods in the Context of Global Environmental Law, *EJIL* (2012), Vol. 23 No. 3, pp. 743–767.

14 Judges below expressed their support for the idea of organized international community sharing common values reflected in obligations *erga omnes*: Individual and Dissenting Opinions of Judges Arnold McNair and Alvarez in *International Status of South-West Africa,* Ad. Op., ICJ Rep. 1950, p. 128, at p. 147 and 176, 177 respectively; Join Dissenting Opinions of Judges Guerrero, Arnold McNair, Read, Hsu Mo in *Reservations to the Convention on the Prevention and Punishment of the Crime of Genocide,* Ad. Op., ICJ Rep. 1951, p. 15, at p. 46; Opinions of Judges Ammoun, pp. 73, 79, Padilo Nervo, pp. 103, 106, 112, 114, 123 and Gross, p. 329 in *Legal Consequences for States of the Continued Presence of South Africa in Namibia Notwithstanding Security Council Resolution,* Ad. Op., ICJ Rep. 1971, p. 16; Judge Bedjaoui, pp. 270–271, Judge Shi, pp. 277–278, Ranjeva, p. 296, Carl-August Fleischhauer, p. 310, Judge Shahabuddeen, pp. 394, 399, Weeramantry, pp. 487, 490, 532 in *Legality of the Threat or Use of Nuclear Weapons,* Ad. Op., ICJ Rep. 1996, p. 226; Judge Koroma, p. 205, Kooijmans, p. 231, Elaraby, p. 258 in *Legal Consequences of the Construction of a Wall in the Occupied Palestinian Territory,* Ad. Op., ICJ Rep. 2004, p. 136; Cançado Trindade, p. 552 in *Accordance with International Law of the Unilateral Declaration of Independence in Respect of Kosovo,* Ad. Op., ICJ Rep. 2010, p. 403, at p. 552; Cançado Trindade in *Questions Relating to the Obligation to Prosecute or* Extradite (Belgium v Senegal), ICJ Rep. 2012, p. 422, at pp. 557–558; Diss. Op. of Judge Koroma in *Case Concerning Armed Activities on the Territory of Congo* (Democratic Republic of Congo v Rwanda) (*Jurisdiction and Admissibility*), ICJ Rep. 2006, p. 6, at pp. 58, para. 14, 63, para. 26. Sep. Op. of Judge Ranjeva in the context of arguments that *erga omnes* rules override the *Monetary Gold* rule in *Case Concerning East Timor* (Portugal v Australia), ICJ Rep. 1995, p. 90, pp. 130–131; Diss. Op. of Judge Weeramantry, pp. 153, 154, 205, Diss. Op. of Judge Skubiszewzki, pp. 206, para. 103. Sep. Op. of Judge Petren in *Nuclear Tests* case (Australia v France), ICJ Rep. 1974, p. 253, at pp. 303, 305.

15 For instance, Friendly Relations Declarations refers to all States as "equal members of the international community". Declaration on the Principles of International Law Concerning Friendly Relations and Cooperation among States in accordance with the Charter of the United Nations (Declaration on Friendly Relations), 24 October 1970, GA Res. 2625, 25 UN GAOR Supp. (No. 28) at 121, UN Doc. A/8028 (1970). See also, Letter dated 26 March 2007 from the Secretary-General addressed to the President of the Security Council (Report of the Special Envoy of the Secretary-General on Kosovo's Future Status)

(common interests)[16] and "public conscience"[17] that bind together states or all members of the international community.[18] This feature distinguishes the international community from international society, which merely represents an "aggregation of its members, the sovereign States that interact in the international arena as unitary, hermetic and coequal units".[19] Perception of international community goes beyond merely aggregation of States, which

---

[S/2007/168). The Report states: "The time has come to resolve Kosovo's status. Upon careful consideration of Kosovo's recent history, the realities of Kosovo today and taking into account the negotiations with the parties, I have come to the conclusion that the only viable option for Kosovo is independence, to be supervised for an initial period by the international community", paras. 3 and 5.

16 Abi Saab notes that "Only if this society is welded together by a sense of community, even to very different degrees, over a broad range of matters (that is to say of interests and values), can be aggregately designated a 'community'. G Abi-Saab, Whither the International Community? (1998), 9 *EJIL*, p. 249.

17 Judge Weeramantry noted in his dissenting opinion: "The public conscience of the global community has thus been greatly strengthened and sensitized to 'considerations of humanity' and 'dictates of public conscience'" and elimination of nuclear weapons is in "general interests of the community of nations" *Legality of the Threat or Use of Nuclear Weapons,* Ad. Op., ICJ Rep. 1996, p. 226, at pp. 490 and 532.

18 Tasiulas notes that international community perceives itself as a coherent community by "acknowledgment of shared values", 'In Defense of Relative Normativity: Communitarian Values and the *Nicaragua* case', 16 *Oxford Journal of Legal Studies,* (1996) 85, pp. 116–117; R Kolb, (2016), p. 96. One of the examples is referred to by Judge Ranjeva who notes: "The law of nuclear weapons is one of the branches of international law which is inconceivable without a minimum of ethical requirements expressing the values to which the members of the international community as a whole subscribe. The survival of mankind and of civilization is one of these values". Separate Opinion, *Legality of the Threat or Use of Nuclear Weapons,* Ad. Op., ICJ Rep. 1996, p. 226, at p. 296. See also Sep. Opinion of Carl-August Fleischhauer, *Legality of Threat...* p. 310. Philip Allot notes: "international society is orientated in the direction of the international public interest, that is to say, it is endlessly creating itself as a structure-system for the survival and prospering of the whole of humanity". Reconstituting Humanity-New International Law, 3 *EJIL* (1992), p. 251. See also G. Abi-Saab, 'The ICJ as a World Court' in V. Lowe and M. Fitzmaurice, Fifty Years of the International Court of Justice: Essays in Honour of Sir Robert Jennings (Grotius, Cambridge, 1996), p. 7.

19 N. Tsagourias, *International Community, Recognition of States and Political Cloning,* in Colin Warbrick & Stephen Tierney (2006), p. 215. Judge Shahabuddeen notes in this regard: "... there have been important developments concerning the character of the international community and of inter-State relations. While the number of States has increased, international relations have thickened; the world has grown closer. In the process, there has been a discernible movement from a select society of States to a universal international community." Dissenting Opinion of Judge Shahabuddeen, *Legality of the Threat or Use of Nuclear Weapons,* Ad. Op., ICJ Rep. 1996, p. 226, p. 394. Judge Shahabuddeen's point concerned the effects of use of nuclear weapons and potential consequences of its use which may lead to "annihilation of mankind and civilization" at p. 399.

have to coexist to achieve their individual interests, to accepting existence of certain common interests that demand cooperation.[20] Trindade argues that "the interests of each individual State cannot make abstraction of, or prevail upon, the pursuance of the fulfilment of the general and superior interests of the international community in matters of direct concern to this latter".[21] Examples of obligations established to protect community interests can be found in various areas of international law. They feature in the context of environmental protection,[22] the uses of the natural resources of international seabed as common heritage of mankind,[23] basic human rights,[24] more specifically, the right to self-determination[25] and prohibition of torture.[26] Also, exercise of universal jurisdiction over international crimes is regarded as recognition of existence of international community[27] and concerted action by states and other members of the international community to set up the International Criminal

20 B. Simma and A. Paulus, "The 'International Community': Facing the Challenge of Globalization," EJIL 9, no. 2, 1998, p. 271.

21 C. Trindade, *International Law for Humankind: Towards a New Jus Gentium,* (2nd ed., The Hague Academy of International Law Monographs, Leiden, 2013), Vol. 8., p. 275.

22 E. Orlando, Public and Private in the International Law of Environmental Liability, in F. Lenzerini & A. Vrdoljak (eds.), *International Law For Common Goods: Normative Perspectives on Human Rights, Culture and Nature,* (Hart Publishing, Oxford, 2014), p. 406. F. Francioni notes that environmental law is now removed "from the narrow confines of private law regulating reciprocal relations between neighbouring States" and has become a "concern of the international community". Realism, Utopia and the Future of International Environmental Law, EU Working Papers, 2012/11, p. 3. On the non-reciprocal character of global environmental protection treaties see A. Boyle, "Saving the World? Implementation and Enforcement of International Environmental Law Through International Institutions", Journal of Environmental Law 3 (1991), p. 230; E. Morgera, Bilateralism (2012), p. 748.

23 C. Joyner, "Legal Implications of the Concept of the Common Heritage of Mankind", 35 *ICLQ* (1986) pp. 191–192. D. Bodansky, *What's in a Concept? Global Public Goods, International Law, and Legitimacy,* EJIL (2012), Vol. 23 No. 3, pp. 653–654. For instance, the common interest in the Area which forms the common heritage of mankind is promoted by the International Seabed Authority under Article 153(1) of UNCLOS. See Y. Tanaka, Protection of Community Interests in International Law: The Case of the Law of the Sea, *Max Planck UNYB* 15 (2011), p. 343.

24 *Barcelona Traction* case (1970), p. 3, at p. 32.

25 *Case Concerning East Timor* (Portugal v Australia), ICJ Rep. 1995, p. 90, at pp. 94, 95.

26 *Questions Relating to the Obligation to Prosecute or Extradite* (Belgium v Senegal), ICJ Rep. 2012, p. 422, at p. 458, para. 103. In the *Furundzija* case, the ICTY regarded prohibition of torture as having *jus cogens* character and producing effects *erga omnes*. IT-95-17/1-T10, Trial Chamber Judgment, 10 December 1998, paras. 137–139, 144 and 160.

27 A. Addis, Imagining the International Community: The Constitutive Dimension of Universal Jurisdiction, *Human Rights Quarterly* 31 (2009), p. 132. See also Separate Opinion of Judge Guillaume in the *Arrest Warrant* case in which he links exercise of universal jurisdiction to the notion of international community (albeit with negative connotation), ICJ Rep. 2002, p. 3, para. 15.

Court may be viewed as an indication of operation of international community.[28] Some commentators even suggest that obligations to protect world cultural heritage also belong to the category of obligations towards international community.[29]

One will not err to say that the discourse regarding community interests is based on such concepts as *jus cogens*[30] and *erga omnes* and *erga omnes partes*.[31] Introducing these concepts into legal discourse solidified rather cautious but steady move towards recognition of communitarian values (interests), but more importantly recognition of importance of enforcement of such norms.[32]

---

28 E. Kwakwa, 'The international community, international law, and the United States: three in one, two against one, or one and the same?, in M. Byers & G. Nolte (eds), *United States Hegemony and Foundations of International Law,* (CUP, Cambridge, 2003), p. 25. Some of these crimes "affect the interests of the world community as a whole because they threaten the peace and security of humankind ..." M. Cherif Bassiouni, *International Crimes: Jus Cogens and Obligation Erga Omnes*, 59 *Law & Contemp. Probs.* (1996), p. 69.

29 R. O'Keefe, "World Cultural Heritage: Obligations to the International Community as a Whole?", 53 *ICLQ* (2004) pp. 190 and 196–197, and pp. 208–209, p. 341, See also J. Noyes, 'The Common Heritage of Mankind: Past, Present, and Future', 40 *Denv. J.Int'l L. & Pol'y* (2011 2012), p. 447.

30 See generally, A. Orakhelashvili, *Peremptory Norms in International Law,* 2006, OUP, Oxford. A Hameed, Unravelling the Mystery of *Jus Cogens* in International Law, *BYIL,* (2014) 84 (1), pp. 52–102. C. Tomuschat, also notes that *jus cogens* violations infringe upon the most fundamental values of the international community as a whole. "Obligations Arising for States without or against Their Will", 241 *RCADI* (1993), p. 224.

31 As Judge Bedjaoui put it: "Witness the proliferation of international organizations, the gradual substitution of an international law of cooperation for the traditional international law of coexistence, the emergence of the concept of "international community" and its sometimes successful attempts at subjectivization. A token of all these developments is the place which international law now accords to concepts such as obligations *erga omnes*, rules of *jus cogens*, or the common heritage of mankind. The resolutely positivist, voluntarist approach of international law still current at the beginning of the century – and which the Permanent Court did not fail to endorse in the aforementioned Judgment – has been replaced by an objective conception of international law, a law more readily seeking to reflect a collective juridical conscience and respond to the social necessities of States organized as a community". Declaration, *Legality of the Threat or Use of Nuclear Weapons,* Ad. Op., ICJ Rep. 1996, p. 226, at pp. 270–271. As regards the obligations *erga omnes partes* the Court in the *Extradition Proceedings* case noted as follows: "That common interest implies that the obligations in question are owed by any State party to all the other States parties to the Convention. These obligations may be defined as "obligations *erga omnes partes*" in the sense that each State party has an interest in compliance with them in any given case". *Questions Relating to the Obligation to Prosecute or Extradite* (Belgium v Senegal), ICJ Rep. 2012, p. 422, at p. 449, para. 69.

32 *Jus cogens* and *erga omnes* are often presented as two sides of the same coin. While the former emphasizes the highest status of the norm in the normative hierarchy the latter concerns the consequences of breaches which are owed to all, i.e. the focus of *erga omnes* is on the "legal interest of all States in compliance". Paragraph 7 of the Commentary to Articles on State Responsibility, Commentary on Articles on State Responsibility. See also

Conklin describes the link between peremptory norms and international community as one former being the *"ethoi"* of the international community.[33] Indeed, peremptory norms presuppose existence of community interests, which implies subordination of "individual state interests to community interests".[34] As Orakhelashvili rightly points out: "the way this works is that through the sources of law the international community articulates its basic values using the channels that reveal the will of the community as a whole".[35] Although importance of such norms[36] has been taken as a criterion for placing them at the top of the hierarchy,[37] strictly speaking, it is the importance of values (or relations) that these norms protect (govern) which puts them in the superior position in the hierarchy of sources. This normative superiority presupposes existence of general (community) interests that such norms seek to protect.[38]

Nevertheless, the concept of international community can be seen as too amorphous a concept to have any practical legal implications for the law of State responsibility and more specifically for the right to enforce community interests by bringing legal suits before international courts and tribunals.[39] In fact state practice shows a rather inconsistent pattern of enforcement of community obligations at a universal level. This may be indicative of the lack of sense of prevalence of community interests over individual interests

C. Bassiouni, International Crimes: *Jus Cogens* and Obligations *Erga Omnes, Law and Contemporary Problems,* Vol. 59, No. 4, pp. 72–73. C. Trindade describes *jus cogens* as norms "identified with general principles of law enshrining common and superior values shared by the international community as a whole…". *Questions Relating to the Obligation to Prosecute or Extradite (Belgium v Senegal)*, ICJ Rep. 2012, p. 422, at pp. 557–558.

33 W. Conklin, The Peremptory Norms of the International Community, EJIL (2012), Vol. 23 No. 3, pp. 855–858.

34 A. Orakhelashvili, *Peremptory Norms of the International Community: A Reply to William E. Conklin,* EJIL (2012), Vol. 23 No. 3, pp. 863–864.

35 Ibid. p. 865.

36 The ICJ in the famous *obiter* in the *Barcelona Traction* case differentiated *erga omnes* obligations from those in the field of diplomatic protection by reference to the importance of the former. (1970), para. 33.

37 A. Tzanakopoulos, The Permanent Court of International Justice and the 'International Community' in M. Fitzmaurice, P. Merkouris, P. Okowa (eds.), *Legacies of the Permanent Court of International Justice, Queen Mary Studies in International Law,* (Martinus Nijhoff Publishers, Leiden, 2013), Vol. 13, p. 351.

38 A. Tzanakopoulos, (2013), p. 353.

39 N. Politis, *Le Problème des limitations de la souveraintė et de la théorie de l'abus des droits dans les rapports internationaux,* 6 R.C.A.D.I. 1, 6 (1925) *quoted in* N. Berman, *"But the Alternative Is Despair": European Nationalism and the Modern Renewal of International Law, Harv.L.Rev* (1993)106, p. 1807.

of States.[40] At a universal level such enforcement mechanisms (institutions) have been "conservative"[41] and the procedural means of enforcement do not symmetrically correlate to substantive norms established to protect community interests.[42] The latter varies from one international tribunal to another.[43] Conversely, a more consistent attitude can be observed at a regional level.[44] However, the ICJ's recent decisions demonstrate the Court's willingness to step out of the narrow confines of legal interpretation of its standing rules to accommodate community interests. Despite frequent references to community interests in various ICJ decisions, the only two decisions in which the ICJ gave community obligations (*obligations erga omnes and erga omnes partes*) practical effect are *Extradition Proceedings* case in which the Court allowed Belgium to sue to protect collective interests of states parties to the CAT[45] and *Whaling in Antarctica* case where Australia's standing to protect a common interest of States parties to the International Convention for Regulation of Whaling to ensure the optimum level of whale stocks was recognized by the ICJ.[46] Fitzmaurice and Tamada noted in this regard: "the Whaling case can be evaluated as a cornerstone for admitting a wide range of standing where the applicable law contains obligations *erga omnes partes*. This admission of public interest litigation must have a huge impact on future cases before the ICJ, and on the litigation strategy of States".[47]

40 S. Leckie, "Inter-State Complaint Procedure in International Human Rights Law: Hopeful Prospects or Wishful inking?", 10 *Human Rights Quarterly* (1988) pp. 249–301.

41 S. Villalpando, "The Legal Dimension of the International Community: How Community Interests are Protected in International Law", *EJIL* 21 (2010), p. 410.

42 A. Nollkaemper, International Adjudication of Global Public Goods: The Intersection of Substance and Procedure, *EJIL* (2012), Vol. 23 No. 3, p. 770.

43 A. Nollkaemper, (2012), p. 789.

44 Article 33 of the ECHR, Article 45 of the American Convention on Human Rights.

45 B. Simma, The ICJ and Common Goods: The Case of Human Rights, in Federico Lenzerini & Ana Filipa Vrdoljak (eds.), *International Law For Common Goods: Normative Perspectives on Human Rights, Culture and Nature,* (Hart Publishing, Oxford, 2014), pp. 29–35. For a detailed analysis of the cases see pp. 114–125 of the book.

46 For the link between *erga omnes partes* and *jus standi* to enforce such obligations see extensive discussion of Australia's arguments and of the *Whaling* case in C. Tams, Roads Not Taken, Opportunities Missed: Procedural and Jurisdictional Questions Sidestepped in the Whaling Judgment, M. Fitzmaurice & D. Tamada, Introduction, in M. Fitzmaurice & D. Tamada (eds.), *Whaling in the Antarctic: Significance and Implications of the ICJ Judgment,* (Brill, Leiden, 2016), pp. 204–209. For detailed analysis of the case see pp. 122–125 of the book.

47 M. Fitzmaurice & D. Tamada (2016), Introduction, p. 3. For a similar view see H. Sakai, After the Whaling in the Antarctic Judgment: Its Lessons and Prospects from a Japanese Perspective, in M. Fitzmaurice & D. Tamada (2016), pp. 316–317.

However, the journey to recognition of community/collective interests and recognition of the right to enforce such interests has taken almost two centuries. Following sections illustrate in greater detail the origins of community/collective interests, the areas in which such interests are most articulated and eventually links the concept of community interests (and international community) to enforcement of such interests by way of *actio popularis*.

However, before proceeding to analyse the concept of community/collective interests further clarity has to be brought to the use of terms. The literature occasionally uses the terms 'general' and 'community/collective' interests interchangeably. The notion of the 'general interest' in this book is construed narrowly to refer to the interest by States to see that all rules of international law are observed, i.e. interest in protection of the system itself.[48] Riphagen notes: "Whether a particular State has an interest in the performance of its international obligations by another State is a matter of fact. In the long run every state has an interest in the observance of any rule of international law, including the rule of *pacta sunt servanda*. But this by no means authorizes – let alone obliges – every State to demand the performance by every other State of its international obligations".[49]

1 Classification of Obligations in International Law: Bilateralist vs Multilateralist Conceptions of International Norms

The question concerning the nature of obligations in international law and more specifically of collective/community obligations stood at the very centre of the debates throughout the ILC's works on state responsibility and the law of treaties. The debates gained particular prominence in the context of the right to invoke responsibility for internationally wrongful acts. The distinction made in the Articles on State Responsibility between the right of injured States and States other than injured to invoke responsibility was informed by the classification of obligations in international law into 'bilateralist' and 'multilateral', i.e.

48 Rosenne accepted "that there was a general international interest in the continued observance of the rules of international law", however, he expressed scepticism "that every State was entitled at all times to exact observance of all those rules. A State needed something more than general interest; it must show some right which was at the same time direct and specific". See Statement of Rosenne, YbILC, Volume I, 1970, 1980th Meeting (30 June 1970) (AC/CN.4/233), para. 62, p. 220. See also Statement of Mr. Bartos, who claimed that an internationally wrongful act injured international order and States 'had interest in maintaining that order'. YbILC, 1973, Vol. I, 1206th Meeting, 15 May 1973, para. 24. p. 25.

49 Fourth Report by Riphagen, YbILC, 1983, Volume II, Part I, para. 113, p. 21.

obligations established to protect collective interests of the group and those owed to the international community as a whole.[50]

Bilateralist conception of inter-state relations, which dominated the international legal discourse, viewed the relations of responsibility as established between the "pairs of States" parties to the multilateral treaty or the custom.[51] This was for many years the traditional approach in international law. According to this approach international law represented a normative structure consisting mainly of bilateral relations between States.[52] The bilateralist conception of international law postulates that international treaties, whether bilateral or multilateral, represent reciprocal undertakings whereby the states parties aim to achieve the "equilibrium of commitments".[53] This also applies to obligations under customary law. The primary emphasis in these relations is made on the existing correlation between 'subjective' rights and obligations arising from treaties or custom, i.e. to every right there is a correlative duty.[54]

Bilateralist conception of international law also finds its support in the case law of international courts and tribunals. In its decision in the *Phosphates in Morocco* case the Permanent Court of International Justice noted that the act of a State must be 'contrary to the treaty rights of another State'.[55] In the same

50 YbILC, 2001, vol. II, Part 2. See Articles 42 and 48 respectively.

51 Fourth Report on State Responsibility by Riphagen, para. 115, p. 22. Riphagen notes that international norms, whether treaty or customary, are of reciprocal nature, save in cases of objective regimes, exceptions prescribed under the UN Charter and the notion of international crimes. For Riphagen's classification of objective regimes (three types of objective regimes) see paras. 116–121, pp. 22–23.

52 P. Weil, 'Towards Relative Normativity in International Law?', (1983), 77 *AJIL*, pp. 413–422; See also J. Crawford, 'The Standing of States: A Critique of Article 40 if the International Law Commission's Draft Articles on State Responsibility', in M. & D. Fairgrieve (eds.), *Judicial Review in International Perspective*, (The Hague, Kluwer Law International, 2000), p. 24.

53 First Report of Hersch Lauterpacht on the Law of Treaties, YbILC, 1953, vol. II, para. 7, p. 127. However, Lauterpacht maintained that this conception of treaties applies only to treaties of economic nature. Ibid (p. 127).

54 In the *Right of Passage Over the Indian Territory* case, Judge Wellington Koo stated 'it means that with the right on each side there also exists an obligation that of India to accord passage and that of Portugal to respect rules of procedure respecting the application for, and grant of, passage. In other words, the rights and obligations of both sides are concomitant and correlative'. (Portugal v India), (Merits), ICJ Rep. 1960, Separate Opinion, p. 63. On the correlativity of rights and duties see N. Hohfeld, *Fundamental Legal Conceptions*, (New Jersey, The Lawbook Exchange Ltd, 2000), pp. 5–6.

55 *Phosphates in Morocco* case, (Italy v France) (Preliminary Objections), (1938), *P.C.I.J., Series A/B, No. 74*, p. 10, para. 22. Italian-United Nations Conciliation Commission in the Armstrong Cork Company case noted that wrongful actions "produce the responsibility

Phosphates in Morocco case, the Permanent Court of International Justice affirmed that when a State commits an internationally wrongful act against another State international responsibility is established "immediately as between two States".[56] It is submitted that such a wrongful act amounts to infringement of the "subjective" rights of others.[57] There are numerous examples of bilateralist international treaties, but the ones which are most often referred to are, international treaty instruments in the area of trade and commerce[58] as well as Conventions on Diplomatic and Consular Relation.[59] These treaty instruments, although multilateral, but are bilateralizable and establish obligations between the sending and the receiving States. Such treaties are also called

---

of those performing such actions and allowing the State which has suffered or whose subjects suffered damage to demand reparation". United Nations, *Reports of International Arbitral Awards*, Vol. II (United Nations Publication; Sales No.: 65.V.4, p. 163) quoted in the Second Report of Roberto Ago, para. 15, YbILC, 1970, vol. II, p. 180. The Chorzow Factory approach is reaffirmed by Ago in his Third Report. YbILC, 1971, Vol. II, Part 1, para. 30, p. 187.

56 Ibid. See also *Factory at Chorzow,* (Germany v Poland), (Merits), (1928), P.C.I.J., Series A, No. 17, p. 29.

57 A. Tanzi, 'Is Damage a Distinct Condition for the Existence of an Internationally Wrongful Act?' in M. Spinedi, B. Simma (eds.), *United Nations Codification of State Responsibility,* (New York, Oceana Publications, Inc., 1987), p. 4. It has to be noted that Crawford's explanation of the term "subjective" in his Third Report clearly suggests that he did not mean to confine the meaning of the term as referring to exclusively bilateral relations between states. He suggests that the term does not exclude the reliance on collective interests. In support of his contention he refers to *South West Africa* cases and notes that in that case it was "subjective" interests of peoples which were involved rather than the State. It follows that the scope of the term "subjective" was meant to be broader. See paragraphs 84–85 of Crawford's Third Report on State Responsibility, DOCUMENT A/CN.4/507 and Add.–4. Crawford himself was critical of the term "subjective" because it implied that there could be "non-subjective" obligation or right. He stated that the term was "therefore unnecessary as well as potentially misleading". Ibid, para. 84. The principle of correlativity of rights and duties does not preclude States from invoking responsibility when they are not specially affected by the breach. The ICJ's statement in the *Barcelona Traction* case that 'responsibility was the necessary corollary of a right' was made after the Court's statement on the *erga omnes* obligations, suggesting that the correlativity of rights does not preclude responsibility beyond purely bilateral relations. Third Report on State Responsibility. Ibid para. 85.

58 Second report on the law of treaties, by Sir Humphrey Waldock, YbILC, 1963, vol. II, DOCUMENT A/CN.4/156 and Add.1–3, para. 23, p. 58. James Crawford also notes that Convention on Diplomatic Relations is bilateralizable. Third Report, para. 100. This distinction is endorsed by the Articles on State Responsibility which proposes two separate Articles 42 (injured States) and 48 (States other than injured states). See comment of Ian Sinclair on Riphagen's Fifth Report, YbILC 1984, Volume I, 1865th meeting, paragraph 5, p. 304.

59 UN Treaty Series, vol. 500, p. 95, entry into force 24 April 1964 and vol. 596, p. 261, entry into force 19 March 1967.

"synallagmatic contracts".[60] When a party to the treaty commits an internationally wrongful act against a party to the bilateralizable treaty the interests of other States parties to such treaties are not specially affected.[61]

However, despite the dominance of bilateralist view, international law has seen a noticeable shift away from exclusively bilateralist conception of international law towards recognition of "multilateral" obligations i.e. obligations established to protect collective interests. The view that States can conclude international treaties to protect interests beyond purely bilateral, and which can be allocated to groups of States or the international community as a whole, seems to be beyond any doubt. Such treaties are set to protect interests, which cannot be allocated exclusively to individual States parties to the treaties and which do not consist of exchange of benefits.[62] Whether a treaty or custom is established to protect collective interest is a question of interpretation of a given legal instrument.[63] Broadly speaking, all obligations can be said to be established in pursuit of some collective interest shared by the parties.[64] In fact behind the very idea of the object and purpose of the treaty lies the extra-legal

60 Third Report on State Responsibility, by Riphagen, YbILC, 1982, Vol. II, Part 1, paragraph 123, p. 13.

61 Ushakov noted in this regard: "An internationally wrongful act engaged the responsibility of the subject of international law who committed it, because it harmed someone's interests and there was therefore injury". YbILC, 1973, Volume I, 1203rd Meeting, 10 May, 1973, paragraph 41, p. 12.

62 Third Report by Willem Riphagen, YbILC, 1982, Vol. II, Part 1, para. 52, p. 30. See also views of Marina Spinedi who argues that certain norms establish "general" or "collective" interests. Given that these are legally protected interests all States are vested with *rights* to protect these interests. She mentions obligations in the field of disarmament, human rights, environment as examples. M. Spinedi, '*Les consequences juridiques d'un fait internationalement illicite causant un dommage a l'environment*', in F. Francioni and T. Scovazzi (eds.), *International Responsibility for Environmental Harm,* (London, Graham and Trotman, 1991), pp. 88–89.

63 Riphagen notes in this regard: "It was sometimes difficult to ascertain from the text of a multilateral treaty in favour of which State an obligation had been stipulated. That was the case, for example, with the rule in the Conventions on the Law of the Sea, which limited the right of the coastal State with regard to the drawing of straight baselines. The obligation not to draw baselines so as to cut off another State from the high seas – or from an economic zone – clearly affected not only another coastal State, but also third States, and flag-States in particular. The same would be true in regard to obligations arising from the rule governing straits which connected two parts of the high seas, or from treaty regimes governing inter-oceanic canals". See para. 15 of Riphagen's comment on the Draft Articles submitted in his Fifth Report on State Responsibility, Yearbook of International Law Commission, 1984, Volume I, 1858th Meeting, p. 262.

64 Crawford, Fourth Report, para. 40. On the nature of 'common interest' as an accumulation of individual interests of States see Van Hoogh, *Theoretical Inquiry into Obligations Erga Omnes,* (The Hague, Kluwer, 1996), p. 16.

aspect.[65] However, there are treaties, which are concluded with the primary purpose of attaining a collective interest. Violation of such treaties produces different consequences in terms of the right of action against the wrongdoing State. Such action does not aim to vindicate individual (special) interests of States but rather collective interests. The following section aims to identify such interests in international law.

2 Towards Identification of Collective Interests[66]

The indication that International Law Commission was willing to acknowledge the existence of collective interests started with the proposal by some of its members to distinguish between States directly and indirectly injured as a result of the internationally wrongful act. Ushakov was amongst the ILC members who were one of the first to underline this distinction.[67] To exemplify the point Ushakov referred to acts of aggression where the direct injury is caused

65 Third Report by Willem Riphagen, YbILC, 1982, Vol. II, Part 1, para. 52, p. 30. See also Higgins who is very sceptical of the proposition that *Barcelona Traction case* entitled all States to take legal action. She notes in this regard: "There is surely a general legal interest, in the broadest sense, in the maintenance of legal obligations which admit of diplomatic protection. These are part of the reciprocal fabric of international law, in which there is understandably a collective interest. Is it really correct, as the Court seems to imply, that obligations *erga omnes* entitle any State to claim against the alleged wrongdoer? If in the Court's example, State A engages in racial discrimination against a national of State B, is State C entitled to espouse his claim on the grounds that the obligation of non-discrimination is *erga omnes?* It seems bizarre for the Court to be suggesting this when in 1966 it declined to pronounce on whether racial discrimination was prohibited under general international law". 'Aspects of the Case Concerning the Barcelona Traction, Light and Power Company Ltd.', (1970–1971), (11), *Va.J.Int'l L.*, p. 330.

66 Tams defines collective interests as "fundamental values as well as interests shared by groups of States collectively". C Tams, 'Individual States as Guardians of Community Interests' in U. Fastenrath, R. Geiger, D.-E. Khan, A. Paulus, S. von Schorlemer and Ch. Vedder (eds.), *From Bilateralism to Community Interests, Essays in Honour of Judge Bruno Simma*, (OUP, Oxford, 2011), p. 380.

67 See Arangio-Ruiz who in his Third Report on State Responsibility speaks of different consequences which may ensue for states injured directly or non-directly, however, expresses scepticism about the accuracy of the distinction and the use of terminology. For discussion YbILC, 1991, Vol. II, Part 1, paras. 93–95, pp. 27–28. See also Fourth Report by Arangio-Ruiz where he provides reasons which underlie his and ILC's unwillingness to adopt the idea of directly and indirectly injured States. Fourth Report, YbILC, 1992, Vol. II, Part 2, paras. 127–129, p. 43. Arangio-Ruiz refers to the human rights obligations as example allowing to reject the classification of states into directly and non-directly injured. He notes: "Any violation of its obligation (human rights obligation) by State A will constitute a simultaneous infringement of the corresponding right of States B, C, D and

to one State but others are affected indirectly. Ushakov suggested that the indirect injury was inflicted on the international community as a whole rather than on other States.[68]

The view that States may be affected in different ways as a result of internationally wrongful acts was also expressed in Articles on States Responsibility (hereinafter ASR). According to Article 48 of the ASR "Any State other than an injured State is entitled to invoke responsibility of another State in accordance with paragraph 2 if: a) the obligation breached is owed to a group of States including that State, and is *established for the protection of a collective interest of the group*; or b) the obligation breached is *owed to the international community as a whole*. Despite explicit reference to collective interests in the Commentary to Articles on State Responsibility it falls beyond the scope of ASR to provide the list or the definition of 'collective interest'.[69]

However, a careful study of various fields of international law reveals that collective obligations have now permeated many of its different areas. Environmental law, human rights, law of the sea and other areas of international law contain obligations, which are established to protect collective interests.[70] Support for the view about existence of community obligations can be found in the writings dating back to nineteenth century. Vattel was amongst the early proponents of the right to enforce collective obligations.[71] According to Vattel fishing and navigation in the open sea do not cause injury to anyone 'and the sea is in these two respects, is sufficient for all mankind' and he notes that failure to comply with the law of nations justifies action by all.[72]

One of the early examples of treaty instruments, which contained provisions aimed at protection of collective interest, was Clayton-Bulwer Treaty of

---

E respectively. The rights of all the latter States being the same –namely the right to have State A respect the human rights of those under its jurisdiction – no one of them is more or less directly affected by the violation than any other" (ECHR is mentioned as example). See Arangio-Ruiz's Fourth Report on State Responsibility, para. 134, pp. 44–45.

68 See YbILC, 1984, Volume I, 1861st meeting, Comments to the Draft Articles of Riphagen, Comment by Ushakov, paras. 3–4. Despite Ushakov's acceptance of the concept of *erga omnes* obligations his conception of inter-state relations was limited to exclusively bilateral. See 1929th meeting, YbILC, 1985, vol. I, p. 310.

69 See para. 7 of the Commentary to Article 48 of the Articles on State Responsibility, 2001.

70 E. Hey, 'Global Environmental Law: Common Interests and the (Re)constitution of Public Space' (2009) 1 *Iustum Aequum Salutare*, p. 42.

71 For Vattel the right of passage through international straits is a right "enjoyed by all mankind". V. Emerich De, "The Law of Nations; or Principles of the Law of Nature, Applied to The Conduct and Affairs of Nations and Sovereigns", translated by Joseph Chitty, (Sweet and Maxwell, London, 1834), p. 129.

72 Ibid, pp. 125–126.

19 April, 1850 between the United States and the United Kingdom on the construction of the Panama Canal[73] and the Treaty of Constantinople which established the regime for Suez Canal.[74] Article VI of the Clayton-Bulwer Treaty states that "… for the purpose of more effectually carrying out the great design of this convention, namely, that of constructing and maintaining the said canal as a ship communication between the two oceans, for the benefit of mankind, on equal terms".[75]

Lauterpacht's classification of treaties into purely consensual and contractual and those of international legislative character also supports the view that international law has moved beyond the classical conception of the nature of obligations in international law.[76] Lauterpacht's first example referred to the

73 T. Lawrence, *Essays on Some Disputed Questions in Modern International Law* (Cambridge, 1885, Deighton, Bell and Co.), pp. 145–146. However, Lawrence contends that Clayton-Bulwer Treaty, as far as neutralization of the Isthmus of the Panama Canal is concerned, does not and cannot affect rights and duties of third States because the US cannot 'legislate for all the world'. On the international importance of straits and the interest of the international community of States in using them see E. Brüel, *International Straits,* (Sweet and Maxwell, Ltd., London, 1947), Vol. 1, p. 37, 42, and 43; See also B. Jia, *The Regime of Straits in International Law,* (Clarendon Press, Oxford, 1998), pp. 35–36.

74 Article 1 of the Convention states: "The Suez Maritime Canal shall always be free and open, in time of war as in time of peace, to every vessel of commerce or of war, without distinction of flag. Consequently, the High Contracting Parties agree not in any way to interfere with the free use of the Canal, in time of war as in time of peace". Waldock also maintains that the Treaty of Constantinople establishes an *erga omnes* regime of navigation for Suez canal. See para. 10 of the Draft Article 63 (Treaties providing for objective regimes) of Waldock's Third Report of Law of Treaties. YbILC, 1991, 1964, Vol II, p. 29. See in general C. Selak, "Suez Canal Base Agreement of 1954 its Background and Implications", (1955) 49, *AJIL*, p. 487. Mr. Gladstone, the then Prime Minister, was most careful to acknowledge in his speech of July, 1883 the right of all the powers: "I wish to announce that we cannot undertake to do any act inconsistent with the acknowledgment, indubitable and sacred in our eyes, that the canal has been made for the benefit of all nations at large, and that the rights connected with it are matters of common European interest" *quoted in* T. Lawrence, *Essays on Some Disputed Questions in Modern International Law* (Cambridge, 1885, Deighton, Bell and Co.), p. 54.

75 An argument is made that treaties concerning the status and navigation of international straits and canals are viewed as treaties conferring rights or benefits on third States. Whether a treaty grants benefits or vests rights in third parties can be determined by interpretation of the treaty provisions. See M. Villiger, *Commentary on the 1969 Vienna Convention on the Law of Treaties*, Commentary to the Article 36 of the VCLT, (Brill, Leiden, 2009), p. 484.

76 First Report of Hersch Lauterpacht on the Law of Treaties, YbILC, 1953, vol. II, para. 1, p. 93. McNair also distinguishes between contractual and law-making treaties. 'The Functions and Differing Legal Character of Treaties', (1930) 11 *BYIL*, p. 105. In 1930 Lord McNair referred to the distinction between the contractual and law-making treaties as embryonic and 'at its infancy' pp. 106–107. See however, Ago who was very sceptical about the proposed differentiation of the regime of state responsibility based on the distinction

objective nature of the legal personality of the UN and the 1856 Convention on Demilitarization and Neutralization of Aaland Islands.[77] He maintained that the Convention of 1856 between Russia, UK and France embodying the principle of demilitarization of these islands was in the nature of "a settlement regulating European interests" and that, as such, it "constituted a special international status for the Aaland Islands" with the result that every interested State had the right to insist upon compliance with them.[78] He further noted that the Convention "creates a so-called public law of Europe".[79] The Committee of Jurists established under the League of Nations maintained that the Convention did not create rights in favour of Switzerland which was a non-party, for such right must have been clearly vested by the conventional provisions.[80] In the absence of the intent to create rights in favour of third States by the States parties to the Convention, it was by virtue of the objective nature of the Aaland Islands Convention that the Committee concluded that Switzerland had an interest in ensuring Finland's compliance with obligation to demilitarize. The Committee noted in this regard:

> Nevertheless by reason of the objective nature of the settlement of the Aaland Islands question by the Treaty of 1856, Sweden may, as a Power directly interested, insist upon compliance with the provisions of this Treaty in so far as the contracting parties have not cancelled it. This is all the more true owing to the fact that Sweden has always made use of it [the right] and [it] has never been called in question by the signatory Powers." The Committee further noted: "These provisions were laid down in European interests. They constituted a special international status relating to military considerations, for the Aaland Islands. It follows that

between so-called legislative and contractual treaties or fundamental and constitutional norms. Although he expressed sympathy with the distinction as a theoretical concept, however, he did not find it useful for the purposes of invocation of responsibility of States and rejected differentiating the regimes of responsibility based on the source of the obligation (i.e. constitutional, legislative etc.). The emphasis, in his view, must be placed on the content of the obligation, i.e. which interests the norm protects, rather than its source. Fifth Report by Roberto Ago, YbILC, 1976, Vol. II, Part 1, paras. 30–32, pp. 12–13.

77 For extensive analysis of the status of Aaland islands under the 1856 Convention see H. Rotkirch, 'The Demilitarization and Neutralization of the Aaland Islands: A Regime 'in European Interests', Withstanding Changing Circumstances'. (1986) 23(4), *Journal of Peace Research,* pp. 357–376. It has to be noted that Finland rejected the view that the 1856 Convention was binding upon it. p. 367.

78 First Report of Hersch Lauterpacht on the Law of Treaties, YbILC, 1953, vol. II, para. 1, p. 94.

79 Ibid, para. 5, p. 98; See also R. Roxburgh, *International Conventions and Third States,* (London: Forgotten Books, 1917), pp. 60–61.

80 See para. 11 of Waldock's Third Report of Law of Treaties. Commentary on Article 63, p. 30.

> until these provisions are duly replaced by others, every State interested has the right to insist upon compliance with them.[81]

The foregoing statement suggests that the regime-creating treaties create rights and obligations to protect collective interests. Waldock notes with respect to the nature of aforementioned treaties:

> The common elements which are present in the several categories of treaties discussed in the preceding paragraphs are that in all of them the parties intend *in the general interest to create a regime of general obligations and rights for a region, territory or locality which is subject to the treaty-making competence of one or more of them.* It is the fact that one or more of the parties has a particular competence with respect to the subject-matter of the treaty which differentiates these cases from the case of general law-making treaties. In the latter case no one State has any greater competence than another with respect to the subject-matter of the treaty; and for this reason it is not possible to attribute the same measure of objective effect to the treaty.[82]

The gist of the debate concerning the legal effects of regime creating treaties is vividly articulated by McNair.[83] He refers to communication between France and Britain on the binding effect of General Treaty of Vienna of 1815 on neutralization of two provinces of Sardinia, provinces of Chablais and Faucigny.[84]

---

81 *League of Nations Official Journal,* Special Supplement No. 3 (October 1920), p. 18) *quoted in* para. 11 of Waldock's Third Report of Law of Treaties. Commentary on Article 63, p. 30.

82 See para. 13 of Waldock's Third Report of Law of Treaties. Commentary on Article 63, p. 31. Waldock also mentions another category of treaties, which is also considered in the academic writing as having objective character and opposable *erga omnes*. However, this type of treaties is distinguishable from others in that they do not vest in other non-party States rights and privileges and they do not aim at establishing a regime in general interest of non-party States. See para. 15 of Waldock's Third Report on Law of Treaties. Commentary on Article 63, p. 32. Their opposability to other States is 'incidental' and stems from the established legal fact, e.g. cession of territory. Examples are 'treaties for cession of territory, boundary treaties' etc. See para. 13 of Waldock's Third Report on Law of Treaties, Commentary on Article 63, p. 31. Under such treaties the right of standing to demand compliance is limited to States parties only. See para. 15 of Waldock's Third Report on Law of Treaties. Commentary on Article 63, p. 32.

83 A. McNair, "Treaties Producing Effects *Erga Omnes*", *in Scritti di Diritto Internazionale in Onore di T. Perassi*, vol. II, (Milano, Giuffrè, 1957), pp. 23–36. McNair seems not to consider objective regimes in the context of the principle *pacta tertiis nec nocent nec prosunt.*

84 A. McNair(1957), p. 24. For the view that States cannot legislate for the world (statement in the context of neutralization of the Ithmus of the Panama Canal by the guarantee of the USA) See Lawrence (1885), pp. 145–146.

The debate took place in the context of the war between France and Sardinia on the one hand and Austria on the other. Britain claimed that Sardinia which allowed passage of French troops through its territory acted in breach of the regime of neutralization established under the General Treaty of Vienna. According to Britain both Sardinia's and Switzerland's regime of neutrality was established in the European interest and even as non-parties to the Treaty of Vienna these two States could not have permitted French troops to pass through their territory, lest they could damage the 'European interest'.[85] McNair contends that these treaties create "objective law" which produced *erga omnes* effect.[86] McNair further argues that the treaties establishing objective regimes are concluded whenever "some public interest is involved".[87] With reference to the principle of "sacred trust of civilization" enshrined in Article 22 of the Covenant of the League of Nations McNair notes: "… the new regime established in pursuance of this "principle" has more than a purely contractual basis…"[88] He continues:

> the Mandate transferred to the mandatory, or created and recognized in the hands of the mandatory, certain rights of possession and government (administrative and legislative) which are valid *in rem-erga omnes,* that is, against the whole world, or at any rate against every State which was a Member of the League or in any other way recognized the Mandate; moreover, there are certain obligations binding every State that is responsible for the control of territory and available to other States.[89]

---

85 Extract from the Report of the Law of Officers of May 18, 1859 quoted in McNair (1957), p. 24. France, on the other hand, maintained that provisions of the Treaty of Vienna were not opposable to Sardinia or Switzerland as States non-parties to the treaty. p. 24.

86 McNair too bases his conclusion on the PCIJ's decision in the *Wimbledon* case. Ibid. p. 29. McNair further points out: "It may be that in addition to the semi-legislative power exercised by these States there is another juridical element which is significant, namely, the creation by Germany of certain rights *in rem* in regard to a strip of her territory for the public benefit, which finds a parallel at any rate in the common law in the process of dedicating land or the right to use it for public purpose". p. 29. This point McNair made with respect to Article 380 of the Treaty of Versailles.

87 Separate Opinion, Arnold McNair, *International Status of South West Africa* (Advisory Opinion), [1950], ICJ Rep. p. 153.

88 Ibid, p. 154.

89 Ibid, p. 156. The ICJ also noted that "The 'Mandate' had only the name in common with the several notions of mandate in national law. The object of the Mandate regulated by international rules *far exceeded that of contractual relations* regulated by national law. The Mandate was created, in the interest of the inhabitants of the territory, and of humanity in general, as an international institution with an international object of sacred trust of civilization". Ibid, p. 132.

Fitzmaurice too refers to treaties established to protect collective interests. He categorized treaties into reciprocal, interdependent[90] and absolute (integral).[91] Although this classification did not as a whole make into the final text of the VCLT some provisions of the VCLT suggest the applicability of the classification.[92] According to Fitzmaurice reciprocal treaties constitute reciprocal exchange of rights and benefits between the contracting parties. Conversely, interdependent treaties form a system of mutually dependent commitments, 'whereby performance of obligations by one state is dependent on the 'equal or corresponding' performance of all other States".[93] Treaties on disarmament, which have the sole and 'common' objective of disarming, are examples of such treaties.[94] This objective can only be attained through 'interdependent performance of obligations to disarm'.[95] Antarctic and Outer Space Treaties are also viewed as establishing interdependent obligations.[96] Violation of such treaties by a State party 'prejudices the treaty regime applicable

90 Second Report on the Law of Treaties, Gerald Fitzmaurice, YbILC, 1957, Vol. II, p. 30.

91 Gerald Fitzmaurice, Second Report, YbILC, 1957, Vol. II, para. 115, p. 53.

92 See for instance Article 60 of the VCLT. J. Pauwelyn (2003), p. 59.

93 Gerald Fitzmaurice, Second Report, YbILC, 1957, vol. II, p. 31.

94 Ibid, para. 126, p. 54. B. Simma, The Antarctic Treaty as a Treaty Providing for an "Objective Regime", (1986), 19, *Cornell Int'l L.J.*, p. 197.

95 Reuter refers to a different example and notes: "in a case of a treaty limiting fishing rights, with a view to protecting stocks, failure by one party to perform obligations affected all the parties. In some cases, however, the obligations of States were not invariably symmetrical. It was possible to envisage a disarmament treaty imposing the obligation to disarm on one State only". See comment of Reuter on Riphagen's Fifth Report, YbILC 1984, Volume I, 1861st meeting, para. 15, p. 279. Riphagen notes in this regard: "On the one hand, some multilateral treaties recognize or create, as between the States parties to them, a *collective* (in contradistinction to a merely common or parallel) interest of those States, for the protection or promotion of which those States enter into obligations". Sixth Report by Riphagen, para. 21 of the Commentary on Article 5 of the Draft Articles on State Responsibility, YbILC, 1985, Volume II, Part I, p. 8. See Third Report of Arangio-Ruiz, YbILC 1991, Vol. II, Part 1, para. 81, p. 25. Ruiz draws on the Fitzmaurice's report on the law of treaties when he refers to the divisible and integral (indivisible) obligations.

96 It has to be noted that Crawford uses the term "integral obligations" in the same sense as Fitzmaurice uses the term "interdependent obligations". Crawford, Fourth Report, para. 38. Also, it has to be noted that Antarctic treaty is not exclusively limited to integral obligations. It contains all three types of obligations, reciprocal (Article 3-exchange of information), interdependent (Articles 1 and 5 – measures of military nature and explosions), and integral (in the sense used by Fitzmaurice) (Article 2 – Freedom of scientific investigation). See Second Report on the Law of Treaties, by Sir Humphrey Waldock, Special Rapporteur, YbILC, 1963, vol. II, DOCUMENT A/CN.4/156 and Add.1–3. Simma denies *erga omnes* effect of Antarctic Treaty by virtue of customary law too. He maintains that the general interests which States parties to Antarctic Treaty aspire to protect do not warrant reactions

between them all and not merely the relations between the defaulting State and the other parties'.[97] The third category of international treaties, i.e. 'integral' (absolute) or 'regime-creating' or of 'social' nature[98] do not require corresponding performance of other States and hence are not dependent on the performance by others.[99] Amongst the examples of such obligations Fitzmaurice mentions 'obligations concerning maintenance of certain standards of working conditions or to prohibit certain practices arising under ILO[100] conventions, or under the maritime conventions as regards standards of safety at sea', Genocide Convention, Human Rights Conventions and Geneva Conventions of 1949,[101] 'treaties imposing an obligation to maintain a certain regime or system in a given area, such as the regime of the Sounds and the Belts at the entrance to the Baltic Sea' etc.[102] According to Fitzmaurice obligations under such treaties 'are not owed to the parties to the treaty but rather to the entire world'.[103] Nevertheless, Fitzmaurice contends that even this fact does not preclude applicability of the principle of *res inter alios acta* to States non-parties to the treaty.[104] Such treaties become binding on all other States by virtue of their transformation into the customary rules of *erga omnes*

---

of third States. Third States were simply indifferent, hence unwilling to react. The indifference continued until the issue of resources of Antarctic became subject of debates. Hence no practice was available to make a conclusive statement that *erga omnes* effect of Antarctic Treaty materialized through customary law. B. Simma, *The Antarctic Treaty,* (1986) 204 205.

97 Second Report on the Law of Treaties, by Sir Humphrey Waldock, Special Rapporteur, YbILC, 1963, vol. II, DOCUMENT A/CN.4/156 and Add.1–3, para. 23, p. 58.

98 Gerald Fitzmaurice, Second Report, YbILC, 1957, vol. II, para. 115, p. 53.

99 Ibid, p. 54.

100 For the brief discussion of complaints filed to ILO by way of *actio popularis* see L. Scott, The Inter-State Complaint Procedure in International Human Rights Law: Hopeful Prospects or Wishful Thinking? (1988), 10(2), *Human Rights Quarterly,* pp. 278–281. However, Scott maintains that of all six complaints filed to the ILO Commission only the first case involving Ghana and Portugal represented a pure case of *actio popularis* not motivated by political interests or interests of the nationals of the claimant State. p. 282.

101 Although human rights treaties are sometimes put in the category of obligations of integral character, their breach, unlike the violation of other integral obligations, does not authorize other States parties to suspend the treaty. Crawford, Fourth Report, para. 38.

102 Fitzmaurice, Second Report (1957), para. 125, p. 54.

103 Ibid, para. 126, p. 54.

104 Third Report on the Law of Treaties, Fitzmaurice, YbILC, 1958, v. II, Para. 77, p. 41. Although sceptical about the "objective regimes" because they set up obligations applicable to third States. See Fourth Report by Riphagen, para. 85, YbILC, 1983, Vol. II, Part 1 p. 16. Riphagen maintains that such regimes are established to attain a collective interest. Objective regimes, according to Riphagen, represent aggregation of interests of States forming their collective interest. Fourth Report, para. 97, p. 18. Riphagen defines objective regimes as follows: "In essence it is the "normative" character – in contradistinction

nature.[105] There are also rules which aim to establish and protect collective interests of a particular group but which may also extend beyond the immediate interests of the group members and apply to wider international community.[106] These obligations are referred to as obligations *erga omnes partes.*[107] Interests protected by such obligations cannot be allocated to one particular State party to the convention. Under treaties of this kind it is rare for one State to be specially affected. As a rule, no state's interest is any different from the interest of other States parties to the convention. Therefore, all of them are equally interested in compliance with the obligations. Nevertheless, it is possible that one State is affected specially, however, such instance does not preclude the interests of other States parties in compliance with the treaty obligations.[108] *Wimbledon case* exemplifies this point.[109] This case was brought before the PCIJ under Articles 380 and 386 of the treaty of Versailles. Article 380 stipulated that "the Kiel Canal and its approaches shall be maintained free and open to the vessels of commerce and war of *all nations* at peace with Germany on terms of entire equality'. According to Article 386 "in the event of violation of any of the conditions of Articles 380–386, or of disputes as to the

to both the quid pro quo character and the "cooperative procedure" character – of the rule of international law which determines its objectivity in the present context. The parties to the regime create the collective interest which requires that each of them fulfill its obligations irrespective of the fulfillment of the obligations by another party. In this sense the objective regime is the opposite of a *si omnes* clause of a treaty as requiring just that". Fourth Report, para. 98, p. 18. Examples of such treaties include International Tin Agreement and the International Sugar Agreement which foresee mechanisms to ensure compliance with the provisions of the treaty. Similarly, the agreements which envisage preserving the food stuff. Under such agreement, failure by one State party to comply with the provisions of the treaty (e.g. to make contributions of food which it owes under the agreement) affects all other parties to the treaty. Amongst other examples of treaties establishing collective interests is the Law of the Sea Convention which introduced the concept of the "common heritage of mankind" with respect to the natural resources of the deep seabed beyond national jurisdiction. See para. 23 of the ILC's comments on Riphagen's Draft Article 5 in his Sixth Report. YbILC, 1985, Volume II, Part 2, p. 27.

105 Third Report on the Law of Treaties, Fitzmaurice, YbILC, 1958, v. II, Para. 77, p. 41.

106 Articles on Responsibility of States for Internationally Wrongful Acts, para. 7 of the commentary on Article 48. Example to which the commentary refers is the *Wimbledon case.*

107 Articles on Responsibility of States for Internationally Wrongful Acts, paras. 6–7 of the commentary on Article 48. See also Third Report by Crawford, paras. 92 and 106 of the commentary on Draft Article 40.

108 See para. 106 of Crawford's Third Report. Crawford notes that integral obligations (he refers to Article 60(2)(c) as example of such obligations) form sub-category of obligations *erga omnes partes.*

109 *Wimbledon case* (UK, France, Italy, Japan, Poland intervening v Germany), Series A, August 17, 1923.

interpretation of these articles, *any interested Power* can appeal to the jurisdiction instituted for the purpose by the League of Nations". In this case the PCIJ found admissible the complaints of four Applicants: Italy, Japan, UK, and France against Germany despite the fact that only UK and France could claim material injury. UK could do so as the state of nationality of the SS Wimbledon, and France as a State whose national time-chartered a steamship to transport war materials to Poland through the Kiel Canal. Japan and Italy had no material interest in the case. The applicants maintained that Germany's denial of access to the Kiel Canal with reference to its neutrality orders with respect to Russo-Polish war was in breach of the relevant provisions of the Treaty of Versailles.[110] The Permanent Court of International Justice stated that 'each of the four Applicant Powers has a clear interest in the execution of the provisions relating to the Kiel Canal, since they all possess fleets and merchant vessels flying their respective flags'.[111] The Court further noted:

> The Court considers that the terms of article 380 are categorical and give rise to no doubt. It follows that the canal has ceased to be an internal and national navigable waterway, the use of which by the vessels of states other than the riparian state is left entirely to the discretion of that state, and that it has become an international waterway intended to provide under treaty guarantee easier access to the Baltic *for the benefit of all nations of the world*. Under its new regime, the Kiel Canal must be open, on a footing of equality, to all vessels, without making any distinction between war vessels and vessels of commerce, but on one express condition, namely, that these vessels must belong to nations at peace with Germany.[112]

Based on Article 380 of the Treaty the Court declared that the parties *intended* to allow access to the Kiel Canal to all seafaring nations at peace with Germany and noted that narrow interpretation of the relevant provisions of the Treaty contradicted the plain language of the Treaty of Versailles.[113] Further examples of obligations *erga omnes partes* include obligations in the field of 'environment or security' for a particular region and regional human rights protection

110 *Wimbledon* case, (1923), pp. 16–17.

111 Series A, No. 1, p. 20.

112 Series A, p. 23.

113 Series A, pp. 24–25; Also M. McDougal, H. Lasswell, and J. Miller, *The Interpretation of Agreements and World Public Order: Principles of Content and Procedure*, (Yale University Press, New Haven, 1967), pp. 227–228.

mechanisms.[114] Conventions on Biological Diversity, Ozone Depletion, World Heritage, Trade in Endangered Species, Climate Change, the Law of the Sea, Dumping at Sea are also amongst such conventions. Some of these treaties do not have particular beneficiaries (obligees).[115] For instance, failure to comply with provisions of the Vienna Convention for the Protection of the Ozone Layer[116] does not specially affect any state or other person.[117] The Convention imposes a general obligation under Article 2 "to take appropriate measures ... to protect human health and the environment against adverse effects resulting or likely to result from human activities which modify or are likely to modify the ozone layer". Failure to take appropriate measures by a State party will not affect an individual state party to the Convention but rather the collective interest of protection of ozone layer, which the States parties aimed to attain.

3 Absolute Obligations: Nature of Human Rights Obligations

Another category of obligations established to protect interests not specific to particular States parties to a given treaty instrument are referred to as absolute obligations. These obligations, unlike reciprocal, have a primary objective of attainment of 'the general good'.[118] Such treaties are established to protect those 'imperative', higher international interests out of sense of moral

114 The principle of common heritage of mankind usually encompasses outer space and deep seabed, and high seas i.e. areas which do not fall within national jurisdiction of any given State. See E. Franckx, The International Seabed Authority and the Common Heritage of Mankind: The Need for States to Establish the Outer Limits of their Continental Shelf, *The International Journal of Marine and Coastal Law* 25 (2010), p. 544. Article 136 of the UNCLOS states: "The Area and its resources are the common heritage of mankind". J. Noyes, 'The Common Heritage of Mankind: Past, Present, and Future', (2011–2012) 40 *Denv.J.Int'l L. & Pol'y* 447. K. Baslar, *The Concept of the Common Heritage of Mankind in International Law* (Martinus Nijhoff, Dordrecht, the Netherlands: 1998); E. Egede, The Common Heritage of Mankind and the Sub-Saharan African Native Land Tenure System: A "Clash of Cultures" in the Interpretation of Concepts in International Law? (2014) *Journal of African Law*, pp. 1–18; See also C. Tomuschat, Collected Courses of the Hague Academy of International law (Recueil des Cours, 1993, IV) 226. J. Heredia, 'The Heritage Dimension of the Climate System and Its Protection for the Benefit of Mankind', in M. Fitzmaurice, S. Meljean-Dubois and S Negri (eds.), *Environmental Protection and Sustainable Development from Rio to Rio +20*, (Brill, Leiden, 2014), pp. 72–76.

115 para. 108 of Crawford's Third Report.

116 22 March 1985, (1987) 26 ILM, p. 1529.

117 para. 108, Crawford's Third Report.

118 However, the objective of attainment of 'the general good' does not completely remove the reciprocal element from such treaty instruments. Fitzmaurice notes with regards to such treaties that 'these treaties are reciprocal in a sense that each party has a right to

obligation or international solidarity.[119] Examples include humanitarian or human rights treaties.[120] Protection of individuals was originally limited to the field of diplomatic protection. Garcia Amador devoted significant part of his work to the question of diplomatic protection in the context of the rights of aliens.[121] The right of the State of nationality of the alien to diplomatic protection was undisputable and in exercising the right of diplomatic protection, the state was in "reality asserting its own right – the right to ensure, in the person of its subjects, respect for the rules of international law".[122] International treaty instruments in the field of human rights detached the protection of rights of individuals from the state of nationality.[123] Now, the nature of the

---

claim performance of the obligations from other parties in return of its performance of the same obligations'. Fourth Report on the law of Treaties, Fitzmaurice, YbILC 1959, v. II, para. 21, p. 54. Commentary on Article 5: 'Obligatory character of treaties: relationship of obligations to rights'.

119 First Report of Hersch Lauterpacht on the Law of Treaties, YbILC, 1953, vol. II, para. 7, p. 127. (para. 7 of the Commentary to the Alternative Draft Article A on Reservations. p. 127).

120 The ICCPR's Human Rights Committee has stated that human rights treaties 'are not a web of inter-State exchanges of mutual obligations' and that the 'principle of inter-State reciprocity has no place' in human rights. ICCPR Human Rights Comm., General Comment 24(52), 52d Sess., 1382d mtg. at 10, UN Doc CCPR/C/21/Rev.I/Add. 6 (1994)). See also J. Watson, 'The Limited Utility of International Law in the Protection of Human Rights,' (1980) 74 *Proceedings of the ASIL,* 3–4. See also Third Report by Riphagen, para. 94. The Mandate Agreement was also said to be established to protect rights of the inhabitants of the Mandated territory and did not form the synallagmatic contract with the 'real balance of obligations and rights of the parties'. See Separate Opinion of Judge Bustamante, *South West Africa case,* (Judgment) 1962, ICJ Rep. p. 357.

121 Third Report, YbILC, 1958, Vol. II, p. 47.

122 *Mavrommatis* case (1924), p. 12.

123 Slavery Convention, art. 8, 60 L.N.T.S. at pp. 285–267, *entry into force* 9 March 1927; 1933 Convention for the Suppression of Traffic in Women Working of Full Age, Article 4, 150 L.N.T.S. *entered into force* 1 November 1936; 1948 Convention on the Prevention and Punishment of the Crime of Genocide, Article 9, 78 U.N.T.S. p. 277, General Assembly Resolution 260 A (III) of 9 December 1948 *entry into force* 12 January 1951; 1950 Convention for the Suppression of Traffic in Persons and Exploitation of Prostitution of Others, Article 22, 96 U.N.T.S. p. 271, General Assembly Resolution 317 (IV) of 2 December 1949 *entry into force* 25 July 1951; 1951 Convention Relating to the Status of Refugees, Article 38, 189 U.N.T.S. p. 137, General Assembly Resolution 429 (V) of 14 December 1950, *entry into force* 22 April 1954; 1953 Convention on the International Right of Correction, Article 5, 453 U.N.T.S., p. 191, General Assembly Resolution 630 (VII) of 16 December 1952 *entry into force* 24 August 1962; 1953 Convention on the Political Rights of Women, Article 9, 193 U.N.T.S., p. 135, General Assembly Resolution 640 (VII), *entry into force* 7 July 1954; 1954 Convention relating to the Status of Stateless Persons, Article 34, 360 U.N.T.S., p. 117, Economic and social Council Resolution 526 A (XVII), *entry into force* 6 June 1960; 1956 Supplementary Convention on the Abolition of Slavery, the Slave Trade, and Institutions and Practices Similar to Slavery, Article 10, 266 U.N.T.S., p. 3, Economic and Social Council Resolution

rights protected under the human rights instruments began to dictate a conception of rights of individuals the violation of which becomes an interest of every party to the treaty instrument.

Unlike regular treaties which consist of reciprocal exchange of benefits between the States parties, human rights treaties aim at protecting the rights of persons.[124] Parties to human rights treaties are not driven in their compliance with obligations by reciprocity. Some argue that unlike regular treaties, human rights treaties do not constitute a set of reciprocal undertakings but are rather "pledges".[125] According to Brilmayer, characterization of human rights and environmental treaties as pledges allows States not directly affected by the breach to invoke responsibility of the wrongdoing State.[126] Judge Weeramantry argued along similar lines. He noted in this regard:

> Human rights and humanitarian treaties do not represent an exchange of interests and benefits between contracting States in the conventional sense, and in this respect, may also be distinguished from the generality of multilateral treaties, many of which are concerned with the economic, security or other interests of States. Human rights and humanitarian treaties represent, rather, a commitment of the participating States to certain norms and values recognized by the international community.[127]

However, although it is true that human rights treaties are established to protect the rights of individuals rather than States, they also constitute binding reciprocal commitments, which allow States parties to hold each other responsible for the breach.[128] This can take the form of *actio popularis* i.e. a claim which is motivated by interests other than self-interest.[129] This follows from the logic of the decision of the ECHR in the *Ireland v UK* case where the Court

---

608 (XXI), *entry into force* 30 April 1957; 1957 Convention on the Nationality of Married Women, Article 10, 309 U.N.T.S., p. 65, General Assembly Resolution 1040 (XI), *entry into force* 11 August 1958; 1961 Convention on the Reduction of Statelessness, Article 14, General Assembly Resolution 896 (IX), *entry into force* 13 December 1975; 1965 Convention for the Elimination of All Forms of Racial Discrimination, Article 22, 660 U.N.T.S. p. 195, General Assembly Resolution 2106 (XX), *entry into force* 4 January 1969, texts are available at http://www.unhchr.ch/html/intlinst.htm.

124 L. Brilmayer, From 'Contract to Pledge': The Structure of International Human Rights Agreements, (2006) *BYIL*, pp. 164–165.

125 Ibid.

126 Ibid. pp. 177–178.

127 Weeramantry's Separate Opinion in the *Case Concerning Application of the Convention on the Prevention and Punishment of the Crime of Genocide*, (1996), p. 646.

128 L. Scott, (1988), p. 256.

129 Ibid.

spells out the purposes of the drafters of the Convention, which the Court saw as protection of the rights of individuals.[130] The Court stated as follows:

> However, the Irish Government's argument prompts the Court to clarify the nature of the engagements placed under its supervision. Unlike international treaties of the classic kind, the Convention comprises *more than mere reciprocal engagements* between contracting States. It creates, over and above a network of mutual, bilateral undertakings, objective obligations which, in the words of the Preamble, benefit from a 'collective enforcement'. By virtue of Article 24 (art. 24), the Convention allows Contracting States to require the observance of those obligations without having to justify an interest deriving, for example, from the fact that a measure they complain of has prejudiced one of their own nationals.

It follows that the attainment of the 'common good' is inherent in the European Convention on Human Rights.[131] Similarly the Court in its decision in *France et al. v Turkey* case also noted with reference to the *Pfunders case* that the Convention 'gives rise to obligations of "objective" character'.[132] The Court based its conclusion on the argument that the applicants were "not exercising their right of action under Article 24 for the purpose of safeguarding any rights of their own, but for the purpose of contributing to upholding the public order in Europe".[133] The Commission further noted that the generally accepted principle of reciprocity under Article 21 of the VCLT does not apply to the obligations under European Convention on Human Rights.[134] According to the Court these obligations are "essentially of an objective character, being designed rather to protect the fundamental rights of individual human beings from infringement by any of the High Contracting parties than to create subjective and reciprocal rights for the High Contracting Parties themselves".[135]

---

130 *Ireland v UK*, (18 January, 1978, Judgment, application number: 5310/71), para. 239.

131 In *Soering v UK* the Court noted in interpreting the ECHR: 'regard must be had to its special character as a treaty for the collective enforcement of human rights and fundamental freedoms… Thus the object and purpose of the Convention as an instrument for the protection of individual human beings require that its provisions be interpreted and applied so as to make its safeguards practical and effective.' *Case of Soering v United Kingdom,* Application No. 14038/88, Judgment 7 July, 1989, paragraph 87.

132 *Application No.* 9940-9944/82 (joined), Decision of 6 December 1983.

133 Ibid. p. 158.

134 *Austria v Italy,* Yearbook 4, 116, at p. 140.

135 Ibid. The European Court on Human Rights has similarly referred to the "objective obligations" created by the Convention over a network of mutual, bilateral undertakings". para. 239 of its judgment in the *Northern Ireland* case.

The Commission further recalls that the enforcement machinery provided for in the Convention is founded upon the system of "a collective guarantee by the High Contracting Parties of the rights and freedoms set forth in the Convention", and that a High Contracting Party, when referring an alleged breach of the Convention to the Commission under Article 24, "is not to be regarded as exercising a right of action for the purpose of enforcing its own rights, but rather as bringing before the Commission an alleged violation of the public order of Europe".[136]

The preceding analysis prompts a conclusion that the supervision mechanisms established under human rights treaties do not aim to protect special interests which can be allocated to States parties to the ECHR in their individual capacity. Such mechanisms are set to achieve the effective compliance with the human rights. The legal nexus established between States parties to the human rights treaty through the mechanism of enforcement of obligations available to all States parties is said not to suffice to view States parties to the human rights treaty as possessing rights. The rights are rather vested in individuals. State interests are thus not immediate and specific under such treaties. The interests of States under these instruments are general and limited to ensuring compliance of obligations by other States.[137] The same is true of other human rights treaties[138] and international agreements which are established to protect extra-state interests.[139] For instance, agreements in the field of protection of global environment,[140] human development or world heritage can

136 Para. 40, p. 169 with reference to *Austria v Italy* decision. The ECtHR in cases *Chrysostomos and others against Turkey* called ECtHR as a 'constitutional instrument of European public order in the field of human rights'. The Court noted that the treaty benefits from the 'collective enforcement'. Application No. 15299/89, para. 22, March 4, 1991.

137 See Crawford, Third Report, para. 88.

138 'The Convention and the other human rights treaties are inspired by a set of higher common values (centered around the protection of the human person), are endowed with specific supervisory mechanisms, are applied as a collective guarantee, embody essentially objective obligations, and have a special character that sets them apart from other treaties…". *Case of Constitutional Court v Peru, Inter-Am.Ct. H.R.*, 8 BHRC 522, (1999) paras. 41–45.

139 See the Ad. Opinion on the *International Status of South West Africa* where the Court noted: "The mandate was created, in the interests of the inhabitants of the territory, and of humanity in general, as an international institution with an international object – a sacred trust of civilization", ICJ Rep. 1950, p. 132.

140 B. Oxman, The Rule of Law and the United Nations Convention on the Law of the Sea, (1996), 7, *EJIL*, pp. 363–364.

be named amongst such legal instruments.[141] That States do not have special interest in human rights treaties was also confirmed by the by the International Court of Justice in the Genocide Advisory Opinion. The Court noted:

> It is indeed difficult to imagine a Convention that might have this dual character to a greater degree, since its object on the one hand is to safeguard the very existence of certain human groups and on the other to confirm and endorse the most elementary principles of morality. In such a Convention the contracting States do not have any interests of their own; they merely have, one and all, a common interest, namely, the accomplishment of those high purposes which are the *raison d'être* of the Convention. Consequently, in a Convention of this type one cannot speak of individual advantages or disadvantages to States, or of the maintenance of a perfect contractual balance between rights and duties. The high ideals which inspired the Convention provide, by virtue of the common will of the parties, the foundation and measure of all its provisions.[142]

The passage clearly imparts the view of obligations extending beyond purely 'contractual' and established to protect interests common to a wider group rather than individual States parties to the Convention.

The foregoing analysis suggests that international law has departed from the purely bilateralist view of obligations and is leaned towards recognition of collective and community obligations. This shift/departure marks a fundamental change in the way States enforce obligations against each other. A strongly held view that the right to enforce obligations (the right to invoke responsibility) belongs only to 'specially' affected States has been revisited in favour of

141 Conventions for the Protection of World Cultural and Natural Heritage, 16 November 1972, UN Treaty Series, Vol. 1037, p. 152; Convention on international trade in endangered species of wild fauna and flora (with appendices and Final Act of 2 March 1973), UN Treaty Series, Vol. 993, p. 244; Vienna Convention for the Protection of the Ozone Layer, 28 September 1988, UN Treaty Series, Vol. 1513, p. 293; United Nations Framework Convention on Climate Change, 21 March 1994, UN Treaty Series, Vol. 1771, p. 107; Convention on Biological Diversity, 29 December 1993, UN Treaty Series, Vol. 1760, p. 107. See P. Birnie, A. Boyle, C. Redgwell, (2009), pp. 233–234.

142 Advisory Opinion, ICJ Rep. [1951], p. 23. For the view that the Genocide Convention, including other three categories of multilateral treaties discussed in Judge Alvarez's dissenting Opinion, forms 'an indivisible whole' and do not constitute reciprocal exchange of benefits see pp. 51–54 of the ICJ Reports, 1951. UK also argued that the Genocide Convention, unlike commercial or other multilateral conventions, was not 'reciprocal' or

recognition of community responses to breaches of obligations established to protect collective interests of a group or those owed to the international community as a whole. The following section seeks to explore the possibility of protecting/enforcing such interests by way of instituting *actio popularis* claims before competent international courts and tribunals.

'fundamentally contractual' but 'social, law-making, or status, regime or system-creating'. See pp. 62–63 of the UK Written Statement in the Genocide Advisory Opinion. However, Israel contended that the Genocide Convention contained both normative and contractual provisions. Article 1 of the Convention expressed its contractual nature and reservations were only permissible as far as contractual provisions of the Convention were concerned. See pp. 200–202 of the Israeli Statement in the Genocide Ad. Opinion.

CHAPTER 3

Enforcing Community Obligation

1 Responsibility for Violation of Collective Obligations: Debates within the International Law Commission

Elihu Root noted that "there must be a change in theory, and violations of the law of such a character as to threaten the peace and order of the community of nations must be deemed to be a violation of the right of every civilized nation to have the law maintained and a legal injury to every nation ... [therefore] ... [e]very State has a direct interest in preventing those violations which, if permitted to continue, would destroy the law".[1] Root's statement is a serious departure from the bilateralist conception of international obligations. It is not only premised on recognition of community obligations but also on the recognition of the right to take action in protection of such obligations. Indeed, the importance of classifying obligations in international law has gained greater prominence in the context of law of state responsibility but more specifically for the purpose of enforcement of collective/community obligations.

Article 48 of the International Law Commission's Articles on State Responsibility represents the most recent attempt to introduce the pathways for enforcement of collective/community obligations.[2] Dupuy was right to note that the merit of Crawford's work as the ILC's special rapporteur on State Responsibility lied in his ability to apply Fitzmaurice's classification of obligations to the law of State responsibility thereby laying ground for various avenues of

1 E. Root, '*The Outlook for International Law*', (1917) 10 *AJIL*, pp. 7–9.

2 For scholarly support of responses against breaches of community obligations E. Vattel (1834), p. 126. For Bluntchli any wrongful act which endangered the entire community justified response from any member of that community to protect the legal order. J. Bluntschli, *Das moderne Völkerrecht der civilizierten Staaten als Rechtsbuch dargestellt,* (Nordlingen, Beck, 1872), p. 264. A. Hall, *Treatise on International Law,* (2nd ed., Oxford, 1909), p. 22; See also Eagleton, who however entertained hopes that the bilateralist nature of international law would transform. He thus notes: "the law of responsibility was not conceived of in terms of duties to the community of nations; there was no thought that an injury to one State might be an injury to the whole community of nations... The responsibility of State (legal person) to State (legal person) will not disappear; but I hope, it will be more clearly delimited, and that procedures will appear, so that we move in the direction of a legal order able to punish disobedience in the name of the organized community of nations". "International Organization and the Law of Responsibility", *Recueil des cours de l'Académie de droit international,* 1950, I, p. 423.

 | DOI:10.1163/9789004380981_005

responses to breaches of obligations by injured States (Article 42) and States other than injured (Article 48).[3]

During the ILC's almost half a century long work on Articles on State Responsibility we have witnessed divergent views on the question of enforcement of community obligations. Some of these views were as progressive as to suggest that the rights of aliens were not the matter reserved exclusively to the jurisdiction of the State of nationality but also concerned other States members of the international community.[4] Much wider support for the community responses against certain breaches of international obligations was expressed by the ILC members in the post *South West Africa and Barcelona Traction* period of the work on the law of state responsibility.[5] The first to broach the question of collective enforcement of treaty obligations during the work of the ILC on the law of State responsibility in 1967 was Tammes. He acknowledged the existence of treaties which vested rights in all parties to the treaty to ensure compliance, yet he was curious whether "there was a collective interest of a community of parties in the integrity of a treaty, and, consequently, a collective active subject of responsibility".[6] Ustor in support of Ushakov's proposition[7] stated that in

3 P. Dupuy, (2002), p. 1072.

4 In his statement Sir Gerald Fitzmaurice noted: "If the Special Rapporteur meant to suggest that a State had a right to intervene only when it had some direct interest in a claim, in other words, only in cases where it had suffered an injury distinct from that done to its national, his formulation constituted an excessive restriction of the right of a State to intervene. ... As a matter of fact, *all States* might be said to have a general interest in the treatment of aliens". YbILC, 1956, Volume I, 372nd Meeting – 21 June 1956, para. 43, p. 244, (A/CN.4/96). See, however, *The Panevevezys-Saldutiskis Railway* case in which PCIJ noted that "In the opinion of the Court, the rule of international law on which the first Lithuanian objection is based is that in taking up the case of one of its nationals, by resorting to diplomatic action or international judicial proceedings on his behalf, a State is in reality asserting its own right, the right to ensure in the person of its nationals respect for the rules of international law. ... Where the injury was done to the national of some other State, no claim to which such injury may give rise falls within the scope of the diplomatic protection which a State is entitled to afford nor can it give rise to a claim which that State is entitled to espouse". PCIJ Series A./B. Judgment of February 28th 1939, p. 16.

5 For careful examination of views of the ILC members see, M. Spinedi, "From One Codification to Another: Bilateralism and Multilateralism in the Genesis of the Codification of the Law of Treaties and the Law of State Responsibility," *EJIL* (2002), Vol. 13 No. 5, pp. 1110–1111. Amongst the examples of violations which could 'directly affect the community of nations' Tabibi mentioned violations of "human rights, the self-determination of peoples and nations, armed attacks, and slavery". See para. 23, p. 183, YbILC, 1970, Volume I, 1075th Meeting (23 June, 1970) (A/CN.4/233).

6 Statement of Tammes, para. 79, p. 225, YbILC, 1967, Volume I, 934th meeting, 6 July 1967 (A/CN.4/196).

7 934th Meeting, YbILC, 1967, Volume I, para. 82, p. 225.

the event of violation of the "regime of the high seas" not only the 'injured State' "but other States should also intervene, because an international rule had been broken" and "the nature of legal interest … should be something in international law similar to *actio publica* in Roman law". He further noted that this "was a burning question, especially in the light of the *South West Africa* cases".[8] Sir Humphrey Waldock also lent unwavering support to the idea of obligations owed to the international community as a whole, which he maintained, emanated from the Charter provisions.[9] Particular emphasis was made on the UN's primary objective of maintaining international peace and security which vests interests in all UN members and entitles them to act to protect such interests.[10]

However, Riphagen, who recognized the obligation to act against the international crime (most probably, at least not to recognize its consequences and cooperate with other States to bring the breach to an end), yet stood against the right to react against international crimes by individual members of the international community.[11] He rejected the possibility of decentralized reactions by individual States taking the role of the "policeman" for the international community. Riphagen recognized such possibility in exceptional circumstances.[12]

Ago's reply to the ILC members contained implicit suggestion that the question raised by the ILC members required revisiting the 'classical' bilateralist conception of international norms.[13] Addressing the issue in the context of international crimes of States, he contended that such a move would open door for the concept of the international responsibility towards the international

8 935th Meeting, YbILC, 1967, Volume I, para. 2, p. 226.

9 YbILC, 1970, Volume I, 1076th meeting, para. 34, p. 190. For support of this view, see also Statement by Ustor, YbILC, 1970, Volume I, para. 10, p. 210, 1079th Meeting (29 June 1970).

10 For instance Abi-Saab maintains that the UN Charter (Article 1) sets as a one of its main objectives attainment and maintenance of international peace and security. This, he notes, constitutes a "common and indivisible good in which everyone, and above all the Organization itself, has an interest, hence a standing to act in order to protect it, through the system of pacific settlement of disputes set out in Chapter 6 and the system of collective security set out in Chapter 7". G. Abi-Saab, (1998), pp. 257–258.

11 Third Report by Willem Riphagen, para. 140, p. 45.

12 Ibid. para. 141, p. 45 with reference to the *Namibia Advisory Opinion* which prompts a conclusion that States may resort to decentralized responses before the UN takes action. Such action was taken by the UN in Namibia case. The UN SC declared the South Africa's acts as unlawful. See however, Arangio-Ruiz who argued that in the absence of the "public prosecutor" to institute proceedings before the ICJ for *erga omnes* breaches this role can only be taken by each member of the international community *ut singuli*. Arangio-Ruiz, Fifth Report, para. 216, p. 49.

13 Ago, 935th Meeting, YbILC, 1967, Volume I, para. 6, p. 227.

community for crimes under international law.[14] He nevertheless expressed scepticism whether recognition of the right of action in collective interest was possible at that stage of development of international law. Ago discarded the possibility of relations of responsibility between the wrongdoing state and the international community, without 'personification' of the latter.[15]

It is evident that the departure from strictly bilateralist conception of inter-state relations in favour of multilateral relations transformed the nature of the law of State responsibility. The latter has left the straightjacket of bilateralism and shifted its focus to the 'global common interest and the rule of law'.[16] These developments raised questions concerning the forms of implementation of responsibility for breaches of collective/community obligations.[17] Akin to decentralized responses in the form of countermeasures, institutional responses to such breaches were amongst the viable avenues to implement responsibility of States for breaches of collective obligations and obligations owed to the international community.[18] UN collective security system may be said to exemplify the point.[19] The final text of the Articles on State Responsibility tried to accommodate concerns raised during the ILC's work regarding gradual recognition of community obligations and the need to effectively protect such obligations.[20] However, during debates in the ILC concerning entitlement to invoke responsibility in the general interest States raised concerns regarding the need for injury/damage as a precondition to invoke responsibility. The new text of the Articles on State Responsibility drew a distinction between the injured States (Article 42) and States other than Injured (Article 48). While the former Article requires injury as a condition to invoke responsibility the latter precluded the requirement of injury to invoke responsibility to enforce collective interests

14 YbILC, 1970, Volume I, 1074th meeting, Statement of Roberto Ago, para. 13, p. 177.

15 Such approach, according to the ILC, would have been similar to the relations which form between the culprit and the State in domestic law. The latter view, however, was without prejudice to the already existing developments in international law of treaties where the breach of obligations by one party to the treaty could warrant lawful responses from all other parties. Second Report of Roberto Ago, para. 22 YbILC, 1970, vol. II., p. 184. Crawford also rejected the idea that the phrase "international community as a whole" implied the "legal personality", para. 37 of his Fourth Report.

16 A. Peters, 'Global Constitutionalism Revisited' (2005)11, *Int'l Legal Theory*, p. 49.

17 P. Dupuy, (2002), pp. 1065–1066.

18 C. Eagleton, (1928), pp. 224–226.

19 P. Dupuy, (2002), pp. 1066–1067. See also A. Gattini, 'A Return Ticket to 'Communitarisme', Please', (2002) 13(5) *EJIL*, p. 1182. Bruno Simma views Covenant of the League of Nations and the UN Charter as first attempts to secure community interests. B. Simma, 'Bilateralism and Community Interest…' (1989), p. 823.

20 Article 48 of the Articles on State Responsibility was meant to serve this purpose.

and interests owed to the international community as a whole. The following two sections provide an analysis of whether injury should be required as a precondition to invoke responsibility and the significance of this requirement in the context of invoking responsibility for breach of collective/community obligations.

2 Invoking Responsibility to Protect Collective Interest: Distinguishing between Injured and Non-injured States

Depending on the nature of the obligation breached the right to invoke responsibility by way of bringing action before international court or tribunal may belong to one State, group of States or all States.[21] It is maintained that in either case the right to invoke responsibility for the internationally wrongful act will be based on the premise of correlativity of rights and obligations, which does not know of any exception.[22] Such correlation 'precludes the possibility of abstract responsibility, that is to say, of responsibility in vacuum'.[23]

---

21 Ago, Second Report, 1970, vol. II, para. 46, pp. 192–193. Ago notes that it is by virtue of the importance of the obligation that its violation affects the interests of all States and not just those which are directly and specifically injured. YbILC, 1976, Vol. I, 1361st Meeting, 4 May 1976, para. 11, p. 8. See also views of Rossides, para. 14, (Ibid), p. 9. Yasseen, para. 4, p. 10, Bedjaoui, para. 9, p. 11, YbILC, 1976, Vol. I, 1362nd Meeting, 5 May who backed Ago's idea of introducing different regimes of responsibility depending on the importance of the obligation breached. However, these debates centered primarily on the distinction between responsibility for what would be international crimes and delicts. See pp. 44–67. The debate centered on this distinction because such distinction was introduced in Article 18 of Ago's Fifth Report. One will not err to say that drafting of Article 18 was profoundly influenced by the decision in the *Barcelona Traction* case. See para. 22 of Ago's statement, YbILC, 1976, Vol. I, pp. 57–58.

22 Ago, Second Report, 1970, vol. II, para. 46, pp. 192–193. In the commentary to Draft Article 3 the ILC noted: "In international law the idea of breach of an obligation can be regarded as the exact equivalent of the idea of infringement of the subjective rights of others ... The correlation between legal obligation on the one hand and subjective right on the other admits of no exception". YbILC, 1973, vol. II, p. 182, para. 9.

23 See ILC's Report on State Responsibility, YbILC 1998, Volume 2, Part Two, para. 342, pp. 78–79. Riphagen states: "In many cases the obligation of a State is merely the counterpart or mirror-image of a right of another State; the obligation is not to infringe that right". Sixth Report by Riphagen, para. 3. Crawford notes, in reply to the comments from governments that Draft Article 1 left the question as to the subjects of responsibility open (French comments in particular) that the wording of Article 1 was deliberately left broad to encompass all possible forms of obligations and forms of responsibility, paras. 119–123 of the First Report by Crawford. Crawford notes that such a broad formulation of Article 1 does not aim to suggest that responsibility may 'exist in a vacuum'. He notes with

The State which is willing to invoke responsibility of the wrongdoing State relies on the 'impairment of the subjective right" which is owed to it.[24] In the *Reparations case,* the ICJ stated that 'only the party to whom an international obligation is due can bring a claim in respect of its breach'.[25] This finding is based on the principle of correlativity of rights and duties, i.e. to every duty there is a correlative right to demand performance of the duty.[26] However, the Court's statement may be given dual meaning. The first meaning is that the principle of correlativity of rights and duties precludes invoking responsibility except in cases when the obligation is owed specially/individually and the States which invoke responsibility of the wrongdoing State do so as injured States. Second meaning which can be accorded to the principle of correlativity rests on the premise that the collective obligations are owed to all States and imply existence of correlative (corresponding) collective rights/interest of all States to enforce such obligation.[27]

Crawford's explanation of the term "subjective" in his Third Report on State Responsibility clearly suggests that he did not mean to confine the meaning of the term as referring to exclusively bilateral relations between states. He suggests that the term does not exclude reliance on collective interests. In support of his contention he refers to *South West Africa* cases and notes that there it was the subjective interests of peoples which were involved rather than the State thus implicitly suggesting that the scope of the term "subjective" was broader.[28]

It is worth noting that the idea of distinguishing between injured States and States other than injured had been taken on board as an alternative to the view that all States had to be treated as injured as a result of violation of community obligations. For instance, special rapporteur Arangio Ruiz proposed to view all

---

reference to Commission's commentary on Article 3 that "all cases of State responsibility have as a correlative an infringement of the actual rights of some other person". See First Report by Crawford, para. 123.

24 Ago, Second Report, 1970, vol. II, para. 46, pp. 192–193. Tams attributes the idea that the term "subjective" limits the scope of responsibility relations to exclusively bilateral to Crawford. Tams (2005) pp. 33–34.

25 *Reparations for Injuries Suffered in the Service of the United Nations,* (Advisory Opinion), ICJ Rep. (1949) 181–182.

26 Hohfeld calls such rights a 'claim right'. (2000), p. 11.

27 See Dissenting Opinion of Judge Weeramantry in *Case Concerning East Timor, Portugal v Australia,* [1995] ICJ Rep. 209.

28 See paras. 84–85 of Crawford's Third Report. However, Crawford himself was very critical of the term "subjective" because it implied that there could be "non-subjective" obligation or right. He stated that the term was "therefore unnecessary as well as potentially misleading". para. 84, Third Report.

states as injured when violation of *erga omnes* or *jus cogens* obligations were involved.[29] However, Arangio Ruiz's proposal was rejected. In its comments on paragraph 3 of Draft Article 40 Germany proposed to differentiate between States which can claim all forms of reparation from those who can only claim cessation of the wrongful act. This proposal sought to classify injured States for the purposes of various forms of reparations available to various categories of states depending on the nature of the injury (damage) they suffered. German objection was motivated by the fact that Draft Article 40 viewed all States as injured as a result of international crime failing to distinguish between States which are specially affected by the violation from those whose interest in invoking responsibility was general. For instance, in case of an act of aggression the interests of the target of an armed attack and of other States fundamentally differ. While the former is specially affected and will be entitled to invoke responsibility as an injured State the latter will invoke responsibility in general interest. The approach taken in Draft Article 40 drew criticism from governments also because by considering in Draft Article 40(2) (e) (iii) all States parties to human rights treaties as injured the Article failed to acknowledge the extra state aspect of human rights obligations.[30] Conversely, in the event of gross human rights violations the interests of States are equally affected and there are no States with more immediate (specific) interests than any other.[31] This follows from the nature of human rights obligations which are not established to protect State interests in any way.[32] The idea of distinguishing between States based on the effects of the violation of community obligations

29 Fourth Report on State Responsibility by Arangio-Ruiz, YbILC, 1992, Volume II, Part One, paras. 92–93, p. 34.

30 See Crawford, Third Report, para. 88. See comments of Japan, para. 6 of Japan's comment on Article 19, Document A/CN.4/492 Comments and observations received from Governments, 10 February 1999.

31 The ICJ in the *Legality of the Threat or Use of Nuclear Weapons* case noted that "a great many rules of humanitarian law applicable in armed conflict are so fundamental to the respect of the human person and 'elementary considerations of humanity' …" that they must "be observed by all States whether or not they have ratified the conventions that contain them, because they constitute intransgressible principles of international customary law". ICJ Rep. 1996(I), para. 79, p. 257. The Court in the *Israeli Wall* case qualified these obligations as being 'essentially of an *erga omnes* character', para. 157, p. 199. See Separate Opinion of Higgins who finds it unnecessary to refer to the *erga omnes* concept because, as the Court itself notes, the obligations under humanitarian law are binding under customary international law. See para. 39, p. 217. On the point that humanitarian law treaties should no more be considered as reciprocal or conditional see T. Meron, *The Humanization of International Law,* (Martinus Nijhoff Publishers, Leiden, 2006), pp. 10–11.

32 Comments of McCaffrey, YbILC, 1985, Vol. II, Part II, 1892nd meeting, para. 6, p. 96.

also featured in Riphagen's third report on State responsibility. According to Riphagen not all States could be viewed as "injured" in their individual capacity even if the breach of an obligation affects 'a fundamental interest of the international community as a whole'.[33] As an example he drew analogy with Article 60, para. 2 of the VCLT, which distinguishes between specially affected and other parties to the treaty. Riphagen suggests that such distinction prompts a conclusion that being a party to the treaty by itself does not suffice to be considered an injured State affected by the breach of the treaty.[34] Crawford notes in this regard that the position of 'specially affected' parties under Article 60(2) of the VCLT differs from the position of other States in that the former acts in its individual interest while the latter do so in collective interest.[35]

The distinction between injured and non-injured States raises salient questions regarding the very concept of "injury", and very often, interchangeably used notion of "damage". As noted above, draft Article 40 did not distinguish between the injured and non-injured States. Under this Article all States were considered injured. The decision to classify States into injured and non-injured revived the discussion on whether the injury or damage must be a necessary

33 See Third Report on State Responsibility by Riphagen, footnote to para. 87, p. 35 of the Report.

34 The same logic, he contends, applies to customary rules of international law. See Third Report by Riphagen, para. 90, p. 36.

35 Para. 114, Third Report by Crawford, p. 37 of the Report. However, both VCLT and Articles on State Responsibility envisage a possibility when all States to the treaty are considered as equally injured. Breach of interdependent obligations "necessarily affects the enjoyment of the rights or the performance of the obligations of other States parties". Crawford, Third Report, para. 91, but with reference to Fitzmaurice's Report in the YbILC, 1957, vol. II, p. 54. Also K. Sachariew, 'State Responsibility for Multilateral Treaty Violations: Identifying the 'Injured State' and its Legal Status' (1988) 35 *NYIL*, p. 281. Note, that Crawford prefers to use the term "interdependent" as opposed to "integral" in the context of article 42 of the Article on State Responsibility. See J. Crawford, *The International Law Commission's Articles on State Responsibility: Introduction, Text and Commentaries*, (CUP, 2002, Cambridge), p. 257, footnote 706. Article 60 (2) (c) of the VCLT refers to the obligations of this kind (the breach of which radically changes position of all other States parties). Hence, all States parties to interdependent obligations are entitled to invoke responsibility as injured States. See para. 112 of Crawford's Third Report. Interdependent obligations are not severable. They "operate in an all-or-nothing fashion". Crawford, Fourth Report, para. 38. Article 42(b)(ii) of Articles on States Responsibility refers to obligations of similar nature. It stipulates: A State is entitled as an injured State to invoke the responsibility of another State if the obligation breached is owed to: (a) that State individually; or (b) a group of States including that State, or the international community as a whole, and the breach of the obligation: (i) specially affects that State; or (ii) is of such a character as radically to change the position of all the other States to which the obligation is owed with respect to the further performance of the obligation.

condition to invoke responsibility. The following analysis aims to address this question.

3 Injury and Damage as a Precondition to Invoke Responsibility: a Bar to Invoke Responsibility to Protect Collective Interests (a Bar to *actio popularis*)

Traditionally damage/injury was seen as a precondition to invoke responsibility.[36] Indeed, the question whether injury/damage constitutes a precondition to invoke responsibility, including by bringing claims before international courts and tribunals, has been central to answering the question regarding legality of *actio popularis*. Classification of States into injured (Article 42) and other than injured States (Article 48) in the Articles on State Responsibility suggests that there are cases when States may invoke responsibility without showing that they suffered an injury or damage. These cases include violations of obligations owed to a group of States or the international community as a whole. However, the proposition that responsibility may be invoked in the absence of injury/damage has had its own critics both amongst the States and the commentators.

The starting point of the analysis regarding requirement to show injury/damage is that neither term (injury or damage) is consistently defined in international law.[37] The meanings of these terms are defined contextually.[38] During the prolonged discussions of the notions of 'injury' and 'damage' and their types in the ILC these terms were understood to refer primarily to material and moral damage or injury.[39] However, quite often 'injury' and 'damage' were used interchangeably.[40] Those who held the view that the terms "injury" and

36 C. Tams, 'Do Serious Breaches Give Rise to Any Specific Obligations of the Responsible State?' (2002) 13(5) *EJIL*, p. 1151. Also, E. Wyler, 'From "State Crime" to Responsibility for Serious breaches under Peremptory Norms of General International Law', (2002) 13 *EJIL*, pp. 1151–1152.

37 Fifty-third session, Geneva, 23 April–1 June, 2 July–10 August 2000, A/CN.4/517, para. 30 of Crawford's Fourth Report.

38 Para. 30 of Crawford's Fourth Report.

39 See also C. Dominice, 'The International Responsibility of States for Breach of Multilateral Obligations', (1999) 10(2) EJIL, pp. 359–360; K Sachariew, (1988), pp. 274–276; C. Eagleton (1928), p. 22.

40 Garcia Amador, Responsibility of the State for Injuries Caused in its Territory to the Person or Property of Aliens – Reparation of the Injury, Sixth Report, YbILC, 1961, Vol. II, pp. 3–14.

"damage" had divergent meanings argued that the former referred to impairment of a right while the latter also included material or moral damage ("in the ordinary sense of the word").[41] The distinction was introduced by Arangio-Ruiz who used the terms "injury" and "damage" as referring respectively to concepts of a "legal injury"[42] or *injuria* (legal wrong) and 'material or other loss'.[43] The Articles on State Responsibility recognize the distinction and use the term "injury" as a broader notion. According to Article 31(2) 'injury' includes 'any damage, *whether material or moral*, caused by the internationally wrongful act of a State'. According to paragraph 2 of the Commentary to Chapter 1 of Part Three of the ASR an 'injured State' is the "State whose individual right has been denied or impaired by the internationally wrongful act or which has otherwise been particularly affected by that act". Paragraph 5 of the Commentary to Article 31 describes material damage as 'damage to property or other interests of the State and its nationals which is assessable in financial terms'. The same paragraph defines moral damage as including such things as 'individual pain and suffering, loss of loved ones or personal affront associated with an intrusion on one's home or private life'. It also includes a moral damage to a State i.e. 'the affront or injury caused by a violation of rights not associated with actual damage to property or persons'.[44] It follows that the concept of injury is broader than damage. However, injury does not always arise from damage. For instance, failure to enact domestic legislation in accordance with international treaty obligations does not cause any damage to parties to the treaty. Therefore, one would not err to say that whether damage is a prerequisite for existence of an internationally wrongful act depends on the primary norm.[45] Crawford notes: "It may be that many primary rules do contain a requirement of damage, however defined. Some certainly do. But there is no warrant for the suggestion that this is necessarily the case, that it is an *a priori* requirement".[46]

41 Third Report by Riphagen, footnote to para. 81 at p. 35 of the Report. On the contrary, Garcia Amador maintained that the words "injury" and "damage" were synonymous in English and different languages used different words to refer to the same notion. See Amador, Sixth report, para. 28, p. 8.

42 J. Barboza, 'Legal Injury: the Tip of the Iceberg in the Law of State Responsibility' in M Raggazi (eds.), *International Responsibility Today: Essays in Honour of Oscar Schacter* (Martinus Nijhoff Publishers, Boston 2005) p. 9.

43 See para 99 of Crawford's First Report.

44 Garcia Amador used the term 'political injury' to refer to moral injury to a State. See Garcia Amador, Responsibility of the State for Injuries Caused in its Territory to the Person or Property of Aliens – Reparation of the Injury, Sixth Report, YbILC, 1961, p. 7, para. 27.

45 Para. 113 of Crawford's First Report. See also Fourth Report by Riphagen, para. 74, p. 14.

46 Para. 113 of Crawford's First Report. J Crawford, Fourth Report on State Responsibility, ILC, 'Report of the International Law Commission on the Work of its 53rd Session (23 April–1

Articles on State Responsibility adopt the same logic.[47] Amongst the examples of obligations the breach of which does not produce any damage Crawford mentioned international human rights, or other obligations which States commit to uphold with respect to their own citizens, 'protection of environment, disarmament or other "preventive" obligations in the field of peace and security, and development of uniform standards or rules in such fields as private international law".[48] These are obligations established to protect collective interests and the absence of the material or moral damage or of any special interest of a State party is the very essence of such obligations.[49] The States are interested in protection of human rights not because they suffer particular form of damage (moral or material) but because violations of those rights are 'specifically prohibited by international treaties or general international law'.[50]

On the other hand, "the term "injury" is used only when referring to infringement of the subjective right of another, which was exactly equivalent to failure to fulfill a legal obligation to another".[51] According to Ago the injury was

---

June, 2 July–10 August 2000) A/CN.4/517, para. 28. For strong support of this view see C. Dominice, 'The International Responsibility of States...' (1999), pp. 359–360.

47 Paragraph 9 of the commentary to Article 2 of the ASR states that whether element of damage is required for existence of an internationally wrongful act depends on the 'content' and 'interpretation' of the primary norm. YbILC, 2001, p. 36. This notwithstanding, the commentary to Articles on State Responsibility notes that certain breaches of obligations produce no damage at all. By way of example, paragraph 9 refers to failure of a State to implement a domestic act in accordance with its international obligations. See para. 12 of the Commentary to article 12 of the ASR regarding instances of a legislation resulting in breach of an international obligation. See also para. 3 of the Commentary to Article 14 of the ASR on the legislative measure as an example of a continuing wrongful act. YbILC, 2001, Vol. II, Part Two, pp. 57 and 60 respectively. For a view that failure to take legislative actions in breach of international obligations causes moral and material injury see remarks of ILC Chairman Jorge Castaneda, para. 32, YbILC 1973, Vol. I, p. 26.

48 Para. 114, First Report by Crawford. Preservation of environment or equitable use of natural resources do not normally affect individual interests of a particular State. All members of international community are equally affected by a breach of norms concerning preservation and equitable use of environment and natural resources. R. Lefeber, 'The Existence of Jurisdiction in the Antarctic Region and the Changing Structure of International Law: The International Community and Common Interests', (1990), 21 *NYIL*, p. 91.

49 See First Report on State Responsibility by James Crawford, YbILC, 1998, Volume II, Part One, para. 22 (although it is possible that one or more States may be materially injured as a result of *erga omnes* breach).

50 Crawford, First Report, para. 116.

51 Second Report on State Responsibility, YbILC, 1970, vol. II, p. 194. For the views of individual ILC members see also YbILC, 1970, Vol. I for remarks of Rosenne, p. 220, para. 61; Alcivar, p. 217, para. 27; Nagendra Singh, p. 211, paras. 21–22; Eustathiades, p. 191, para. 43; Reuter, pp. 188–189, para. 12; Carsten, p. 186, para. 48. YbILC, 1970, Volume I, para. 33, 1081st Meeting (2 July 1970). Carsten also expressed support for Ago's position. YbILC, 1970,

inherent in 'every impairment of a subjective right".[52] Hence, he maintained, that existence of the internationally wrongful act, albeit not producing any material or moral damage, suffices to invoke responsibility by way of seeking declaratory judgment from the court.[53]

Nevertheless concerns were also expressed that damage should be treated as a separate element (external event) required for existence of an internationally wrongful act.[54] In its comments on Article 3 (Elements of an Internationally wrongful act) of the 1996 Draft Articles Argentina noted that in order to exercise its claim a State which invokes responsibility should be able to show damage (moral or financial).[55] Argentina noted in this regard: "The damage requirement, is in reality, an expression of the basic principle which stipulates that no one undertakes an action without an interest of a legal nature".[56] France too, in its comments on the same draft Article, stated that 'without damage, there was no international responsibility. This means that a State cannot file a

Volume I, 1075th Meeting, para. 48, p. 186. See Also Reuter lending support for this view. YbILC, Volume I, 1970, 1976th Meeting (24 June 1970) (AC/CN.4/233), paras. 12–13, p. 188 and Alcivar, YbILC, 1970, Volume I, 1080th Meeting, para. 27, p. 217.

52 Second Report by Roberto Ago, YbILC, 1970, Vol. II, para. 54, p. 195. He mentioned failure by a State to enact legislation as one of the examples of internationally wrongful act not producing any injury. YbILC, 1973, Vol. I, 1205th Meeting, 15 May, 1973, para. 16, p. 20.

53 Sixth Report by Garcia Amador, YbILC, 1961 (Document A/CN.4/134), para. 15, p. 5. For the view that third parties, i.e. interested States, cannot ask for pecuniary damage but can only ask for declaratory judgment see D. Hutchinson, Solidarity and Breaches of Multilateral Treaties, *BYIL*, 1988, pp. 159–162.

54 It has to be noted that the Articles on State Responsibility finally adopted in 2001 discard existence of damage as a separate condition necessary to invoke responsibility. This conclusion follows from Article 2 of the ASR and the commentaries thereto. Under this Article an internationally wrongful act of a State exists when conduct constitutes a breach of an international obligation of a State and is attributable to that State. YbILC, 2001, Vol. II, Part Two, para. 34.

55 YbILC, 1998, Vol. II, Part One, para. 4, p. 103, ibid, para. 4, p. 101. Argentina did not exclude the possibility of damage being a necessary condition to invoke responsibility in various contexts. Argentina maintained with reference to the ILC's comments on Draft Article 3 that it was possible to invoke responsibility when breach does not produce 'economic injury to other States…' or cause injury to 'their honour or dignity'. YbILC, 1973, vol. II, p. 183, para. 12. Human rights and labour conventions were mentioned amongst those obligations which did not require injury. See para. 2 of comments by Argentina on Draft Article 1, Document A/CN.4/488 and Add. 1–3; For a view that breach of human rights obligations causes moral injury see comments of Argentina on Article 3 (Elements of an internationally wrongful act of a State) of the 1996 Draft Articles. YbILC, 1998, Vol. II, Part One, para. 5, p. 103. See O. Schacter who mentions human right and labour standards as examples of breaches not causing 'non-material injury'. (1991), p. 206.

56 Reproduced in First Report on State Responsibility of James Crawford, p. 28, para. 108, Argentinian Comments on Draft Article 3.

claim without having an identifiable, specific legal interest'.[57] France opposed Draft Articles 1 and 3 because it felt that they created "international public order". For France, international responsibility must aim at protecting subjective rights of States.[58] France believed that a specific legal interest may serve as a basis to invoke responsibility and such an interest may only arise if a State which is willing to invoke responsibility suffers some form of damage, i.e. material or moral.[59] This position was informed by France's caution that any other approach could have led to the extension of law of state responsibility to the '*protection of international law as such*', i.e. introduce *actio popularis*.[60] France's position also echoed with some of the ILC members.[61] The United States took a more moderate approach denying the requirement of the existence of injury in the context of human rights conventions and other conventions of similar nature.[62]

France's comments must be viewed in the context of the nature of obligations in international law. French conception of injury in effect amounts to denial of community obligations which envisage that all States may have an interest in ensuring compliance with such obligations.[63]

---

57 YbILC, 1998, Vol. II, Part One, para. 4, p. 101.

58 See para. 1 of comments by French Government. Document A/CN.4/488 and Add. 1–3.

59 See also French position in the *Rainbow Warrior* (*New Zealand/France*), UNRIAA, vol. XX, (1990), p. 217 at pp. 272–273, para. 107.

60 See para. 4 of French comments on Article 1, Document A/CN.4/488 and Add. 1–3. See also B. Stern, 'A Plea for 'Reconstruction' of International Responsibility Based on the Notion of Legal Injury' in M. Raggazi (2005), p. 102. For a view that collective interests stem from the international 'duty' violation of which does not cause injury to any State and all States are interested in protection of those interests see C. Lorens 'Deberes jurídicos y responsabilidad internacional' (Legal Duties and International Responsibility), *Hacia un nuevo orden europea e internacional. Homenaje al Profesor Manuel Díez de Velasco*, (Civitas, Madrid 1993,) pp. 147–166. See, Review of the Spanish Literature in the Field of State Responsibility by Carlos D. Esposito http://www.lcil.cam.ac.uk/projects/state_responsibility_document_collection.php.

61 See Statement of Thiam. YbILC, 1970, Volume I, para. 33, p. 233, 1079th Meeting (29 June 1970). See also similar statements of Bartos, YbILC, 1970, Volume I, para. 50, p. 215, 1079th Meeting (29 June 1970); Kearney, YbILC, 1970, Volume I, paras. 42–43, p. 218, 1080th Meeting.

62 See US Comments on Article 19, para. 2, quoted in First Report by Crawford, para. 24, p. 7 of the Report.

63 See See comments by France, quoted in First Report by Crawford, para. 22, p. 7 of the Report. See however comment of Italian government that "…in the case of the breach of what are referred to as *erga omnes* obligations all States addressed by the norm should be regarded as having had a subjective right injured and, consequently, as having suffered *legal damage*" (emphasis added). YbILC, 1998, Vol. II, Part One, para. 5, p. 104.

The foregoing analysis illustrates that indeed the concepts of injury and damage had not been consistently used. However, regardless of meaning the terms injury and damage may have, the central point is that for some States the right to invoke responsibility could only arise if the obligation was owed individually to that State, i.e. if that State is injured. As was already stated Article 48 of the Articles on State Responsibility obviates the need to show injury in order to invoke responsibility of the wrongdoing State for violation of collective/community obligations under international law in general. However, requirement of injury or damage as a condition to invoke responsibility features in the context of judicial claims and manifests itself as a procedural issue in the form of a requirement to show interest/legal interest to bring a claim.[64] The following analysis explores the ways in which the requirement to show interest affects the claimant's *locus standi* to judicially enforce collective/community obligations.

---

64 However, this requirement does not apply across all international courts and tribunals. These exceptional cases will be dealt with as we proceed with the analysis.

CHAPTER 4

Judicial Enforcement of Community Obligations

1 Ineffectiveness of "Bipolar" Litigation in Protection of Collective Interests

Dispute settlement both in domestic and international law is ordinarily confined to bilateral disputes, i.e. disputes in which parties seek to protect their private/individual/special interests/rights.[1] However, there are claims which may extend beyond purely bilateral/private interests and involve interest of groups, collectivities and entire communities. In this situation, the traditionally 'bipolar' litigation proves to be inadequate. Therefore, the need to ensure effective protection of the collective interests makes it necessary to introduce new forms of litigation and create procedural channels through which the *utilitas publica* could be protected.[2] *Actio popularis* claims (public interest litigation) can be devised as one of such means of litigation.

As a rule, *actio popularis* claims are resorted to protect vulnerable groups (human rights of certain groups unable to protect themselves) and commons, such as environment[3] or simply to ensure compliance with law.[4] A more relevant feature of *actio popularis* is that claimant's interest does not differ (stand out) in any way from the interest of any other community member.[5] In these proceedings public, as a whole, becomes interested in the outcome of the proceedings and no member of the public has an interest in protection of such interests paramount to that of any other member of the public.[6] However, it

1 A. Chayes, The Role of the Judge in Public Law Litigation, 1976(89)(7), *Harvard Law Review,* p. 1282.

2 Ibid, pp. 1282–1284 and 1294–1295. G. Samuel, 'The Notion of an Interest as a Formal Concept in English and in Comparative Law before the Court' in Guy Canivet, Mads Andenas, and Duncan Fairgrieve (eds.), *Comparative Law Before the Courts,* (The British Institute of International and Comparative Law, London, 2004), p. 281. See also R. Jenks, *The Prospects of International Adjudication* (Oceana Publications, 1964), p. 184.

3 H. Hershkoff, Public Law Litigation: Lessons and Questions, (2009)10, *Human Rights Review,* pp. 157–181.

4 M. Thio (1971), pp. 2–3.

5 M. Taggart, Rugby, the Anti-apartheid Movement, and Administrative Law in R. Bigwood (eds.), *Public Interest Litigation: New Zealand Experience in International Perspective,* (LexisNexis, Wellington, Limited, 2006), p. 77.

6 C. Schall, 'Public Interest Litigation Concerning Environmental Matters before Human Rights Courts: A Promising Future Concept?' – (2008) 20(3) *Journal of Environmental Law,* p. 43.

 | DOI:10.1163/9789004380981_006

is possible that public interests receive protection through enforcement of the claimant's special interests.[7] This becomes possible when the claimant's individual interest affected by the breach of an obligation is inseparable from the general interest of the international community protected by the same obligation.[8] For instance, a claim by a State which is injured by the oil spill in the high seas will seek to redress the personal injury, however, it also will indirectly provide a redress to the general community of States by obtaining a declaration (in addition to the request for award of damages/compensation) from the court concerning the legality of the wrongdoer's conduct. Although there are examples of States which declare intend to protect both the special and the interest of the international community, yet when the claimant does not make such intention clear the interests of the international community become protected by proxy and become a positive 'side effect' of protection of special interests.

Relaxation of the rules of standing to the extent that the claimant does not need to show any interest in the subject matter of the claim has been viewed as a means of adjusting the procedural norms to the changing nature of substantive norms of international law.[9] This approach is adopted in the context of broadly invoking responsibility of States for violation of international community obligations. Article 48 of the Articles on State Responsibility which obviates the need to show any injury on the part of the State which invokes responsibility for violation of collective/community obligations exemplifies the point very well. The analysis of the debates in the context of the ILC's work on State responsibility conspicuously illustrates the concerns which some States had as regards the ILC's decision to drop the requirement of injury as a precondition to invoke responsibility. Those concerns explain the determined view of majority of ILC members that Article 48 of the Articles on State Responsibility did not reflect existing state of positive international law. It has already been noted that the question whether injury (legal interest/interest) should be

7 On the broader societal importance of certain claims see J. Goldston, 'Public Interest Litigation in Central and Eastern Europe: Roots, Prospects, and Challenges', 28 (2006), *Human Rights Quarterly*, p. 496.

8 This is also characteristic of public interest litigation in domestic law. For instance, claims brought to challenge statutes or executive orders may involve questions, which albeit affect the immediate/private/individual interests of the claimant, yet have much wider implications for the public at large. A. Chayes, (1976), p. 1294. See also J. Jolowitz, 'Protection of Diffuse, Fragmented and Collective Interests in Civil Litigation: English Law', (1983) 42(2) *Cambridge Law Journal*, p. 223.

9 D. Gruner, 'Accounting for the Public Interest in International Arbitration: The Need for Procedural and Structural Reform', (2003) 41 *Columbia Journal of Transnational Law*, p. 924.

a precondition to invoke responsibility is also raised in the context of claims to protect general/collective interests before international courts and tribunals. However, the treatment of this question before international courts and tribunals needs a more nuanced approach. The reason lies in the fact that the difference in the constitutive instruments and the rules of standing of various international courts and tribunals will require an answer based on a seriatim analysis of the standing rules of individual international courts and tribunals which may exclude a definitive conclusion as to whether requirement of injury/damage (legal interest/interest) precludes claims to protect collective interests, i.e. *actio popularis* claims.

2 Injury/Damage (Legal Interest/Interest) as a Condition to Bring a Claim before International Courts and Tribunals

It has already been pointed out that the requirement of injury or damage before international courts and tribunals is expressed in the claimant's ability to show interest/legal interest in the case. In other words, the claimant's interest arises from the injury or damage it suffers. Traditionally claims brought before both domestic and international tribunals have been contingent on the claimant's ability to demonstrate some sort of individual injury/interest.[10] *'Point d'intérêt – point d'action'* is a legal adage, which preconditions an action before a court on the claimant's ability to show an interest in the case.[11]

The claimant's interest in the case may arise both from the violation of the obligations owed to the claimant, but also as a result of the damage done to the claimant in the absence of a violation of any legal obligation and the corresponding legal right.[12] WTO law exemplifies the latter. For instance, Article

10 According to Winiarski, the requirement that any claimant must have demonstrated individual interests was the requirement of the 'general rule of procedure' which the Applicants must have met before submitting a claim before any court, whether municipal or international. He even went further to suggest that the requirement to show interest is a 'principle of international law…". Dissenting Op. of Winiarski, *South West Africa* case, 1962, ICJ Rep. p. 456.

11 P van Dijk, *'Judicial Review'* (1980), p. 369.

12 That the 'interest' to sue may derive both from the conduct which violates legal rights but also from damage not arising from a breach of legal rights see the statement of the Tribunal in the *Lac Lanoux* arbitral award. The Tribunal noted: "It must be determined what are the 'interests' which have to be safeguarded. A strict interpretation of Article 11 would permit the reading that the only interests are those which correspond with a riparian right. However, various considerations which have already been explained by the Tribunal lead to a more literal interpretation. Account must be taken of all interests, of

XXIII (1)(b) of the GATT entitles 'any contracting party' to resort to procedures in paragraph (1)(C) and paragraph 2 of Article XXIII if it "should consider that any benefit accruing to it directly or indirectly under this Agreement is being nullified or impaired or that the attainment of any objective of the Agreement is being impeded as the result of … the application by another contracting party of any measure, *whether or not it conflicts with the provisions of this Agreement…*" Subject to such exceptions in the nature of *lex specialis* it is cogent to argue that ability to show a legal interest/interest represents a general principle of law, which preconditions claims before courts.[13] Despite international courts and tribunals routinely addressing the question of the claimants' *jus standi* and engaging in construction of the rules of standing it is still hard to find any authority, which would provide a conclusive and uniformly applicable definition of 'interest/legal interest'. Neither constitutive instruments nor the rules of procedure/standing of the international courts and tribunals define this notion. The analysis of the case law of international courts and tribunals does not reveal a consistent pattern of application and interpretation of the notion either.[14]

For the purposes of the analysis, the term 'interest' is used as a generic term referring to any cause of action arising from a damage or injury (may be arising from a violation) caused to the claimant by violation of the international obligation or in the absence of such violation.[15] Examination of the standing provisions of international treaty instruments on standing reveals that terms, which refer to 'interest to sue' as defined above differ. For instance, the notions of "victim" in Article 34 of the European Convention on Human Rights and Fundamental Freedoms, or "direct and individual concern" in Article 263

---

whatsoever nature, which are liable to be affected by the works undertaken, even if they do not correspond to a right. Only such a solution complies with the terms of Article 16, with the spirit of Pyrenees Treaties, and with the tendencies which are manifested in instances of hydroelectric development in current international practice". *Lac Lanoux*, See English translation of the decision in ILR 1957, vol. 24, para. 22, pp. 138–139.

13 See para. 15 of the WTO Appellate Body Report in European Communities-Regime for the Importation, Sale and Distribution of Bananas, AB 1997-3, WT/DS27/AB/R, 9 September 1997.

14 This precludes cases in which the interest constitutes merely an expression of subjective desire which is distinguishable from an interest which is protected by a rule of law. The Court in the *Northern Cameroons* case confirmed that there is no 'common meaning' of the term "interest" and that it is meaning is contextually defined. (1963), p. 28.

15 However, 'interest' also has a specific meaning distinct from 'interest' which justifies a claim before a court. The difference will be highlighted as we proceed with the analysis. The distinction was drawn in the *Barcelona Traction* case between the "rights" of the company and the shareholders' "interests".

of the Treaty on the Functioning of the European Union, or "benefit" under Article XXIII of the GATT, or a "legal dispute" in Article 36(2) of the Statute of the International Court of Justice, all refer to the claimant's ability to show 'interest' to sue before a relevant competent court or tribunal. Traditionally, the condition to show interest has served the sole objective of avoiding the flood of 'by-passer' claims and to circumscribe the circle of claimants to those whose interests were specially affected.[16] In effect, the very purpose of applying the rules of standing and require demonstrating interest was to avoid *actio popularis*. Unlike ordinary claims (*actio*), actions brought before courts by way of *actio popularis* are not contingent upon the claimant's satisfaction of the requirement to show individual interest.[17] However, analysis of the case law of various international courts and tribunals which is illustrated hereafter prompts a conclusion that even in cases where the claimant was required by the treaty norms (rules of standing) to show 'interest' these rules have been interpreted and applied by courts in a way that *de facto* introduced *actio popularis* and made requirement to show individual interest redundant.

The following analysis aims to illustrate the ways in which divergent interpretations of the 'interest' may affect the issue of standing and the claimants' ability to institute *actio popularis*.

16 Van Dijk (1980), p. 45.

17 For instance, Article 44 of the American Convention on Human Rights states: "Any person or group of persons, or any nongovernmental entity legally recognized in one or more member States of the Organization, may lodge petition with the Commission containing denunciations or complaints of violation of this Convention by a State party".

CHAPTER 5

Actio popularis before the ICJ

1 Deconstructing the "Legal Dispute"

The International Court of Justice is compelled to address the question of applicants' *locus standi* almost in every case. In doing so ICJ invariably ensures that the applicant is able to show interest/legal interest in the case. ICJ does so by determining whether there is a legal dispute between the parties in accordance with Article 36 of the ICJ's Statute, terms of the compromissory clauses of various international treaty instruments, as well as optional clause declarations.[1]

The ICJ's decisions concerning existence of a legal dispute and exercise of jurisdiction have been primarily limited to claims arising from the breach of bilateralist obligations. Usually, in such cases the question of standing is decided with little or no controversy. However, controversy arises when the claim is brought to protect collective/ community interests.

It has already been noted that judicial enforcement of collective interests is subject to procedural constraints. Even where a primary norm (whether treaty or customary) is established to protect collective interests judicial enforcement of such interests is only possible in accordance with the terms of the compromissory clauses of the relevant treaty instrument or the optional clause declarations in accordance with Articles 36 paragraph 1 and 36 paragraph 2 of the ICJ Statute.

According to Article 36 paragraph 1 of the Statute of the International Court of Justice "the jurisdiction of the Court comprises all cases which the parties refer to it and all matters specially provided for in the Charter of the United Nations or in treaties or conventions in force". This article applies to cases, which can be brought before the ICJ in accordance with the compromissory clauses of international treaty instruments.[2] Examples of such treaties are countless. However, international conventions, which are established to protect collective

1 Analysis of optional clause declarations revealed that they all require the existence of a legal dispute in Accordance with Article 36 of the ICJ's Statute. Full texts of optional clause declarations are available at http://www.icj-cij.org/jurisdiction/index.php?p1=5&p2=1&p3=3.

2 C. Tams, 'Continued Relevance of Compromissory Clauses as a Source of ICJ Jurisdiction', in T. Giegerich, (eds.), *A Wiser Century? – Judicial Dispute Settlement, Disarmament and the Laws of War 100 Years After the Second Peace Conference* (Duncker & Humbolt, Berlin 2009), p. 50.

 | DOI:10.1163/9789004380981_007

interests and contain compromissory clauses are also abundant and these are of direct interest for us.[3] The wording of the compromissory clauses in such treaties is almost identical. For instance, Article IX of the Genocide Convention stipulates that "Disputes between the Contracting Parties relating to the interpretation, application or fulfilment of the present Convention, including those relating to the responsibility of a State for genocide or any of the other acts enumerated in Article 3, shall be submitted to the International Court of Justice at the request of any of the parties to the dispute".

The key word here is "disputes" which refers to legal disputes. As noted, both the ICJ Statute, and the UN Charter as a whole, make references to the term "legal dispute".[4] However, neither the treaty instruments nor the ICJ Statute provide for a definition of "dispute" or a "legal dispute". This has prompted both the ICJ and its predecessor the Permanent Court of International Justice, from the early days of their creation, to elaborate definitions of these terms.

In its decision in the *Mavrommatis Palestine Concessions* case[5] the Permanent Court of International Justice defined the dispute as follows: "A dispute is a disagreement on a point of law or fact, a conflict of legal views or of interests between two persons".[6] This definition of a 'dispute' is very loose. Literal

3 See p. 52 for the list of treaty instruments in human rights field with jurisdictional clauses. Article XI of the Antarctic Treaty, December 1, 1959; Article 37 of the ILO Constitution; Article 287 of the Law of the Sea Convention exemplify jurisdictional clauses not related to human rights treaties.

4 Article 36(3) of the UN Charter, 36(2) of the ICJ Statute.

5 The *Mavrommatis Palestine Concessions* case involved direct injury done to Greece through its nationals on whose behalf Greece was espousing the claim against United Kingdom. PCIJ, Series A – No 2, August 30th, 1924, pp. 11–12. 'Whoever ill-treats a citizen indirectly injures the State, which must protect its citizen. 3 E. De Vattel, Classics of International Law: The Law of Nations or the Principles of Natural Law, p. 136, *quoted in* McDougal, M. Chen, H. Rassel, *Human Rights and the World Public Order,* (Yale University Press, London, 1980), p. 867.

6 In the *Interpretation of Peace Treaties with Bulgaria, Hungary and Romania* the Court in defining the dispute noted that "the two sides hold clearly opposite views concerning the question of the performance or non-performance of certain treaty obligations" and stated that "international disputes have arisen". In the absence of record of views of the parties or if one of the parties makes no responses to the claims of the other party the opposing attitudes of the parties are sufficient to establish a dispute between parties. *Interpretation of Peace Treaties with Bulgaria, Hungary and Romania,* First Phase, ICJ Rep. 1950, p. 65, at p. 74. See also *Northern Cameroons case,* ICJ Rep. 1963, p. 27. In addressing the UK's first preliminary Objection that no dispute arose between itself and Cameroon the Court noted: "… the opposing views of the Parties as to the interpretation and application of relevant Articles of the Trusteeship Agreement, reveal the existence of a dispute … between the Republic of Cameroon and the United Kingdom at the date of the Application. *Northern Cameroons case,* ICJ Rep. p. 27. See also *Consular Staff* case in which the Court found that there was a dispute between the US and Iran based on the US claims that the Iran's actions amounted to breach of its

reading of this definition suggests that the ICJ may consider any 'disagreement on a point of law or fact', involving any conflict of interests, whether this conflict involves claimant's special or general interests. The words "conflict of legal views" also point to this conclusion. The definition of a 'dispute' in the *Mavrommatis* case seems to suggest that a requirement to show an individual/special interest/legal interest is not a precondition to bring a claim before the ICJ. In other words, such reading of the definition opens the door for *actio popularis*.[7] Nevertheless, the ICJ's subsequent practice indicates that the Court, for many years, had been rather cautious to allow for very liberal interpretation of the definition in the *Mavrommatis* case so as to open the door for claims in the absence of special/individual interest. Most prominent of the cases, which are widely recognized as providing a restrictive interpretation of the 'dispute' and the claimants' interest in the case are the *South West Africa cases*.[8] Firstly, these cases are important because they define more clearly the scope of the definition developed in the *Mavrommatis* case.[9] Secondly, they illustrate how construction of a 'legal dispute', in conjunction with interpretation of the substantive norms, determines the circle of States (subjects) entitled to institute proceedings before the Court and possibly open the door for *actio popularis*.

In the *South West Africa cases* the problem of a definition of a 'dispute' under compromissory clause of the Mandate Agreement was quickly and perhaps inadvertently transformed into a much more complex and broader question of the legality of *actio popularis* in international law. The ICJ, when seized of

---

obligations. Despite Iran did not oppose US's claims Iran's contrary attitude led to the rise of a dispute as between the parties. ICJ Reports 1980, pp. 24–25, para. 46.

7 View supporting this proposition was voiced by Judge Bustamente who stated: "Whenever Great Britain as Mandatory performs in Palestine under the Mandate acts of a general nature affecting the public interest, the Members of the League – from which she holds the Mandate – are entitled, provided that all other conditions are fulfilled, to have recourse, to the Permanent Court". *Mavrommatis Palestine Concessions*, Dissenting Opinion of Judge Bustamante, PCIJ., Series A, No. 2, p. 81.

8 (1966).

9 PCIJ, Series A – No 2, August 30th, 1924, p. 11. The ICJ in the 1962 South West Africa decision noted: "… it is not sufficient for one party to a contentious case to assert that a dispute exists with the other party. A mere assertion is not sufficient to prove the existence of a dispute any more than a mere denial of the existence of the dispute proves its non-existence. Nor is it adequate to show that the interests of two parties to such a case are in conflict. It must be shown that the claim of one party is positively opposed by the other". *South West Africa* decision, ICJ Rep. 21 December, 1962, p. 319, at p. 328. See also C. Tomuschat, Commentary on Article 36 of the ICJ Statute, in A. Zimmermann, C. Tomuschat, K. Oellers-Frahm, (eds.), *The Statute of the International Court of Justice: A Commentary*, (OUP, Oxford, 2006), p. 597.

the case, could not have possibly foreseen that it would deliver one of its most controversial and criticized decisions ever.[10]

The case was brought before the ICJ by the governments of Ethiopia and Liberia which filed separate applications on November 4, 1960 against Union of South Africa.[11] The applicants relied on Article 7(2) of the Mandate Agreement as a jurisdictional basis of their application. Article 7(2) of the Mandate Agreement stated:

> The Mandatory agrees that, if any dispute whatever should arise between the Mandatory and another Member of the League of Nations relating to the interpretation or the application of the provisions of the Mandate, such dispute, if it cannot be settled by negotiation, shall be submitted to the Permanent Court of International Justice provided for by Article 14 of the Covenant of the League of Nations.

The Applicants contended that there was a dispute between themselves and the Respondent under Article 7 of the Mandate Agreement because the Respondent denied the Applicants' claims of violation of Article 22[12] of the Covenant of the League of Nations and Articles 2 (failure to promote to the utmost the material and moral well-being and social progress of the inhabitants of the Territory), 4, 6 (failure to submit to the Council of the League of Nations

10 The following passage reflects the view widely shared about the ICJ's decision in the *South West Africa* cases: "The Court's Judgment on the Second Phase of the *South West Africa cases* was given on 18 July 1966. The Twenty-First Session of the General Assembly commenced in September 1966, p. 427. The Judgment, the Court, and individual Members thereof *were* immediately made the targets of near-hysterical abuse and vilification. The Judgment was variously described as "deplorable", "shocking", "shameful", "a distortion of law", "a denial of justice", "an insult to the international conscience and to mankind", one of the most flagrant denials of justice in its [the Court's] history", "scandalous", "a scandal without precedent", an "infamy", "disgraceful", "perverse", "scandalous and wicked", "iniquitous", "a veritable scandal", "shameful", "grotesque", "travesty of justice" and "tangential and devious". Written Statement of South Africa, Namibia Advisory Opinion, para. 7, pp. 427–428 of the Statement.

11 By Order of May 20, 1961 the Court consolidated the two Applications in one case and requested the parties to submit separate memorials. ICJ Rep. 1961, p. 13.

12 Article 22 of the Covenant of the League of Nations stipulates: "To those colonies and territories which as a consequence of the late war have ceased to be under the sovereignty of the States which formerly governed them and which are inhabited by peoples not yet able to stand by themselves under the strenuous conditions of the modern world, there should be applied the principle that the well-being and development of such peoples form a sacred trust of civilisation and that securities for the performance of this trust should be embodied in this Covenant".

an annual report ... containing full information with regard to the territory, and indicating the measures taken to carry out the obligations assumed under Articles 2, 3, 4 and 5), and 7 of the Mandate Agreement.[13]

The Applicants maintained to derive their legal interest from the "right to invoke the compulsory jurisdiction of the PCIJ" under Article 7(2)[14] and to submit to the PCIJ a "dispute concerning Respondent's conduct of its obligations toward the inhabitants of the Territory". The Applicants noted that they had a "legal interest in seeing it through the judicial process that the sacred trust of civilization created by the Mandate is not violated".[15] Basically, the Applicants argued that Article 7(2) of the Mandate Agreement served as a jurisdictional clause (i.e. a procedural norm) to enforce substantive rights/obligations which were expressed in Article 22 of the Mandate Agreement and other provisions of the Mandate Agreement and which materialized in the concept of the 'sacred trust of civilization'. For the Applicants, the latter concept envisioned "obligations of a legal nature, in accordance with the expressed objective of the organized international community to afford legal protection to the well-being and social progress of the inhabitants of mandated territories...".[16] The Applicants noted in this respect:

> In instituting these proceedings, Applicants have moved to protect not only their own legal interests but the legal interests of the United Nations (which itself, may not be a party to contentious proceedings), as well as the legal interests of every other Member State similarly situated.[17] The Applicants further noted: "While it (the dispute) affects the interests of Applicants in assuring compliance with international undertakings, in furthering the principles of the Charter, and in promoting the welfare and human rights of the inhabitants of the Mandated Territory, *it is not*

13 See Application of Ethiopia, ICJ, Pleadings, Oral Arguments, Documents, South West Africa cases (*Ethiopia v South Africa; Liberia v South Africa*), Volume I, 1966, paras. 4–8, 6–14. Also see Written Memorial of Ethiopia, submitted on 15 April 1961, *South West Africa* cases, 1966, Volume I, p. 32, at pp. 32, 90–91.

14 Written Memorial of Ethiopia, submitted on 15 April 1961, South West Africa cases, 1966, Volume I, p. 33.

15 Ibid, p. 92.

16 See *Reply of the Government of Ethiopia and Liberia*, 20 June 1964, pp. 237–238.

17 Observations of Governments of Liberia and Ethiopia, 1 March 1962, p. 456. The Applicants further stated: "In disputing and negotiating with Respondent in the United Nations during the past several years, Applicants, therefore, have been upholding their own legal interests in the proper exercise of the Mandate; but they have been doing more than that. They have also been upholding the collective legal interest of the Members of the United Nations and the interests of the Organization itself". p. 456.

> *a matter* of *sole* or *exclusive* interest to Applicants and Respondent. The dispute is of *concern and interest to all States*, at least those which are Members of the United Nations.[18]

According to Applicants such a conception of 'interest' stemmed from Article 22 of the Covenant and the Mandate Agreement itself and was clearly vested in them by virtue of the compromissory clause of the Mandate Agreement (Article 7(2)).[19] In advancing an argument that the Applicants had a dispute between themselves and a Union of South Africa as required by Article 7(2) of the Mandate Agreement Applicants relied on the definition of a dispute spelled out by the PCIJ in the *Mavrommatis Palestine Concessions* case.[20] Ethiopia maintained that it had disagreement of legal views and the conflict of interests with South Africa concerning the interpretation and application of the Mandate Agreement, but more specifically, the questions of violation by the Mandatory of its duties under the Mandate, whether UN had supervisory powers over the Union or whether the Applicant had a legal interest in the way in which the Mandatory administered the Territory.[21] According to the Applicants the "dispute" between the parties came into existence by virtue of South Africa's rejection of each of the Applicants claims.[22]

What is interesting is that the Respondent did not in principle deny existence of a dispute (conflict of interests) between the parties *on the points of law* subject to the Court's decision in favour of the Applicant on the third preliminary objection. The Respondent classified its disagreements with the Applicants into two groups. The first group included conflict on the points of law and the second referred to the disagreements on the point both of law and the fact. The former category included the issues as to 'whether the Mandate was still in force, whether the UN had supervisory powers in respect of SWA, and whether the Applicants had a legal right or interest in the administration of that territory'. The latter related to the question whether Respondent was in breach of the Mandate.[23] However, despite the Respondent admitted that

18 See Observations submitted by Applicants, p. 455. *Observations of Governments of Liberia and Ethiopia, 1 March 1962,* p. 456 of Observations.

19 Ibid, p. 441.

20 Written Memorial of Ethiopia, submitted on 15 April 1961, *South West Africa* cases, 1966, Volume I, p. 89.

21 Ibid, p. 89.

22 Ibid, p. 89. According to Applicants the dispute came into existence "inasmuch as for more than ten years Applicants and Respondent have been expounding and urging conflicting points of view concerning the issues of law and contract". See Observations, p. 451.

23 Pleadings, South West Africa Cases, (Ethiopia v South Africa; Liberia v South Africa), Pleadings, Oral Arguments, Documents (Volume VII, 1966, CR 1962/35), p. 240.

the parties disagreed on certain points of law and fact, it refused to admit that such disagreement amounted to the 'dispute' as required specifically by the terms of Article 7 of the Mandate inasmuch as the conflict of interests or disagreement, which the Applicants alleged to have existed, "did not affect any material interests of the Applicant States or their nationals".[24] The counsel for the Respondent argued that the interpretation of Article 22 of the League Covenant and Article 7 of Mandate Agreement emphatically excluded the possibility of a claim brought without the Applicant being able to demonstrate legal right or legal interest.[25] Respondent contended that the question of Applicants' *locus standi* could not have been decided by reference to Article 7 alone.[26] Respondent maintained that in the absence of an enforceable legal right opposable to the Applicants no legal interest could arise to institute proceedings before the Court.[27] According to Respondent, the League Members' rights vis-à-vis the Mandatory could have been claimed and enforced only under the 'open door' obligation stipulated by A and B Mandates which imposed on the Mandatories obligations to allow 'equal opportunities for the trade and commerce of other Members of the League'. These obligations were intended

24 See Third preliminary objection of the Respondent, para. 1, p. 376, Preliminary Objections submitted by the Government of the Union of South Africa on 30 November 1961.

25 Pleadings, South West Africa Cases, (Ethiopia v South Africa; Liberia v South Africa), Pleadings, Oral Arguments, Documents (Volume VII, 1966, CR 1962/35), Arguments of Mr. Muller, Counsel for the Government of South Africa, p. 203. For the interpretation of Articles 22 and 7 see Pleadings, Muller, pp. 205–206.

26 Rejoinder submitted by the government of South Africa, 22 December 1964 (Parts/Books – I–III). In support of their contention, the Respondent refers on p. 95 to the opinion of Sir Percy Spender in the *Northern Cameroons* case. Thus in referring to a jurisdictional clause almost identical to the present one, Sir Percy Spender said: "Such a clause would normally refer to disputes which relate to rights and obligations between the parties which exist and are to be found *outside the terms of the clause itself*; disputes in which a State claims to be aggrieved by the infraction, on the part of another State, of an existing right or interest otherwise possessed by it. Such a clause, in short, normally does not confer any additional right or interest upon a State other than a right to have recourse to the tribunal once the conditions imposed by the clause are complied with. A dispute within the meaning of such a clause normally would relate to a legal right or interest in the State claiming to be aggrieved, which resides or is to be found elsewhere than in such a clause itself. It would indeed be unusual to find in a jurisdictional clause a substantive right which itself could be made the subject of a dispute". *Northern Cameroons Judgment,* p. 15, at p. 83. Respondent further referred to opinion of Judge Fitzmaurice in the *Northern Cameroons case*. See p. 96 of the Respondent's Rejoinder, "In the same case, Sir Gerald Fitzmaurice noted: "…the universally accepted principle that, whatever the apparent generality of its language ('any dispute whatever' relating to 'the provisions' of the Agreement), a purely jurisdictional clause … cannot confer *substantive* rights". *Northern Cameroons,* Judgment, 1963, p. 115.

27 See Preliminary Objections of South Africa, (Oral Proceedings), Volume VII, 1966, pp. 236–240.

for the benefit of other member States of the League.[28] However, C Mandates which contained conduct provisions were envisioned for the benefit of the inhabitants of the Mandated Territories.[29] Because the obligations under A and B Mandates envisaged benefits for the League members and their nationals the League Members would have been regarded as 'co-parties' in whose favour the League Council established certain limited rights.[30] The same was not true of C Mandates. The Respondent maintained that as far as the rights (benefits) established in favour of inhabitants were concerned the Applicants could not have been viewed as 'co-parties' and hence could not have had legal interest with respect to these rights (benefits) in the same way as they had as regards the 'open door' obligations of the Mandate.[31] Based on this interpretation of the substantive provisions of the Mandate Agreement and the Covenant the Respondent in its third preliminary objection to the ICJ's jurisdiction stated: "As a matter of logic, conflicts between parties are generally justiciable only when their rights or legal interests are involved. Courts of law are not concerned with conflicts, differences of opinion or opposite views unconnected with the rights or legal interests of the litigants".[32] The Respondent further submitted that *'in the broad sense'* welfare of the inhabitants of the mandated territories concern all states in the world.[33] The Respondent maintained that the only interest, which the Applicants claimed to possess was the general interest in the welfare of the inhabitants of the Mandated territory but such interest could be attributed to every member of the 'inter-related community of nations'.[34] For Respondent the only meaningful construction of the term 'dispute' in Article 7 of the Mandate Agreement suggested that the term could only

28 South Africa, Preliminary Objections, 30 November 1961, Third Preliminary Objection, p. 388.

29 Ibid, pp. 312, 358, 359.

30 Ibid, 311. It must be noted that the Mandate Agreement was introduced by the Resolution of the League Council and replicates the text of the original agreement concluded between the Principal Allied and Associated Powers.

31 Ibid, p. 312.

32 Third preliminary objection of the Respondent, para. 2, p. 376, Preliminary Objections submitted by the Government of the Union of South Africa on 30 November 1961. It is worth noting that it is very hard to define *'a priory'* the character of the interest which would serve as a basis to bring a claim before the Court. It is for the Court to determine in each and every case whether the claimants have sufficient interest to move the Court. For the list of authors who thought that all States Members of the League had a legal interest to bring a claim before the Court see pp. 467–469 of the Applicants' Observations.

33 Pleadings, South West Africa Cases, (Ethiopia v South Africa; Liberia v South Africa), Pleadings, Oral Arguments, Documents (Volume VII, 1966, CR 1962/35), p. 237.

34 Pleadings, South West Africa Cases, (Ethiopia v South Africa; Liberia v South Africa), Pleadings, Oral Arguments, Documents (Volume VII, 1966, CR 1962/35), p. 237.

mean a disagreement or conflict concerning the legal rights or legal interests of the Applicant States.[35] However, it is important to note that Respondent's conception of Applicants' rights or legal interests was restricted by a further requirement to demonstrate that the violation affected the Applicants' material interests. Respondent noted that Article 7(2) of the Mandate Agreement did not grant *locus standi* before the ICJ in the absence of the material interest of the Applicants.[36] For the Respondent, failure by the Applicants to show 'material interest', though did not preclude existence of a dispute as mere conflict of views or interests, however, made such dispute non-justiciable.[37] Applicants objected to this contention on the basis that the condition to show 'material interest' amounted to an "attempt to insert into Article 7 a requirement which does not exist".[38] In the Respondent's view, however, the requirement of existence of a legal interest was inherent in the term 'dispute' which is required by Article 7, because, it was not the Court's function to express its views "on differences of opinion or on conflicts of views unrelated to the legal rights or legal interests of the litigants".[39] Respondent's argument regarding absence of a legal interest on the part of the Applicants was based on the premise that although the concept of "sacred trust" was legal (i.e. was part of the legal instrument), yet it was unenforceable. The Respondent was convinced that the dispute was of a purely political character and that the 'legal standards' could not be applied and that such legal standards were not even defined in the relevant documents.[40] Conversely, the Applicants in addressing this contention noted that the vague and broad language of Article 2 of the Mandate Agreement and Article 22 of the Covenant did not preclude the Court from applying standards spelled out in various Articles of the Mandate and the Covenant.[41] According to the Applicants "the words used in Article 2 – "material and moral well-being", "social progress" are akin to other words such as "due process" and

35 Third preliminary objection of the Respondent, para. 2, p. 377, Preliminary Objections submitted by the Government of the Union of South Africa on 30 November 1961.

36 Pleadings, South West Africa Cases, (Ethiopia v South Africa; Liberia v South Africa), Pleadings, Oral Arguments, Documents (Volume VII, 1966, CR 1962/35), Preliminary Objections (Oral Proceedings), p. 210.

37 Pleadings, South West Africa Cases, (Ethiopia v South Africa; Liberia v South Africa), Pleadings, Oral Arguments, Documents, South Africa's Counter-Memorial, 1966, Vol. II, pp. 178, 193.

38 Observations of the Governments of Ethiopia and Liberia, 1 March 1962, p. 450.

39 Pleadings, South West Africa Cases, (Ethiopia v South Africa; Liberia v South Africa), Pleadings, Oral Arguments, Documents (Volume VII, 1966, CR 1962/35), Arguments of Mr. Muller, Counsel for the Government of South Africa, pp. 200–201.

40 See Respondent's Objections (Oral Proceedings), Vol. VII, 1966 p. 221.

41 Observations of the Governments of Liberia and Ethiopia, 1 March 1962, p. 462.

"equal protection" which national courts are frequently called upon to interpret. Such words are broad in scope, but in the context of the society to which they pertain they embody meaningful norms".[42] For Applicants the Mandate (especially Article 2(2)) embodied commitments of legal nature and that the general character of the terms in which it was coached did not preclude its legal character. According to the Applicants many constitutional provisions are coached in equally broad terms and have been subject to judicial interpretation. Their vague nature or humanitarian character of the provisions does not deprive the Applicants of the legal interests in ensuring their observance by the Mandatory.[43]

Despite the Applicants' contention that Article 7 did not contain any requirement regarding "material interest" the Applicants maintained that "even if Article 7 were interpreted as requiring a so-called 'material interest', such an interest was present in these cases".[44] The Applicants' contention begs an important question as to the definition of "material interest". It appears from the litigants' written and oral submissions that both parties agreed that the 'material interest' was a prerequisite to bring a claim before the Court.[45] However, the parties seemed to be in disagreement on the meaning of the term. The Respondent put its view in the following terms:

> … firstly, that the word "dispute" in a jurisdiction clause such as Article 7 connotes a conflict or disagreement concerning matters in which the Applicant has a legal right or interest. The second is that the Applicants as individual League Members were not intended to have a legal right or interest in matters such as those now before the Court unless their *material interests were affected either directly or through their nationals; and inasmuch as their material interests are not affected, their legal rights or interests are not involved,* and therefore it cannot be said that there is a dispute in terms of Article 7. Finally, that even if it can be said that the Applicants have a legal right or legal interest in the matters presently before the Court, we say it was not intended that such right or interest

42 Ibid.

43 See Reply of the Government of Ethiopia and Liberia, 20 June 1964, p. 482.

44 Observations of the Governments of Ethiopia and Liberia, 1 March 1962, p. 458.

45 For the Respondent the term 'material' pertained in that particular case to 'safety, health, wealth and the like'. However, the Respondent argued that developing a comprehensive definition of 'material interest' was impossible. The definition would depend on the circumstances of every case. Pleadings, South West Africa Cases, (Ethiopia v South Africa; Liberia v South Africa), Pleadings, Oral Arguments, Documents (Volume VII, 1966, CR 1962/35), p. 237.

> could, in the absence of anything affecting the material interests of the Applicants or their nationals, give rise to a dispute envisaged in Article 7 for the adjudication by the Court.[46]

Applicants objected to the Respondent's narrow construction of the term "material interest".[47] For the Applicants the interest in ensuring compliance with the Mandate as members of the international community 'reflect the highest international concern'[48] and this interest itself constitutes what Respondent calls a 'material interest' giving the Applicants the entitlement to bring proceedings before the ICJ under Article 7 of the Mandate Agreement.[49] The Applicants noted that the "legal interests" of the Members embraced the fulfilment of their duties as members of the organized international community and were not confined to their possibilities of material advantage in an immediate and narrow sense".[50] Applicants further stated that the "Respondent's interpretation of the compromissory clause does more than deprive the clause of meaning; it puts into issue the basic nature of the Mandates System. It seeks to transmute the concept of "sacred trust" into a moral principle, rather than one of legal effectiveness".[51] According to the Respondent the supervision under the Covenant was vested in the League Council and Article 22 did not envisage 'judicial supervision' supplementary to the already existing supervision of the League.[52]

The foregoing overview of the litigants' oral and written submissions in the *South West Africa* cases suggests that the ICJ had to address two closely interrelated issues. First and foremost, the Court had to decide whether there was a dispute as between the parties in accordance with the terms of the compromissory clause of the Mandate Agreement. Secondly, the ICJ had to decide on the nature of the Applicants' interest, i.e. whether the obligations were owed to Applicants under the Mandate Agreement and the Covenant of the League of Nations were of such character as to vest in the Applicants the legal right or

46 South West Africa cases, Pleadings, Oral Arguments, Documents, Volume VII, 1966, Preliminary Objections of South Africa (Oral Proceedings), p. 211.

47 Applicants' Observations, p. 472 with reference to Respondent's Preliminary Objections at p. 379.

48 Observations of the Governments of Liberia and Ethiopia, 1 March 1962, pp. 472–473.

49 Ibid.

50 Ibid. p. 441.

51 See Reply of the Government of Ethiopia and Liberia, 20 June 1964, p. 542. The above statement sounds like a proposition in support of *actio popularis*.

52 Third preliminary objection of the Respondent, para. 5, p. 382, Preliminary Objections submitted by the Government of the Union of South Africa on 30 November 1961.

interest to sue the Union of South Africa in the ICJ by virtue of the compromissory clause of the Mandate Agreement.

The question of the Applicants' *locus standi* was dealt with in the 1962 decision of the Court, which is referred to as the first phase of the *South West Africa* cases. The central question before the Court was whether the "dispute" between the parties was the one which was required by Article 7(2) of the Mandate Agreement and was within the meaning of Article 36 of the Statute of the Court".[53]

In its 1962 decision the Court rejected the Respondent's restrictive construction of the term 'dispute' by relying on, what it thought was, a very broad language of the compromissory clause of the Mandate Agreement which permitted any League Member to refer "any dispute whatever' between itself and the Mandatory to the PCIJ. The Court maintained that the Applicants were entitled to invoke compromissory clause (Article 7(2)) of the Mandate Agreement by virtue of Article 37 of the ICJ Statute and that Article 7 did not contain a separate requirement to show legal interest, whether 'particular or general' and irrespective of whether the injury is caused to the Applicants or the people.[54] The Court in its 1962 decision found the claim admissible by establishing a link between the concept of a sacred trust of civilization expressed in Article 22 of the League Covenant (which the Court viewed as sufficient to impose substantive obligations on the Mandatory), the obligation to promote the well-being of the inhabitants (Article 2 of the Mandate Agreement), and Article 7(2) of the Mandate Agreement (procedural clause) as a security for compliance with the Mandate. In the Court's opinion, the language of Article 7(2) of the Mandate agreement was broad enough to cover *any* dispute.[55] The Court noted:

> The language used is broad, clear and precise: ... It refers to any dispute whatever relating not to any one particular provision or provisions, but to "the provisions" of the Mandate, obviously meaning all or any provisions, whether they relate to substantive obligations of the Mandatory toward the inhabitants of the Territory or toward the other Members of the League or to its obligation to submit to supervision by the League under Article 6 or to protection under Article 7 itself. For the manifest scope and purport of the provisions of this Article indicate that the Members of the League were understood to have a *legal right or interest* in

53 *South West Africa case*, 1962 judgment, p. 343.

54 Ibid.

55 Ibid, p. 329.

> the observance by the Mandatory of its obligations toward the inhabitants of the Mandated Territory, and toward the League of Nations and its Members.[56]

The Court further proceeded to state that Article 7(2) of the Mandate Agreement was "… in the nature of implementing one of the securities of this trust, mentioned in Article 22, paragraph 1". It can be inferred from the Court's statements that the legal right or interest, i.e. an entitlement by a procedural rule (compromissory clause) to bring a claim before the Court was inseparable from the substantive obligation to ensure the sacred trust of civilizations under paragraph 1 of Article 22 of the League Covenant or any other substantive provision of the Mandate Agreement.[57] The conflict of interests or a disagreement on the point of fact or law existed by virtue of the interpretation of the concept 'sacred trust of civilization' embodied in Article 22 of the League Covenant as imposing substantive duties, which were opposable to the Mandatory with the correlative (corresponding) right to demand performance of these duties vested in *all* members of the League of Nations. It is by virtue of this interpretation of the sacred trust concept that the Court arrived at the conclusion that all States members of the League had a legal interest to institute proceedings (invoke responsibility) of the Mandatory.

The Court's conclusion that the sacred trust of civilizations under Article 22 of the League Covenant imposed substantive rights and duties upon the parties became one of the central issues which the parties and members of the Court contested.[58] The ICJ noted in the 1962 SWA decision: "The Mandate for South West Africa, like all the other Mandates, is an international instrument of an institutional character, to which the League of Nations, represented by the Council, was itself a Party. It is the implementation of an institution in which all the Member States are interested as such".[59] In such a case the

56 Ibid, p. 343.

57 Judge Wellington Koo maintained that the purpose of the jurisdictional clause in Article 7 of the Mandate Agreement was to ensure that 'each and every Member of the League had a legal right to insist upon' … the performance of the obligations connected with the concept of sacred trust of civilization. According to him the concept of sacred trust cannot be of purely humanitarian or moral character once it was embodied in the legal instrument. Dissenting Opinion, 1966 *South West Africa* case, ICJ Rep. p. 225.

58 See Separate Opinion of Judge Bustamante, 1962 Judgment, ICJ Rep. p. 356. See also Dissenting Opinion of Judge Tanaka who maintains that by becoming part of the mandates system (which happens by virtue of a treaty instrument) the humanitarian or moral interests (like the sacred trust of civilizations) transformed into a legal interest. *South West Africa* case, 1966, ICJ Rep. pp. 289–290.

59 *South West Africa* cases, *Preliminary Objections*, Judgment, ICJ Rep. 1962, pp. 344–345.

legal interest of all States members of the League of Nations would have been affected in the same way and the States willing to bring a claim against the Mandatory would act not in protection of their individual interests but to defend a 'common cause' of protecting human rights of the inhabitants of the Mandated territory.[60] The sacred trust of civilizations which is said to be entrusted in all Members of the League of Nations by virtue of the Article 22 of the League Covenant forms the basis of such legal protection.[61] The Covenant therefore serves as a legal instrument which creates the juridical link between all the States members of the League to achieve the objective of ensuring that the rights of the inhabitants of the Mandated Territory are protected. Hence, the legal interest is vested in all League members.[62] The resort to Court, according to the ICJ, was the ultimate security, along the other mechanisms available to ensure the performance of the sacred trust towards the inhabitants of the mandated territory[63] and the only *effective* way of protecting the rights of the inhabitants of the territory and thereby ensure respect in the sacred trust of civilizations. All other remedies did not provide the same degree of security.[64] Besides, given that the resort to the Court was not available to the League Organs, vesting the right to make claim in the interests of the inhabitants with States was viewed as the 'only *effective recourse for protection* of the sacred trust'.[65] The Court in 1962 took the effectiveness argument one step further. The effectiveness argument was based on the purposive interpretation of the Mandate agreement by the ICJ.[66] In reply to the Respondent's contention that the dissolution of the League of Nations made existence of a dispute between the Mandatory and another Member of the League of Nations

60 Separate Opinion of Judge Bustamante, 1962, ICJ Rep. pp. 361–362.

61 Ibid, p. 378.

62 Ibid, p. 358.

63 See *South West Africa* cases, 1962, p. 336.

64 The unanimity rule precluded the Council from coercing the Mandatory and the possibility of obtaining the advisory opinion from the Court was ineffective due to the nonbinding nature of the opinions. See *South West Africa* cases, 1962, p. 337.

65 Ibid. The 'necessity' argument, which referred to the necessity to ensure effective compliance with the Mandate Agreement by resort to the Court's compulsory jurisdiction was rejected by the Court in the 1966 decision. The Respondent noted in its second objection to the Court's jurisdiction that the Applicants' contention that the judicial supervision was an indispensable aspect of the Mandate system could not as such serve as a basis to confer jurisdiction on the Court. According to the Respondent, the necessity for jurisdiction could not be a substitute for consent to the jurisdiction of the Court. See para. 14, p. 375 of the South Africa's Objections to the Court's Jurisdiction, 30 November 1961.

66 *South West Africa* case, 1962, p. 336.

(as per the wording of the compromissory clause in the Mandate Agreement) impossible, the Court noted that the purposive interpretation of the Mandate suggested that the 'judicial protection of the sacred trust in each Mandate was an essential feature of the Mandates System".[67] Thus the Court by the decision of 8 to 7 found that the parties had a dispute as "envisaged in ... Article 7" and the Court had jurisdiction to decide the case on its merits.[68]

Four years later when it was expected of the ICJ that it would proceed to adjudicate the merits of the *South West Africa* case and that the question of the Applicants' *locus standi* had been conclusively resolved by the Court's 1962 decision, the ICJ decided to revisit the question of its own competence.[69] The Court in the 1966 judgment found that the 1962 decision on the Applicants' *locus standi* did not take into account the absence on the Applicants' part of the interest in the subject matter of the claim.[70] According to the Court's 1966 decision having a legal interest to invoke a jurisdictional clause was not the same as having the interest in the subject matter of the claim.[71] The Court explains the reasons for such a decision as follows:

> In this connection, there was one matter that appertained to the merits of the case but which had an antecedent character, namely the question of the Applicants' standing in the present phase of the proceedings, not, that is to say, of their standing before the Court itself, which was the subject of the Court's decision in 1962, but the question, as a matter of the merits of the case, of their legal right or interest regarding the subject-matter of their claim, as set out in their final submissions.[72]

67 Other securities were the Administrative supervision of the League itself. Ibid, p. 344.

68 Ibid, p. 347.

69 ICJ's reversal in 1966 of the 1962 decision in SWA case should be viewed as a decision, albeit belated, but one on the joinder of the merits and admissibility stages in accordance with Article 62(5) of the Rules of the Court. R Higgins, 'The International Court and South West Africa: The implications of the Judgment', (1966), 42(4) International Affairs, p. 578. Amongst the many reasons advanced to explain the Court's 1966 South West Africa decision one concerns the sudden change in the Court's composition which was due, as representative of Liberia stated, to the 'death, disability and a spurious disqualification apparently engineered by the Court's President…'. Statement of Mr. Grimes of Liberia. See "Les réactions devant l'arrêt de la Cour internationale de Justice concernant le Sud-Ouest africain', *Annuare français de droit international,* vol. XII (1966), p. 154 quoted in Written Statement of South Africa, *Namibia Advisory Opinion,* p. 436 of the Statement.

70 South West Africa case, 1966, p. 36, para. 60.

71 Ibid.

72 Ibid, para. 4, p. 18.

The above statement by the ICJ suggests a distinction between the *jus standi ratione personae* and *jus standi ratione materiae*.[73] The Court in its 1966 decision rejected the Applicants' claim that the jurisdictional clause (Article 7) of the Mandate Agreement in itself 'conferred a substantive right', i.e. the right to see that the conduct provisions are observed by the Mandatory, i.e. it denied the Applicants' *jus standi ratione materiae*.[74] The Court noted as follows:

> The Court can see nothing in it that would take the clause outside the normal rule that, in a dispute *causing the activation of a jurisdictional clause*, the *substantive rights themselves which the dispute is about, must be sought for elsewhere* than in this clause, or in some element apart from it, – and must therefore be established *aliunde vela liter*. Jurisdictional clauses do not determine whether parties have substantive rights, but only whether, if they have them, they can vindicate them by recourse to a tribunal.[75]

The Court further noted: "To hold that the parties in any given case belong to the category of State specified in the clause, – that the dispute has the specified

73 S. Rosenne, *The Law and Practice of the International Court, 1920–2005*, (Martinus Nijhoff Publishers, 2006), Volume II, pp. 878–879. See Dissenting Opinion of Judge Koretsky who rejects the differentiation between the procedural right (i.e. the right to invoke jurisdiction) and a substantive right owed by one State to another. For Koretsky these two aspects coincide in the compromissory clause of the Mandate Agreement. The Applicants derive both procedural right (the right to invoke jurisdiction) and the legal interest in the subject matter of the claim from the compromissory clause. *South West Africa* case, 1966, ICJ Rep. p. 344. However, in his separate opinion, in the *Barcelona Traction case* Judge Morelli notes that Belgium's lack of standing must be understood as an absence of substantive right and not procedural. para. 2 of his Opinion. Morelli notes in this regard: "The point is that any question of capacity can only be raised in relation to a rule of law which is either undisputed or assumed to exist. The question is then as follows: which is the entity, as between the various entities to which that rule is directed, on which, in the actual case, that rule confers the right invoked? More particularly, is it in fact on the Applicant that such a right is conferred? If the very existence of the rule is negated, any possibility of raising problem of capacity is excluded". para. 6 of Morelli's opinion. A year after the *Mavrommatis case* the PCIJ further explained what constitutes a 'difference of opinion'. According to the PCIJ such difference of opinion arose "as soon as one of the Governments concerned points out that the attitude adopted by the other conflicts with its own views". *Certain German Interests in Polish Upper Silesia*, (1925), p. 14.

74 South West Africa case, para. 62, p. 38. See Dissenting Opinion of Judge Tanaka who maintains that no meaningful distinction can be drawn in Article 7, para. 2 (jurisdictional clause) between the procedural and substantive aspect of the Applicants' rights. According to Judge Tanaka, the Article embodies both elements. *South West Africa* case, 1966, ICJ Rep. pp. 255–256.

75 Ibid, para. 65, p. 39.

character, – and that the forum is the one specified, – is not the same thing as finding the existence of a legal right or interest relative to the merits of the claim".[76] The logic of the Court's statement can be better understood by drawing analogy with optional clause declarations under Article 36 paragraph 2 of the ICJ's Statute. Although under the optional clause declarations, States may reciprocally accept the ICJ's jurisdiction the mere existence of the reciprocal declaration of acceptance of the Court's jurisdiction is not sufficient to bring a claim against another State.[77] In the absence of a breach of a substantive right ('the existence of a legal right or interest in the subject-matter of … the claim') owed to that State the mere reliance on the optional clause declaration as a basis of the claim will not suffice.[78] In this sense, in the context of judicial proceedings arising from jurisdictional clauses of international treaty instruments, it is impossible to delink the jurisdictional clause from the substantive obligations and to derive the legal interest solely based on the jurisdictional clause. For this reason the ICJ was compelled to decide on the Applicants' *locus standi* and existence of a legal dispute as part of the question on the legal nature of the obligations under both the Mandate Agreement and the Covenant of the League of Nations.

The starting point of the enquiry whether the Applicants had *locus standi* was the PCIJ's definition of the 'dispute' in the *Mavrommatis Palestine Concessions* case in which the PCIJ very simply defined the "dispute" as a "disagreement on a point of law or fact, a conflict of legal views or of interests between two persons". As noted above, this definition is amenable to very permissive interpretation. For instance, it is not clear what meaning "conflict of interests" purports to have. Does it refer to conflict of litigants' 'individual (special) interests' only,[79] i.e. interests which arise from the breach of obligations owed

76 Ibid, para. 60, p. 37. Higgins relies on this very passage and notes that the Applicants fall within the category of States envisaged by Article 7(2) and by virtue of this they must be qualified to have a legal interest. Therefore, she continues: "to be in the same category of States and have a legal interest in the subject-matter should not be different". R. Higgins, The International Court and South West Africa: The implications of the Judgment, *International Affairs*, 1966, No. 4, vol. 42, p. 580.

77 See Separate Opinion of Judge Van Wyk, *South West Africa* case, 1966, para. 3.

78 *South West Africa* case, 1966, p. 50, para. 97. See Separate Opinion of Judge Van Wyk, South West Africa case, 1966, para. 3.

79 Dissenting Opinion of Judge Van Wyk, South West Africa case, 1962, pp. 613–615. For instance, Judge Forster in his Dissenting Opinion acknowledged the importance of the maxim 'no interest, no action' he nevertheless believed that the term 'interest' must not be interpreted restrictively and include only 'individual interests', i.e. interests owed individually to the Applicant States. South West Africa case, 1966, p. 478. In his dissent to the Court's decision to exercise jurisdiction in the *Mavrommatis Palestine Concessions* case Judge Oda rejected Greece's right to defend private interests before the ICJ. For Oda,

to the claimants specially/individually or it also refers to interests of general nature, which arise from the violation of collective obligations.[80] Furthermore, can the 'legal dispute' be construed even more restrictively (as suggested by Respondents) to involve only claimant's 'material interests' (tangible interests)?

As far as the last question is concerned, it has to be noted that although the Court took note of the Respondent's argument that the dispute under Article 7 of the Mandate Agreement required demonstration of the material interests, the Court in the 1966 decision found it unnecessary to address the possibility of bringing claims in the absence of the material or tangible interest.[81] The Court decided that the Applicants could only assert legal rights or interests in respect of 'special interest' provisions of the Mandate, which were envisioned under A and B Mandates.[82] The Court explicitly noted that such decision was made irrespective of whether the Applicants had material or tangible interests.[83] In the Court's opinion, the right of individual protection existed under A and B Mandates because such right was vested in the Applicants by the Mandate Agreement.[84] The absence of the material or tangible interests did not affect the Court's decision to deny the Applicants the right of protection of the conduct provisions.[85] The right of protection was rejected because "such right or interests, in order to exist, must be clearly vested in those who claim them, by some text or instrument, or rule of law…".[86] Hence, the Applicants' claim could have succeeded only if they could have demonstrated 'the existence of

Article 26 of the Mandate for Palestine implied that "an Application by such a Member (member of the League) must be made exclusively with a view to the protection of general interests and that it is not admissible for a State simply to substitute itself for a private person in order to assert his private claims". PCIJ Series A, No. 2, p. 86.

80 See dissenting opinion of Judge Morelli. *South West Africa* case, 1962, p. 573.

81 *South West Africa* case, 1966, p. 32, para. 44. However, see Jessup who addressed Respondent's arguments that material damage (material interest) was not a precondition to bring claims before the ICJ. He noted: "International Law has long recognized that States may have legal interests in matters which do not affect their financial, economic, or other "material", or, say, "physical" or "tangible" interests". Separate Opinion of Judge Jessup, South West Africa case, 1962, p. 425. To support his statement he draws upon examples from State practice where States reacted to breaches of human rights or humanitarian law under treaty or customary international law. In his opinion, State practice and number of treaty instruments supported the proposition that States could respond against breaches which did not affect their material/tangible interests. Separate Opinion of Judge Jessup, 1962, p. 425.

82 *South West Africa case,* 1966, para. 44, p. 32.

83 *South West Africa* case, 1966, para. 44, p. 32.

84 Ibid. para. 44, p. 32.

85 Ibid.

86 Ibid.

a legal right or interest in the subject-matter of their claim, such as to entitle them to the declarations or pronouncements they seek'... .[87] The Court was not persuaded by the Applicants' argument that such interests were vested in applicants by the concept of 'sacred trust'. According to the Court, the concept was humanitarian and was not susceptible to adjudication akin to provisions of the preamble of the UN Charter.[88] In the Court's opinion, the interest which stemmed from the concept of "sacred trust of civilization" could be allocated to all 'civilized' States in the same way as all States are interested that all rules of international law are observed.[89] However, the Court maintained that such an interest being based on the moral or humanitarian concept of "sacred trust", could have formed the basis of the Applicants' claim only if it is 'given juridical expression and be clothed in legal form'.[90] According to the Court, the concept was devoid of 'juridical content' and could not generate legal rights or interests which could be claimed before the Court, i.e. could be justiciable.[91] The Court's analysis prompts a conclusion that the Applicants' *locus standi* was denied because the Applicants sought to protect general interests which appertained to every UN member and in fact, to every member of the international community and not to the Applicants individually. The Applicants' interests did not stand out in any special way and could not be distinguished from the interests of all other member States of the General Assembly.[92] This view is indicative of the Court's conception of a 'legal dispute' as being limited to conflict of individual/special interests only, unless the jurisdictional clause states otherwise.

It has already been noted that understanding the "legal dispute" as a "conflict of interests" without further qualification of the nature of the interests may open the door for submitting to the Court most abstract claims.[93] As far as the ICJ and the Rules of the Court are concerned they do not explicitly require showing of a legal interest as a precondition for admissibility of a claim.[94] In the *South West Africa* cases such requirement was introduced through the construction of a "dispute" in the jurisdictional clause of the Mandate Agreement. Judge Morelli in his comments on the meaning of a 'legal dispute' explains the gist of the Court's concern regarding the nature of the Applicants' interest in the case. He argues that a disagreement and a dispute are not the same, just

87 Ibid, para. 48, p. 34.
88 Ibid, para. 50, p. 34.
89 Ibid.
90 Ibid. para. 51, p. 34.
91 Ibid. para. 54, p. 35.
92 Ibid. para. 11, p. 20.
93 Dissenting Opinion of Judge Van Wyk, *South West Africa*, 1962, p. 659.
94 S. Rosenne, (2006), p. 1170.

like the conflict of interests should not be equated to existence of a dispute. He notes: "It is sufficient to reflect that international society as a whole is the result of a relationships existing between the interests of different States; interests which are very frequently opposed without it being necessary on that account to suppose that disputes exist between the States concerned".[95] The Court's 1966 decision concerning Applicants' *locus standi* was premised on the same logic. In the Court's view the analysis of the texts of the Mandate Agreement and the League Covenant suggested that states individually were not vested with right of supervision of the Mandatory's compliance with the conduct provisions of the Mandate Agreement.[96] Such right of supervision was reserved for the League itself and States could demand performance of the Mandate only through the League organs.[97] The 'securities' for the performance of the sacred trust were entrusted in the League Council and not in individual members of the League.[98] The Court further noted: "In the light of these various considerations, the Court finds that the Applicants cannot be considered to have established any legal right or interest appertaining to them in the subject-matter of the present claims, and that, accordingly, the Court must decline to give effect to them".[99] The Court and Judge Morelli's above quoted statements seem to reject the point of view that the general/public interest which the Applicants asserted in the observance of the Mandate Agreement as members of the League of Nations was covered by the definition of a 'legal dispute' and that it could serve as a cause of action against the Respondent. The Court proceeded with the following statement:

> For these reasons the Court, bearing in mind that the rights of the Applicants must be determined by reference to the character of the system said to give rise to them, considers that the 'necessity' argument falls to the ground for lack of verisimilitude in the context of the economy and philosophy of that system. Looked at in another way, moreover, the argument amounts to a plea that the Court should allow the equivalent of an *'actio popularis'*, or right resident in any member of a community to take legal action in vindication of a public interest. But although a right of this kind may be known to certain municipal systems of law, it is not known to international law as it stands at present: nor is the Court able to regard

95 Dissent. Opinion, South West Africa case, 1962, ICJ Rep. p. 567.
96 *South West Africa,* 1966, para. 33, p. 29.
97 Ibid.
98 Ibid, 1966, para. 24, p. 25.
99 Ibid, para. 99, p. 51.

> it as imported by the 'general principles of law' referred to in Article 38, para. 1(c) of its Statute.[100]

The ICJ's decision in the *South West Africa cases* raises number of salient questions concerning the place of *actio popularis* in international law. First question concerns the ICJ's statement that *actio popularis* "…may be known to certain municipal systems of law", but "… is not known to international law…". This proposition puts the ICJ in a position of the international court which can decide for the entire international community and raises a question whether the ICJ is competent to decide for all other international courts and tribunals regarding the jurisdictional *locus standi*. Second question is whether *actio popularis* should be conceptualized as a procedural issue and addressed exclusively within the rules of procedure of international courts and tribunals or as a matter of substantive right which can be vested in States by virtue of an express rule of treaty or customary international law. The second question broaches a third question related to sources of *actio popularis*, i.e. whether *actio popularis* is a judge-made right or its existence is invariably subject to the consent by States. The following sections aim to address these questions.

2 *Actio popularis*: Can ICJ Decide for other International Courts and Tribunals?

It is evident that the ICJ in its statement on existence of *actio popularis* in international law was comparing two different legal systems (international and municipal). The Court's generalization that *actio popularis* was alien to international legal system suggests that the Court precluded existence of *actio popularis* under *any* of the sources of international law. The ICJ's statement that *actio popularis* "… is not known to international law as it stands at present" supports this conclusion. This statement raises questions concerning the ICJ's powers to pronounce on the existence/legality of *actio popularis* in international law in general.

100 Ibid, para. 88, p. 47. See also Dissenting Opinion of Judge Winiarski who states: "Reference has been made in this connection to an institution under the old Roman penal law known as *"actio popularis"* which, however, seems alien to the modern legal systems of 1919–1920 and to international law. Is it possible that such can have been the common intent of the framers of the Mandate instruments? There is no evidence for it, it has been asserted without any attempt to show that it was so; on the contrary, it would seem that the circumstances in which the Mandate was established exclude such an eventuality". *South West Africa* case, 1962, p. 452.

Nevertheless, before one proceeds to address this question it has to be noted that the Court's conclusion that *actio popularis* was alien to international law was first of all factually mistaken. The reason lies in the fact that at the time the decision was delivered there were treaties which contained compromissory clauses vesting in States parties the right to enforce general interests. Judge Jessup stated in this regard:

> I agree that *there is no* generally established *actio popularis* in international law. But international law has accepted and established situations in which States are given a right of action without any showing of individual prejudice or individual substantive interest as distinguished from the general interest.[101]

Jessup proceeded to provide ample evidence of treaty instruments which stipulate for the right of States to resort to judicial proceedings without having suffered special injury when another State party fails to comply with its obligations.[102] This right of a State is not contingent upon existence of tangible/material damage to the State or to one of its nationals.[103] Jessup contended that the Mandate Agreement resembled the characteristics of the treaty instruments mentioned in his examples and the interest of States members of the League of Nations extended beyond simple interest of material/tangible

101 Dis. Op., South West Africa case, 1966, pp. 387–388.

102 By way of example Jessup refers to Articles 26 and 423 of the Constitution of the International Labour Organization, Minorities Treaties, Article 11 of the Treaty of St. Germain-en-Laye of 10 September 1919, Article IX of the Genocide Convention. According to Article 26 of the ILO Constitution "Any of the members shall have the right to file a complaint with the International Labour Organization Office if it is not satisfied that any other Member is securing the effective observance of any Convention which both have ratified in accordance with the foregoing articles". Article 423, paragraph 1 of the ILO Constitution states: "Any question or dispute relating to the interpretation of this Part of the present Treaty or of any subsequent convention concluded by the Members in pursuance of the provisions of this Part of the present Treaty shall be referred for decision to the Permanent Court of International Justice". Article 11 of the Treaty of St. Germain-en-Laye states: "The Serb-Croat-Slovene State further agrees that any difference of opinion as to the question of law or fact arising out of these Articles between the Serb-Croat-Slovene State and any of the Principal Allied and Associated Powers or any other Power, a member of the Council of the League of Nations, shall be held to be a dispute of an international character under Article 14 of the Covenant of the League of Nations. The Serb-Croat-Slovene State hereby consents that any such dispute shall, if the other party thereto demands, be referred to the Permanent Court of International Justice". Separate Opinion of Jessup, *South West Africa*, 1962, pp. 425–430.

103 Ibid. pp. 425–430.

nature but applied to general interest in observance of the Mandate by the Mandatory. This was said to be the intention of States who instituted the Mandate System, a conclusion which stemmed from the history of the Mandate System.[104]

As for the ICJ's conclusion and Judge Jessup's confirmation of the Court's view that *actio popularis* did not exist in international law or under general principles of law it has to be noted that by stating this the ICJ exceeded its competence in two ways. Firstly, it has to be noted that the ICJ's pronouncement amounts to statement of law *in abstracto*, the function which the ICJ exercises as part of its advisory jurisdiction. In the *South West Africa* cases the ICJ's primary task, as very simply formulated by the Court itself, had to be confined to whether the "dispute" between the parties was the one which was required by Article 7(2) of the Mandate Agreement and was within the meaning of Article 36 of the Court's Statute".[105] Hence, the ICJ's task was limited to deciding a very specific question as to whether there was a "dispute" and whether the Court had jurisdiction before the ICJ. Secondly, even assuming that the question put before the Court by the claimants was not so narrowly defined the ICJ would still be precluded to decide on the legality of *actio popularis* under international law in general. This is not in line with the ICJ's function which had to be confined to simply stating whether claimants had a right to bring a claim before the ICJ by way of *actio popularis*. Decision on the legality of *actio popularis* can only be made by each and every international tribunal independently of one another and in accordance with its constitutive instrument, the rules of procedure and relevant substantive norms which bind the litigants in the dispute. Therefore, the ICJ's denial of the right to *actio popularis* under international law may not be construed as a pronouncement for all other international courts and tribunals. The International Criminal Tribunal for Former Yugoslavia in *Prosecutor v Tadić* case noted that:

> International law, because it lacks a centralized structure, does not provide for an integrated judicial system operating in an orderly division of labour among a number of tribunals, where certain aspects or components of jurisdiction as a power could be centralized or vested in one of them but not the others. In international law, every tribunal is a self-contained system (unless otherwise provided).[106]

---

104 Ibid. p. 429.

105 *South West Africa*, 1962 Judgment, p. 343.

106 *Prosecutor v Tadić* (1996) 35 ILM, p. 32, at p. 39.

This statement underlines the way in which the proliferation of international courts and tribunals has led to competing approaches to adjudication in terms of interpretation and application of both substantive and procedural norms.[107] This is more so when international courts and tribunals decide on the questions of their jurisdiction (competence). It is a well-established rule of international law that "an international tribunal is a master of its own jurisdiction".[108] Principle of Kompetenz-kompetenz which is embodied in Article 36, paragraph 6 of the ICJ Statute also departs from this premise.[109] This principle reinforces the view that no international court can pronounce on the legality/permissibility/existence of a claim on the jurisdiction of any other international court.

As has been noted, the Statement in the *South West Africa* case also raises a question about sources of *actio popularis*. This question is fundamental to understanding the ways in which *actio popularis* comes into existence, i.e. whether its creation owes solely to the interpretative function of the international court, to states, or to both. The answer to the latter question will be coupled with the inquiry into an inseparable issue of whether *actio popularis* should be treated as a question of procedural/jurisdictional *locus standi* or rather substantive law. Judge Rosalyn Higgins in her Separate Opinion in the *Israeli Wall Case* noted in this respect:

> ... The Court's celebrated dictum in the *Barcelona Traction* case is frequently invoked for more than it can bear. Regrettably, this is now done also in this Opinion, at para. 155. That dictum was directed to a very specific issue of *jurisdictional locus standi*. As the ILC has correctly put it in the Commentaries on ASR (A/56/10 at p. 278), there are certain rights in which, by reason of their importance "all states have a legal interest in their protection.[110]

Judge Higgins did not err in stating that the ICJ by vesting in international community the legal interest to protect community obligations simply intended to define the scope of its jurisdiction in cases involving claims aimed at protection of collective interests. It has already been noted that the *obiter* in the

107 This is particularly the case with treaty rules concerning the right to sue before different international courts and tribunals. See R. Alford, 'The Proliferation of International Courts and Tribunals: International Adjudication in Ascendance'. (2000) 94 *American Society of International Law: Proceedings of the Annual Meeting*, p. 162.

108 S. Rosenne, (2006), p. 812.

109 C. Tomuschat, (2006), p. 643.

110 Para. 37, p. 213.

Barcelona Traction case was an attempt to revisit the decision in the 1966 *South West Africa* case. By looking at the ICJ's *obiter* as a question of jurisdictional *locus standi* it is cogent to argue that the *Barcelona Traction* dictum was also an attempt to revisit the definition of a dispute by extending its scope beyond the special/individual interests of the parties to the dispute and through permissive interpretation of its own rules of standing to devise a procedural tool in the form of *actio popularis* to enforce community obligations. However, *actio popularis* does not always depend on the interpretative function of courts. In cases when right of *actio popularis* is vested in States by the express provisions of treaty instruments the role left for the international courts is that of formal endorsement of the right. Nevertheless, in the absence of such express provisions, court's interpretative function becomes central to the decision to introduce *actio popularis* by inference from the nature of substantive obligations which the parties are bound by and which the court is also bound to apply. Reliance by courts and tribunals both on these substantive rules and on the rules of standing (jurisdictional clause) raises question concerning the sources of *actio popularis*. The following section aims to address this question.

3 Sources of *actio popularis*: Express and Inferred Right to *actio popularis*

Traditionally the question of claimant's *locus standi* under domestic law is considered as a question of procedural character and the decision whether the claimant has an interest in the case is seen as falling within exclusive prerogative of courts. As a rule, it is the court which has a final say on whether there is a legal dispute or whether the claimant can claim to be a victim of the violation and therefore has an interest in the case. Decision on the legality of *actio popularis*, as a question pertaining to the claimant's *locus standi* and the court's jurisdiction is no exception. International courts and tribunals decide on the claimant's *locus standi* through interpretation of constitutive instruments and the rules of standing (rules of procedure) and by assessing whether the claimant satisfies the standing requirements. However, the interpretative process of the rules of standing (rules of procedure) does not take place in isolation from the substantive obligations which an international court or tribunal is bound to apply. The impact of substantive norms on the interpretative process of the rules of standing and court's decision on the legality (admissibility) of *actio popularis* is hard to measure. However, the litmus test for a decision by an international court or tribunal in favour of *actio popularis* is whether the substantive norm which the court or tribunal applies, is established to protect some collective interest, i.e. an interest which extends beyond the claimant's individual/special interest. This notwithstanding, existence of collective interest and the question of the right to enforce such interest before the court should be treated as two distinct issues. One does not automatically lead to another. Therefore, one needs to establish a source of *actio popularis* independently of the substantive obligations which are established to protect collective interests.

Actio popularis under treaty law may exist either by virtue of express treaty stipulation or may be inferred from the nature of the substantive treaty norms established to protect collective interests of the States parties to the treaty instrument.[111] When the right to *actio popularis* is inferred from collective character of treaty norms it means that the court or tribunal have construed the jurisdictional clauses to be able to adjust them to the collective nature of substantive norms.

As far as customary law is concerned *actio popularis* serves simply as a means of enforcing such customary norms, which are established, to protect collective or community interests. In such a case States can bring *actio popularis* claims before the ICJ in accordance with optional clause declarations under Article 36, paragraph 1 of the ICJ Statute. Although optional clause declarations can be used as means of enforcing treaty obligations too, however, they are most effective tools which the ICJ Statute devises to enforce customary norms of international law, including customary norms established to protect collective interests. The right to enforce 'ordinary' customary norms is simply a question of establishing a breach by one State of customary obligations towards another subject to existence of a jurisdictional link between the injured and the wrongdoing States. However, when the ICJ decides whether states can bring *actio popularis* claims before the ICJ to protect collective obligations under customary law, the Court, in the first place, will have to establish or depart from the assumption that the right to invoke responsibility to protect collective/community interests exists in international law as general rule of international law. As a second step the ICJ will have to inquire whether or not its rules of standing as a matter of *lex specialis* preclude invoking responsibility before the Court. In the absence of such a special rule, the ICJ may, by reference to the right to invoke responsibility to protect collective interests under general international law, proceed to construe Article 36, paragraph 2 of the ICJ Statute so

111 Article 33 of the European Convention on Human Rights represents an example of express authorization of inter-state proceedings by way of *actio popularis*. Under this article "Any High Contracting Party may refer to the Court any alleged breach of the provisions of the Convention and the Protocols thereto by another High Contracting Party".

as to allow for *actio popularis* claims. Therefore, the ICJ's decision on existence of *actio popularis* as a means of enforcing customary rules of international law which are established to protect collective interests will be preconditioned on its conviction that the right to invoke responsibility to protect collective interests is a right already established under customary international law. The following analysis aims to expand the foregoing arguments.

3.1 Actio popularis *by Inference under International Treaty Instruments: Establishing a Link between Interpretation of Jurisdictional Clauses and Substantive Norms in Applications Brought before the ICJ*

It has been noted that the right of *actio popularis* before the ICJ can arise by judicial inference. The inference is made from the fact that the norm is established to protect collective interests of the parties in cases when classic compromissory clauses are involved.[112] In the latter case the court plays a decisive role in construing its rules of standing in such a way as to allow enforcement of such collective interests.

It has been noted that the nature of the norm and the right to enforce the norm are two distinct issues. Therefore, the fundamental question is whether international courts and tribunals have the power to introduce *actio popularis* through interpretation of their rules of standing in light of the nature of the substantive obligations or whether they should simply defer the matter for the States to expressly legislate in favour of *actio popularis*. Under the former approach *actio popularis* becomes a question of jurisdictional nature whereby international courts and tribunals have more freedom to accept or reject *actio popularis* claims, while a more deferential approach by international courts and tribunals will make the right of *actio popularis* to be expressly legislated by States.

It has already been noted as part of the analysis of the *South West Africa* cases that the question of standing falls within the prerogative of every international court and tribunal.[113] Claimant's *locus standi* can be decided based on the constitutive instruments, rules of procedure of respective courts and tribunals with due regard to the nature of substantive obligations which the claimant seeks to enforce before an international court or tribunal. However, reliance on the procedural norm alone in order to make a decision on the applicant's *locus standi* to protect collective interests will prove to be meaningless. In fact, if a

112 By classic compromissory clauses we mean those which refer to '*disputes concerning interpretation and application of treaties*'.

113 See extensive discussion on pp. 204–221.

court or a tribunal decides in favour of *actio popularis* by permissively interpreting compromissory clauses of a treaty one can conclude with absolute certainty that the court acted upon a belief that the nature of obligations under the treaty allows to invoke responsibility in to protect collective/community interests. This belief can be informed by variety of different factors. Such factors may include, treaty provisions which allow for inter-State enforcement of conventional rights before dispute settlement bodies other than the ICJ[114] and practice of States within a treaty instrument which shows evidence of States parties invoking responsibility of one another to protect collective interests under the treaty. In any event, the ICJ in interpreting terms of the compromissory clauses to allow for *actio popularis* before the ICJ must depart from the conviction (however formed) that the nature of obligations under the treaty generally allows for one State party to invoke responsibility of another to protect collective interest established by the treaty. In these cases the court simply infers *actio popularis* by relying on the nature of the substantive obligation and liberal interpretation of the compromissory clauses of the international treaty instruments which the claimants relied upon to bring the claim. The following analysis aims to illustrate how the construction of compromissory clauses with reference to the substantive obligations of the claimants which are established to protect collective interests may open the door to *actio popularis* before the ICJ. The analysis will be based on the *Northern Cameroons, Genocide cases, Questions Concerning Extradition, Nuclear Tests cases and Whaling case.*[115] Despite only in one of these cases the ICJ explicitly endorses *actio popularis*, however all decisions (and the arguments raised by the litigants) very well illustrate the link between the nature of the substantive norm which the applicants seek to enforce and the compromissory clauses.

The cases and their analysis will be grouped into those which are brought under international treaty instruments in the field of human rights and other obligations established to protect collective interests. It has to be noted from the outset that the compromissory clauses in all five cases are worded almost identically. All require that there be a dispute between the parties and that the dispute concerns interpretation and application of the treaty instrument. Evidently, neither treaty instrument expressly vested in the States parties the right to bring an *actio popularis* claim. Therefore, in all of the following cases the right of *actio popularis* is inferred from the nature of the substantive norm coupled with the ICJ's interpretation of the terms of the compromissory clauses.

114 Entitlement of States parties to the Torture Convention under Article 21 to bring inter-state complaints to the Committee Against Torture is a good example.

115 See (1996, 2007), (1963), (1974), (2012), (2013).

The starting point of analysis is the *Northern Cameroons* case which in many respects resembles the facts of the *South West Africa* cases. The *Northern Cameroons* case was brought before the ICJ by the Government of Cameroon against the United Kingdom. Cameroon asked the Court to decide that "United Kingdom has, in the application of the Trusteeship Agreement of 13 December 1946, failed to respect certain obligations directly or indirectly flowing therefrom ..."[116] The case was brought before the Court under Article 19 of the Trusteeship Agreement which stated:

> If any dispute whatever should arise between the Administering Authority and another Member of the United Nations relating to the interpretation or application of the provisions of this Agreement, such dispute, if it cannot be settled by negotiation or other means, shall be submitted to the International Court of Justice, provided for in Chapter XIV of the United Nations Charter.

The Government of the UK denied existence of any dispute relating to the interpretation and application of the Mandate Agreement as between itself and Cameroon and rejected the Applicant's interpretation of Article 19 to the extent that it was broad enough to include disputes relating to the discharge of duties by the UK under the Trusteeship Agreement concerning the rights of inhabitants of the Trust Territory.[117] According to UK interpretation, the object of Article 19 was limited to disputes as regards 'obligations specifically undertaken in relation to Member States and their nationals in the Agreement'.[118] The UK maintained that its compliance with obligations towards the inhabitants of the Trust territory could only be monitored by the General Assembly towards which it was accountable and not the individual Members of the UN which could use the Court as a medium.[119] Neither, in the UK's view, was the

116 *Northern Cameroons* case, 1963, p. 18.

117 *Northern Cameroons case,* Counter-Memorial submitted by the UK, para. 28, p. 60 of the Counter-Memorial, 13 August, 1962.

118 Ibid, para. 31, p. 61. 1962. See Dissenting Op. of Judge Bustamante, *Northern Cameroons* case, who notes that Article 19 served as a 'universal guarantee' to settle disagreements between States which produce legal injury to third States. p. 180.

119 *Northern Cameroons case,* Counter-Memorial submitted by the UK, paras. 31–32, pp. 61–62 of the Counter-Memorial. See also Preliminary Objections submitted by the UK government, Oral Pleadings (Northern Cameroons case), CR 1963/1, Arguments of Sir John Hobson, p. 288 of the Objections. Sir Hobson noted that the Articles which concerned the individual interests of Member-States were 9, 10, 11 or 13, the remaining Articles 3, 5, 6 and 7, imposed obligations on the Administering State only as regards the United Nations 'and not to another Member of the United Nations'.

Court entitled to subject to judicial review the UN General Assembly Resolutions or resolutions/declarations of other UN organs.[120] UK therefore maintained that the dispute existed as between the Republic of Cameroon and the UN GA.[121] The Counsel for the UK government, Sir Hobson noted as follows concerning the Applicant's standing to sue:

> … it should be observed that the Republic of Cameroon has not alleged any breach of obligations specifically undertaken by the United Kingdom in the Trusteeship Agreement for its benefit or for the benefit of its nationals. It therefore has no special interest and, in my submission, cannot rely on a merely general interest in the welfare of the territory. Any such interest would be held in common with all Members of the United Nations and would be separate from and additional to the interests, which each already has of dealing with these problems as members of the General Assembly. As I have already submitted, no such purely protective interest exists under the Trusteeship system…[122]

Although the UK government conceded that there existed a difference of opinion, yet, the UK contended that not every divergence of views amounted to a dispute and the difference of opinion between UK and Republic of Cameroon was not of such a nature as to give rise to the dispute.[123] UK further maintained that the PCIJ's definition of a 'dispute' should not be construed as applying to any difference of opinion.[124] Differences of opinions may occasionally be so abstract as to make it impossible to present to the Court a justiciable claim. Therefore, permissive construction of the term "dispute" may prompt an unreasonable conclusion that all debates which represent divergence of views amongst the Members of the UN Security Council under Chapter VI of the UN Charter constitute a "legal dispute" which can be adjudicated by the ICJ.[125] UK's definition of "dispute" was very similar to the definition which the Government of South Africa provided in the South West Africa cases. Both made existence of a dispute subject to existence of a normative link between the claimant and the defendant, i.e. that one owes obligations individually to

120 *Northern Cameroons case,* Counter-Memorial submitted by the UK, para. 32, p. 62.

121 Ibid.

122 *Northern Cameroons case,* Preliminary Objections submitted by the UK government, Oral Pleadings, CR 1963/1, Arguments of Sir John Hobson, p. 289.

123 Ibid. p. 291.

124 Ibid.

125 Ibid. p. 292.

the other and that such substantive obligations were breached.[126] According to UK, the obligations concerning inhabitants of the Trust Territory were owed to the United Nations and not to UN members in their individual capacity. The UK based its contention on the premise that failure to comply with obligations under the Trusteeship Agreement did not affect Cameroon's individual/special interests. In the absence of injury to individual/special interests the UN Members were barred from invoking responsibility of the UK by way of instituting proceedings before the Court.[127] Any claim before the Court must be brought to protect a special interest of the claimant, which is affected by a violation.[128]

Sir Hobson further submitted that: "Unless the parties have conflicting, actual interests, the case is likely to be characterized as one for an advisory opinion and the controversy as academic, a mere difference of opinion or disagreement not involving their legal relations, and hence *not justiciable*".[129]

The legal position of Republic of Cameroon was that the term 'any member' did not require further qualification regarding the requirement of interest.[130] The language of Article 19 of the Trust Agreement was said to be unequivocal and therefore unlike *Wimbledon* case where the Court had to construe the words 'any interested Power" in the Treaty of Versailles the Court in Cameroons case did not have to decide on the question of claimant's legal interest. The Counsel for the Republic of Cameroon noted that a claim under Article 19 by any member of the United Nations did not amount to *actio popularis*. It was noted:

> Ce n'est pas *l'actio popularis* de l'ancien droit romain, car ce ne sont pas tous les États qui peuvent agir: ce sont les États Membres, c'est-à-dire ceux qui font partie de l'Organisation sous l'autorité de laquelle le régime de tutelle a été institué et qui est l'un des co-contractants de cette convention.[131]

---

126 Ibid. pp. 291–292.

127 Ibid. p. 292.

128 Ibid.

129 E. Borchard, *Declaratory Judgments*, (Banks Baldwin Publishing Co., Cleveland, 1941), p. 30, quoted in Preliminary Objections submitted by the UK government, Oral Pleadings (Northern Cameroons case), CR 1963/1, Arguments of Sir John Hobson, pp. 308–309. Justiciability and standing are two different concepts but they may overlap. M. Taggart, (2006), p. 96.

130 *Northern Cameroons case*, Preliminary Objections submitted by the UK government, Oral Pleadings, CR 1963/1, Oral Arguments, Part II, Duplique De M. Weil, 3 Octobre 1963, p. 413.

131 Ibid. However, see Judge Morelli who equates the claim by any State Member of the UN concerning administration of the Territory and treatment of inhabitants to *actio popularis*. This proposition is based on his belief that the rights of protection were not vested

This statement suggests a different conception of *actio popularis*. For Cameroon the membership in the UN precludes the popular nature of its claim before the Court. The claim could be said to amount to *actio popularis* had the claimant State been a non-member State of the United Nations. However, the claim of exactly identical nature brought before the Court by *Ethiopia and Liberia* was considered as *actio popularis* in the *South West Africa* cases. The Court stated that the Republic of Cameroon:

> … in filing its Application on 30 May 1961, … exercised a procedural right (under Article 19) which appertained to it – a procedural right which was to be exercised in the general interest, *whatever may have been the material individual interest* of the Republic of Cameroon. But within two days after the filing of the Application *the substantive interest* which that procedural right would have protected, disappeared with the termination of the Trusteeship Agreement with respect to the Northern Cameroons.[132]

---

in individual members of the UN but on the UN as a legal entity and hence the action by individual member would not concern his 'subjective rights'. See para. 8 of his Sep. Op., in the Northern Cameroons case. In his view to accord UN member States individual right of action may lead to 'conflicting claims' regarding single course of action. Hence, only collective interests of UN Members can be realized through the medium of either the UNGA or the Trusteeship Council. Para. 4 of the Opinion. As far as the scope of Article 19 is concerned Judge Morelli also supports the proposition that States are entitled to protect only obligations which are owed to them individually, i.e. 'subjective rights'. para. 5 of the Sep. Op. *Cameroons* case. He draws upon a hypothetical example of a multilateral treaty which imposes on States parties an obligation to accord particular treatment with respect to each other. Morelli rightly maintains that failure by one State to treat the nationals of another State party in accordance with the treaty does not entitle all States parties to resort to dispute settlement procedures. Only those States parties to the treaty whose nationals are affected have interest to resort to Court. See para. 5 of his Sep. Op., *Northern Cameroons* case. Although Judge Morelli does not deny existence of a dispute as between Cameroon and UK he believes that, because the Applicant does not claim any subjective right owed to it, the dispute cannot relate to the interpretation and application of the Agreement. See para. 6 of the Sep. Op. Judge Morelli further noted: "This second category of substantive provisions (referring to obligations towards inhabitants of the Territory) contemplates interests which are not individual interests of the various States Members of the United Nations but rather collective interests, that is to say interests common to all the States Members (this approach replicates the ECtHR's approach in the *Ireland v UK* case). In general, the rules of international law may protect the collective interests of States by different means. Firstly, these rules may confer substantive rights on all the States concerned so that each of them is individually entitled to demand the conduct provided for". See para. 4 of his Sep. Opinion, Northern Cameroons case.

132 *Northern Cameroons* case, p. 36. For the opinion that the Applicant's interest continued to exist even after termination of the Trusteeship Agreement, see Dissenting Opinion of Judge Badawi, Northern Cameroons case, ICJ Rep. pp. 152–153. Judge Fitzmaurice

The Court's statement affirms the *actio popularis* nature of the claim brought before the Court but also reinforces the view that procedural norms (jurisdictional clauses) cannot independently serve as a basis of *locus standi.* The 1966 *South West Africa* decision adopted the same logic. The ICJ in both cases rejected the Applicants' *locus standi* because the Court believed that the Applicants failed to demonstrate existence of an interest, which was specific to them. However, the *Northern Cameroons* case differs from the *South West Africa* cases in one important respect. Whereas the Court in the *South West Africa* cases decided on the absence of Applicants' interest (i.e. that no interest was vested in the Applicants) by virtue of interpretation of the Mandate Agreement and Article 22 of the League Covenant, in the *Northern Cameroons* case the Court decided that the Applicant seized to have interests as a result of termination of the Trusteeship Agreement, i.e. the Court refused to decide on the non-existent obligations and viewed a possible decision of the Court as a pronouncement on "an academic interest" of Northern Cameroon. It followed that the termination of the Trusteeship Agreement had deprived the Applicant of any interest, which it could have claimed had the Agreement remained in force. If one puts aside the litigants' UN membership in the *Northern Cameroons* case Cameroon's claim would be similar to a claim by any State member of the international community against another State with the sole purpose of upholding the rule of law in cases when the wrongdoing State owes no obligation to the State which invokes responsibility under any legal source.

The fact that the Court in the *South West Africa* cases declined to adjudicate the case based on the absence of a legal interest and the Court's unwillingness to adjudicate simple divergence of views illustrates the limitations which the Court is willing to impose on its judicial function.[133] Had the Trusteeship Agreement remained in force the Court could have rejected Cameroon's application as being incompatible with its judicial function on the basis similar to the one the Court relied on in *South West Africa* cases, i.e. absence of the Applicant's legal interest in the subject matter of the case. Instead the Court preferred to reject the application based on the mootness of judgment.[134] However, it can

---

suggested that the words "the provisions of this Agreement" must have been read as if they were followed by the words "in respect of which that Member enjoys substantive rights under the Agreement". See Sep. Op. of Fitzmaurice, p. 112.

133 See L. Gross, Limitations upon the Judicial Function, (1964) 58(2) *AJIL*, pp. 426–427. See however Judge Bustamante's views whether the Court's decision to find the application admissible in the *Cameroon's* case would be in compliance with the Court's judicial function. ICJ Rep. p. 179.

134 L. Gross, Judicial Function, p. 430. Judge Beb A Don noted in his dissenting opinion: "The Federal Republic of Cameroon maintains that, in respect of the Northern Cameroons,

be cogently argued that the Court's desire to impose limitations on its judicial function or its decision in favour of the claimants' *locus standi* in either of the two cases would have been informed by the Court's belief that the nature of obligations under the Mandate Agreement in the *South West Africa* cases or the Trusteeship Agreement in the *Northern Cameroons* case was such as to vest in all UN member states a general interest in protection of such obligations.

Analysis of the ICJ's more recent case law also prompts a conclusion that in cases when the claimant's *locus standi* to enforce collective interests is not expressly stipulated in a treaty instrument the Court will be compelled to delve into the nature of substantive obligations for persuasive evidence that the States parties to the treaty instrument intended to confer on every member State a general interest in ensuring compliance with obligations. The issue of correlation between jurisdictional clauses and substantive norms also featured in *Genocide Convention* cases which were brought before the ICJ under Article IX of the Genocide Convention. Article IX of the Genocide Convention, to which reference has already been made also requires that a dispute regarding interpretation and application of the Genocide Convention be submitted to the International Court of Justice. It has already been pointed out that in the Genocide Convention "the contracting States do not have any interests of their own; they merely have, one and all, a common interest…".[135] If one were to adopt the logic of the 1966 *South West Africa* decision, the ICJ would not have had jurisdiction over the claims brought under the Genocide Convention or indeed many other international human rights instruments. In fact the view that States do not have a general interest of protection under the Genocide Convention finds its supporters too. For instance, a very strict construction of

the United Kingdom, by its conduct during the exercise of the Trusteeship, failed to respect the stipulations of the 1946 Agreement, and this is denied by the Respondent. There is thus a dispute of a legal character relating to the interpretation and application of the Agreement. Cameroon has brought this dispute before the Court. However important the developments which occurred after the seisin of the Court, there persists between the Parties a legal conflict, an uncertainty which the Court must resolve. The nature of the dispute is not such as to require a material prejudice. The mere conflict of points of view concerning the interpretation of an agreement suffices. The judgment in such a case cannot be anything but declaratory, and examples of such judgments are not lacking in the jurisprudence of the Permanent Court of International Justice and this Court". ICJ Rep. p. 194. See also separate Opinion of Fitzmaurice in the *Northern Cameroons* case who also takes the view that the issue before the Court was "an academic one". ICJ Rep. p. 98. He further notes: "But courts of law are not there to make legal pronouncements in *abstracto*, however great their scientific value as such. … Otherwise, they serve no purpose falling within or engaging the proper function of courts of law as a judicial institution". ICJ Rep. pp. 98–99.

135 ICJ Rep. p. 23.

the term "dispute" in Article IX of the Genocide Convention was proposed by Judge Oda in the *Case Concerning Application of the Convention on the Prevention and Punishment of the Crime of Genocide.*[136] Judge Oda contended that the nature of the rights and duties under the Genocide Convention was such that it was not intended to protect rights of States but rather rights of individuals or groups of persons.[137] Furthermore, Judge Oda noted that "the failure of the other State is itself a violation of the treaty but such a violation alone cannot be interpreted as constituting a dispute between the applicant State and the respondent State relating to that treaty unless it can be shown to have infringed such rights of the former State as are protected thereby.[138] The latter statement is reinforced by the Oda's contention that the obligations under the Genocide convention to "prevent and punish" genocide or genocidal acts do not form specific inter-state obligations of one State party to the Convention to another but are owed *erga omnes*, to all States parties in general or to the international community as a whole.[139] Given this special nature of the Genocide Convention, Oda maintains that no "dispute" can possibly arise between the States parties and to make the wrong good, the resort must be had to Organs of the UN other than the ICJ or to international penal tribunal.[140] Judge Oda continued his line of reasoning by the following statement:

> In order to seize the Court of the present case ... Bosnia and Herzegovina would have to show that Yugoslavia has breached the rights of *Bosnia and Herzegovina as a Contracting Party* (which by definition is a State) that should have been protected under the Convention. This, however, has not been shown in the Application and in fact the Convention is not intended to protect the rights of Bosnia and Herzegovina as a State. Yugoslavia might have been responsible for certain instances of genocide

---

136 (1996).

137 See para. 4, p. 626 of Oda's declaration in the *Genocide Convention* case (Bosnia and Herzegovina v Yugoslavia), Preliminary Objections, Judgment of 11 July 1996.

138 Ibid. para. 3, pp. 625–626.

139 Ibid. para. 4, p. 626.

140 Ibid. However, a different construction of Article IX of the Genocide Convention follows from *travaux préparatoires* of Article IX (Secretariat Draft E/447, Draft Article XIV) which states as follows: "Since the Convention is not intended to regulate the particular relations between States but to protect an essential interest of the international community, any dispute is a matter affecting all the parties to the Convention. Hence, such disputes should not be settled by an authority arbitrating between two or more States exclusively, for then its decision would lack any claim to be binding on other States". H. Abtahi & P. Webb, *The Genocide Convention: The Travaux Préparatoires,* Vol. I, (Martinus Nijhoff Publishers, 2008), p. 251.

> or genocidal acts committed by its public officials or surrogates in the territory of Bosnia and Herzegovina, but this fact alone does not mean that there is a "dispute" between the States relating to the responsibility of a State, as Yugoslavia did not violate the rights bestowed upon Bosnia and Herzegovina by the Convention.[141]

Oda's declaration replicates ICJ's 1966 *South West Africa* decision in adopting a very restrictive construction of the term "dispute" which excludes the possibility of adjudicating cases involving public interests. However, his statement also shows that his narrow construction of a "dispute" is heavily influenced by the hermeneutics of the nature of obligations under Genocide Convention. Furthermore, Judge Oda justifies this approach by a judicial policy concern reflected in the caution that the Court may run the risk of opening the floodgate for numerous cases.[142] It is difficult to tell whether Judge Oda's concern about increase in the Court's case load may have affected his construction of the nature of obligations under the Genocide Convention, however, it is clear that his conception of the nature of obligations under the Genocide Convention was decisive in determining the claimant's *locus standi* before the ICJ to protect collective interest which the Genocide Convention aims to protect.

Shabtai Rosenne's views on the nature of the obligations under the Genocide Convention are similar to that of Judge Oda. He argues that the entitlement to institute proceedings before the ICJ under the Genocide Convention belongs to the injured States only.[143] Such states suffer injury only when their nationals are affected and only these States can become parties to the dispute under Article IX of the Genocide Convention. This argument, in Rosenne's view, precludes claims of *actio popularis* nature.[144] The ICJ's decisions in the Genocide cases neither endorse nor conspicuously reject the views expressed by these two prominent jurists. In these cases the Court in addressing the question of existence of a dispute in the context of its decision on jurisdiction once again relied on the definition of a dispute developed in the *Interpretation of the Peace Treaties* case. These cases involved the Court's definition of the "dispute" in the context of human rights treaties. According to the Court the dispute arises under a human rights treaty if the parties 'hold clearly opposite views concerning the question of the performance or non-performance of certain

141 para. 6, p. 628 of Oda's Declaration, *Genocide Convention case* (Bosnia and Herzegovina v Yugoslavia), Preliminary Objections, Judgment of 11 July 1996.

142 Ibid. para. 10, pp. 629–630.

143 S. Rosenne 'War Crimes and State Responsibility' in Y. Dinstein, M. Tabory (eds.), *War Crimes in International Law*, (The Hague, 1996), p. 81.

144 Ibid.

treaty obligations".[145] The question of performance of obligations was raised in the *Case Concerning Interpretation and Application of the Genocide Convention* (*Bosnia and Herzegovina v Yugoslavia*). In this case Yugoslavia filed seven preliminary objections to the Court's jurisdiction. In its fifth preliminary objection Yugoslavia submitted that no dispute existed as between the parties because "the 1948 Genocide Convention can only apply when the State concerned has territorial jurisdiction in the areas in which the breaches of the Convention are alleged to have occurred".[146] The Respondent State believed that as far the acts complained of were concerned "the Respondent State did not have territorial jurisdiction, either for enforcement purposes or for prescriptive purposes, in the relevant areas in the period to which the Application relates".[147] The Court refused to adopt such a narrow interpretation of the obligations under the Genocide Convention and reinforced the view that the rights and obligations in the Genocide Convention were established to protect collective interests.[148] The ICJ, once again quoting the Genocide Advisory Opinion, reiterated "the universal character both of the condemnation of genocide and of the cooperation required "in order to liberate mankind from such an odious scourge".[149] However, the Court in this case did not address the question whether Bosnia and Herzegovina could espouse a claim on behalf of victims whose nationality was non-Bosnian. Perhaps the reason lies in the fact that the Applicant did not raise this issue in its submissions to the Court. However, the same question was raised again in the *Case Concerning Application of the Convention on the Prevention and Punishment of the Crime of Genocide* between Bosnia and Herzegovina and Serbia and Montenegro.[150] Unlike previous applications before the Court in which Bosnia and Herzegovina did not make any reference to the right to espouse a claim before the ICJ on behalf of non-citizens of Bosnia, in this case the Applicants argued that there existed a 'dispute' under Article IX of the Genocide Convention even where the claim was submitted on behalf of non-Bosnians. The Applicants, with reference to the famous dicta of the *Barcelona Traction* case and the Advisory Opinion on the Genocide Convention stated as follows:

---

145 *Interpretation of Peace Treaties with Bulgaria, Hungary and Romania,* First Phase, ICJ Rep. 1950, p. 74.

146 Preliminary Objections, 1995, p. 129.

147 Ibid, p. 130.

148 *Genocide Convention case* (Bosnia and Herzegovina v Yugoslavia), Preliminary Objections, 11 July 1996, ICJ Rep. p. 616.

149 Ibid.

150 Judgment of 26 February, 2007, ICJ Reports, 2007, p. 43.

> In other words, this means that any State has a 'legal interest' in suing a State committing genocide (provided there exists a jurisdictional link between the two litigant States), whether the victims of the genocide are its own citizens or not and wherever the crime is committed. In the present case, this implies that Bosnia and Herzegovina could even sue Yugoslavia (Serbia and Montenegro) without having to prove that the victims are Bosnian and even if the acts of genocide are committed on the territory of third States or on the Respondent State's territory itself, serving to illustrate the importance of the Convention and its provisions.[151]

This passage gives a broader meaning to the rights and obligations under the Genocide Convention and to the meaning of the 'dispute' under Article IX. In effect, it is an attempt to introduce *actio popularis*. However, in its reply to this submission the Court took a cautious approach and refused to pronounce on the Applicant's right to protect non-nationals based on grounds unrelated to the question of the Applicant's *locus standi* before the Court. The Court noted in this respect:

> In its final submissions the Applicant requests the Court to make rulings about acts of genocide and other unlawful acts allegedly committed against "non-Serbs" outside its own territory (as well as within it) by the Respondent. Insofar as that request might relate to non-Bosnian victims, it could raise questions about the legal interest or standing of the Applicant in respect of such matters and the significance of the *jus cogens* character of the relevant norms, and the *erga omnes* character of the relevant obligations. For the reasons explained in paragraphs 368 and 369 below, the Court will not however need to address those questions of law.[152]

In paragraphs 368 and 369 of the decision the ICJ simply notes that the Applicant was unable to furnish sufficient evidence to support its allegations and failed to address the issue of the Respondent's *dolus specialis*.[153] The Court's statement concerning the Applicant's legal interest illustrates the caution with which it treated the question of protection of the rights of victims other than those who are the citizens of the State, which espouses the claim before the

151 Memorial of the Government of the Republic of Bosnia and Herzegovina, 15 April, 1994, p. 182. *Genocide Convention case* (Bosnia and Herzegovina v Serbia and Montenegro). Judgment of 26 February, 2007, ICJ Reports, 2007, p. 43.

152 *Genocide Convention case* (Bosnia and Herzegovina v Serbia and Montenegro). Judgment of 26 February, 2007, ICJ Reports, 2007, p. 120, para. 185.

153 Ibid. pp. 193–194.

ICJ. However, one would want to believe that the ICJ's repeated affirmation of the collective nature of the rights and obligations under the Genocide Convention precludes the argument against *actio popularis* under this treaty instrument. Otherwise, the ICJ's statements concerning the nature of the rights and obligations in the Genocide Convention becomes devoid of any purpose. The States parties to the Genocide Convention are bound by the normative link of Conventional ties and neither State party has an interest paramount to any other State party when the rights of non-citizens are involved. This is particularly so when the State of nationality of victims refuses to take any action for protection of its nationals. The argument is based on the broader conception of a 'dispute' as extending beyond conflict of litigants' individual/special interests.

The above notwithstanding, the ICJ's recent case law shows a gradual inclination towards recognition of *actio popularis* by creating a clearer link between the collective nature of obligations under treaty instruments and their jurisdictional clauses. The question of judicial enforcement of general interests irrespective of the victim's State of nationality featured once again in the *Questions Relating to the Obligation to Prosecute or Extradite* case.[154] In this case Belgium invoked two basis of jurisdiction: (a) Article 30 of the Convention against Torture and Other Cruel, Inhuman or Degrading Treatment or Punishment; (b) the declarations made by Belgium and Senegal under Article 36, paragraph 2, of the Statute of the Court.[155] Article 30, paragraph 1 of the Torture Convention is a compromissory clause which stipulates:

> Any dispute between two or more States Parties concerning the interpretation or application of this Convention which cannot be settled through negotiation shall, at the request of one of them, be submitted to arbitration. If within six months from the date of the request for arbitration the Parties are unable to agree on the organization of the arbitration, any one of those Parties may refer the dispute to the International Court of Justice by request in conformity with the Statute of the Court.

Belgium submitted to the Court that there existed a 'dispute' in accordance with Article 30, paragraph 1 of the Torture Convention by virtue of Senegal's failure to comply with obligations under the Convention.[156] More specifically, Belgium maintained that Senegal *inter alia* failed to comply with its obligations

154 (2012).
155 Memorial of the Kingdom of Belgium, 1 July 2010, Volume I, p. 34.
156 Ibid. p. 36.

by refusing to prosecute or extradite Mr. Habré within a reasonable period of time.[157] Belgium also argued that the 'legal dispute' existed as between the parties under the optional clause declarations because Senegal, by taking no action against Mr. Habré 'violates Senegal's conventional and customary obligation to prosecute or extradite'.[158] In the Oral Proceedings Belgium argued that it had both under the Torture Convention and customary international law "the right to insist that Senegal fulfils its treaty obligation to ensure that Mr. Habré is brought to justice" or be extradited.[159]

First signs that Belgium claimed protection of interests which extended beyond its individual interests and involved collective interests appeared in the answer of Belgium's legal counsel to Judge Simma's question. Judge Simma asked:

> in the first round of its pleadings, Belgium has emphasized the existence of an obligation on Senegal to prosecute or extradite Mr. Habré based both on conventional and customary international law. Belgium's pleadings have been relatively brief however on the nature and foundation of its right to see the obligation of *aut tradere, aut judicare* performed by Senegal particularly on the basis of customary international law. In the second round and without going too deeply into the merits of the case, could Belgium therefore provide further clarifications on the nature of this right, particularly, its right based on customary international law? And on the nature of the prejudice it would suffer?[160]

In his answer to this question, Belgium's legal counsel, Eric David, noted that Belgium was entitled both under conventional and customary law to "see States fulfill their obligation to prosecute or extradite the perpetrator…". For Belgium this entitlement reflected most 'fundamental and social value' which had the primary objective of removing impunity for the crimes in question.[161] The legal counsel proceeded to argue that, by nature, the injury which Belgium suffered did not differ from the injury which was done to all other States by virtue of Senegal's conduct.[162] Belgium's latter contention was based on its belief

157 Ibid.

158 Ibid. p. 42.

159 Public sitting, Monday 6 April 2009, verbatim record, p. 39.

160 Public sitting, Monday 6 April 2009, verbatim record, p. 58.

161 Second Round of Oral Proceedings (*Belgium v Senegal*), Belgium (Tuesday 7 April 2009 at 4.30 p.m.), para. 12., pp. 7–8.

162 Ibid. para. 13, p. 8.

that the obligation *aut dedere aut judicare* was of an *erga omnes* character.[163] Belgium contended that "the dispute between Belgium and Senegal ... relates to the respective obligations of these States in the context of the fight against impunity for perpetrators of crimes under international law...; this concern is shared by the whole of the international community".[164] Belgium's answer to Judge Abraham's question on whether Belgium had a right to invoke Senegal's responsibility for the alleged breach with respect to victims of non-Belgian nationality and what legal basis Belgium relied upon to exercise this right also reveals the popular nature of the action brought by Belgium before the Court.[165] In its reply to Judge Abraham's question Belgium noted that it had two bases to invoke Senegal's responsibility under international law, Article 42, (*b*) (*i*) or Article 48 of the Articles on State Responsibility.[166] Belgium's reliance on Article 42 was informed by its contention that one of the victims of the alleged violations was a Belgian national of Senegalese origin.[167] However, Belgium's reliance on Article 48 was informed by its belief that the right to invoke responsibility under the Torture Convention extended beyond the State of victim's nationality.[168] Belgium stated that "indeed, it is not the nationality of the alleged victims which is the basis of the entitlement of a State to invoke the responsibility of another State".[169] Belgium proceeded to state: "the treaty ... is a typical example of an obligation *erga omnes partes* or *erga omnes* and not just an obligation owed in a bilateral manner between two States. The rule is aimed at realizing a collective interest concerning all States parties, or all States in the case of general international law".[170] Belgium's submissions before the Court prompt a conclusion that in addition to special interest, which Belgium sought

163 Ibid.

164 CR 2012/2, Public sitting held on Monday 12 March 2012, at 10.20 a.m., at the Peace Palace, President Tomka presiding, in the case concerning *Questions Relating to the Obligation to Prosecute or Extradite* (Belgium *v* Senegal), Merits, Arguments of Belgium, p. 9.

165 CR 2012/5, Public sitting held on Friday 16 March 2012, at 10 a.m., at the Peace Palace, President Tomka presiding, in the case concerning *Questions Relating to the Obligation to Prosecute or Extradite* (Belgium *v* Senegal), p. 32.

166 CR 2012/6, Public sitting held on Monday 19 March 2012, at 10 a.m., at the Peace Palace, President Tomka presiding, in the case concerning *Questions Relating to the Obligation to Prosecute or Extradite* (Belgium *v* Senegal), para, 55, p. 52.

167 Ibid. paras. 60–61, p. 54.

168 Ibid. para. 55, p. 52.

169 Ibid.

170 Ibid. para. 56, pp. 52–53. Belgium noted in this respect: "In the present circumstances, Belgium, like any other State party to the Convention against Torture as regards compliance with that Convention, or any other State as regards compliance with general international law, is entitled to invoke the responsibility of Senegal, simply because they are part of the group to which the obligation is owed, and without further conditions". para. 58, p. 53.

to protect due to Belgian nationality of the some of the victims it also invoked collective interest as a cause of its action before the Court.[171] The latter allows an argument in favour of the *actio popularis* nature of Belgium's claim. Senegal, on the other hand, denied that there existed a dispute as between itself and Belgium because "Senegal has never indicated that it opposed or refused to accept the principle or extent of the obligations implied by the Convention against Torture".[172]

As far as Belgium's claims regarding Senegal's compliance with obligations under customary international law were concerned the ICJ found that no dispute existed as between the parties at the time the Application was filed with the Court.[173] The Court therefore refused to base its jurisdiction on Article 36, paragraph 2 of the ICJ Statute. The Court's decision to deny existence of a dispute under Article 36, paragraph 2 was based on the diplomatic exchanges of the parties regarding their differences, which made references to the Torture Convention only.[174] The Court therefore only had to decide whether it had jurisdiction to decide a dispute under Article 30, paragraph 1 concerning interpretation and application of Article 6, paragraph 2, and Article 7, paragraph 1, of the Convention against Torture.[175]

The Court in dealing with Belgium's arguments concerning the right to invoke responsibility irrespective of victim's nationality noted that the States parties to the Convention had a 'common interest' to prevent acts of torture and to preclude impunity of the perpetrators of these acts.[176] Therefore the obligations under the Convention, more specifically, obligations under Article 6 paragraph 2 of the Torture Convention must be performed provided that the alleged offender remains in the territory of the State party 'regardless of the nationality of the offender or the victims, or of the place where the alleged offences occurred".[177] Other States parties act to protect collective interest in order to ensure compliance by the State which hosts the alleged offender.[178] The Court relied on the *obiter* of the *Barcelona Traction* case to conclude that

171 See Judge Skotnikov's Separate opinion in which he criticizes the Court for failing to decide on the question of Belgium's standing as an injured State, which left the question of legality of Belgium's extradition request untouched. *Questions Relating to the Obligation to Prosecute or Extradite*, p. 481, para. 8.

172 Counter-Memorial of the Republic of Senegal, 23 August 2011, Volume I, para. 135, p. 23.

173 *Questions Relating to the Obligation to Prosecute or Extradite*, p. 445.

174 Ibid. pp. 444–445.

175 Ibid.

176 Ibid. para. 68, p. 449.

177 Ibid.

178 Ibid.

States parties to the Torture Convention had a legal interest in protection and by analogy applied this reasoning to obligations under the Convention on the Prevention and Punishment of the Crime of Genocide.[179] According to the Court the claimants under the Torture convention (therefore Genocide Convention too) were not required to show any 'special interest', for such special interest could have been demonstrated only in rare cases.[180] Hence, Belgium had *locus standi* before the ICJ to invoke Senegal's responsibility for violations of Article 6, paragraph 2, and Article 7, paragraph 1 of the Torture Convention.[181] The Court's decision in effect amounts to introducing *actio popularis* under the Torture convention, a right which the same court denied to Ethiopia and Liberia in the *South West Africa cases*.[182] The Court's decision on Belgium's standing was informed by its conclusion that the Torture Convention was not established to protect individual/special interests of States parties but collective interests. Whether the mere fact that the Torture Convention is established to protect collective interests sufficed, in the absence of express authorization, to entitle States to invoke responsibility for protection of collective interests was called to question. Comparison was drawn with Article 33 of the European Convention, which is also established to protect collective interests of all States parties but the right to bring claims before European Court on Human Rights by States parties to the European Convention is expressly vested in them.[183]

---

179 Ibid. Whether the *obiter* in the *Barcelona Traction* case referred to substantive or procedural rights prompted considerable debates amongst the jurists. It has already been noted that Rosalyn Higgins in the Barcelona Traction *obiter dicta* suggested that the concept of *erga omnes* obligations to be understood as a rule relating to the procedural rather than substantive law. However, in the Belgium v Senegal extradition proceedings case Judge Xue, in her Dissenting Opinion, noted that the *obiter* in the *Barcelona Traction* case was meant to impose a substantive obligation on States and not procedural, i.e. the right to bring information. Dissenting Opinion of Judge Xue, *Questions Relating to the Obligation to Prosecute or Extradite*, paras. 15–17, pp. 574–575.

180 *Questions Relating to the Obligation to Prosecute or Extradite*, p. 450, para. 69.

181 Ibid. p. 450, para. 70.

182 Judge Xue argued that the Court must have confined its decision to the construction of the nature of obligations arising from Article 5, paragraph 1 only, that is, to cases when the State invokes responsibility in the capacity of the injured State (i.e. when it enforces special but not collective interests), *Questions Relating to the Obligation to Prosecute or Extradite*, p. 574, paras. 12–13.

183 Separate Opinion of Judge Skotnikov, *Questions Relating to the Obligation to Prosecute or Extradite*, para. 17, p. 484. Numerous decisions of the European Court and the Commission on Human Rights postulate the objective nature of the obligations enshrined by the European Convention on Human Rights. The Commission in the *Austria v Italy* case (No. 788/60, Dec. 11.01.61, Collection 7, p. 23 at pp. 40–43, Yearbook 4, p. 116 at pp. 136–142) noted that the purpose of the High Contracting Parties to the Convention was "to establish a common public order of the free democracies of Europe" and that obligations

Judge Skotnikov cast doubt on the Court's conclusion that the entitlement of States to invoke responsibility of other States parties to the Torture Convention may be implied (inferred) from the mere fact that the Torture Convention was established to protect collective interest.[184] Skotnikov denied the right to bring claims before the ICJ in the absence of express authorization under the Torture Convention and in light of the absence of the relevant State practice under Article 21 of the Torture Convention.[185] Article 21 of the Torture Convention states that:

> A State Party to this Convention may at any time declare under this article that it recognizes the competence of the Committee to receive and consider communications to the effect that a State Party claims that another State Party is not fulfilling its obligations under this Convention.

---

undertaken by the Parties in the Convention "are essentially of an objective character being designed rather to protect the fundamental rights of individual human beings from infringement by any of the High Contracting Parties than to create subjective and reciprocal rights for the High Contracting Parties themselves". Also, the Commission in the case of *Chrysostomos v Turkey* (March, 1991) noted "the High Contracting Parties in concluding the Convention intended to achieve greater unity by a common understanding and observance of human rights and to take steps for the collective enforcement of the rights and freedoms defined in Section I" (See para. 20 of the Report). The Commission also distinguished between the declaration of acceptance of the ICJ's jurisdiction under Article 36(3) and the basis of inter-state applications under Article 24 of the European Convention. Whereas the former operates on the principle of reciprocity the latter procedure is brought into effect by virtue of ratification of the European Convention (see para. 22 of the Chrysostomos Report). In the *Ireland v UK* case the Court noted: "Unlike international treaties of the classic kind, the Convention comprises more than mere reciprocal engagements between contracting States. It creates, over and above a network of mutual, bilateral undertakings, objective obligations which, in the words of the Preamble, benefit from a "collective enforcement". By virtue of Article 24, the Convention allows Contracting States to require the observance of those obligations without having to justify an interest deriving, for example, from the fact that a measure they complain of has prejudiced one of the their own nationals". para. 239, 18 January, 1978, Judgment, application number: 5310/71.

184 Separate Opinion of Judge Skotnikov, *Questions Relating to the Obligation to Prosecute or Extradite*, para. 18, p. 484, Judge Xue also argued along the same lines discarding the view that the collective interest alone ('the *erga omnes partes* nature of obligations) can serve as a cause of action for States which are willing to invoke responsibility under the Torture Convention. para. 18, p. 576.

185 Judge Xue also maintains that the Court's finding that the *erga omnes partes* nature of the Convention entitles any State to bring claims under the Torture Convention finds no support in the State practice. *Questions Relating to the Obligation to Prosecute or Extradite*, para. 18, p. 576. This point raises an important question regarding relevance of State practice to determination by the ICJ of its jurisdiction (competence) to decide cases. Article 36, paragraph 6 of the ICJ Statute vests this prerogative with ICJ and not States.

> Such communications may be received and considered according to the procedures laid down in this article only if submitted by a State Party which has made a declaration recognizing in regard to itself the competence of the Committee.

Indeed, Skotnikov may be right to state that no State practice exists under Article 21 of the Torture Convention, in the sense, that no State party to the Torture Convention has brought communication against another State party before the Committee Against Torture. However, this argument fails to take into account the difference between, on the one hand, the entitlement to institute proceedings and on the other, State's unwillingness to exercise the right for reasons of political expediency. Even under international treaty instruments which expressly authorize inter-state claims irrespective of the victim's nationality, examples of such claims are very limited. Moreover, when such claims were brought very often the claimant State had a political interest in bringing the case rather than for the purpose of preserving the *ordre public*. Case law of the European Commission/Court on Human Rights very well illustrates the point. Inter-state applications brought before the ECtHR have very often been caused by protracted political differences.[186]

The same logic applies under the Torture Convention. Absence of practice of submitting communications to the Committee Against Torture is immaterial. The very fact that sixty-four States parties to the Torture Convention have made declarations under Article 21, paragraph 1 of the Torture Convention accepting the competence of the Committee Against Torture suffices to argue that the States parties intended to hold each other accountable irrespective of the victim's State of nationality, with the sole purpose of upholding the common objectives of the Torture Convention.[187]

Judge Xue also attempted to refute the argument in favour of claims to protect collective interests before the ICJ based on the fact that Articles 17–21 of the Torture Convention already envisions supervision mechanisms over implementation by the States parties of the Torture Convention.[188] According to Xue, these mechanisms are already designed to enforce collective interests which the Convention seeks to protect and therefore raise questions

186 D. Harris, O'Boyle &Warbrick, *Law of the European Convention on Human Rights*, (OUP, Oxford, 3rd ed.), 2014, p. 117.

187 For the texts of declarations of acceptance of the competence of the Committee Against Torture see https://treaties.un.org/Pages/ViewDetails.aspx?mtdsg_no=IV-9&chapter=4&lang=en.

188 Dissenting Opinion of Judge Xue, *Questions Relating to the Obligation to Prosecute or Extradite*, para. 19, p. 576.

concerning availability/necessity of additional right of resort to the ICJ.[189] However, this argument is hard to accept. Examples of international treaty instruments with several optional dispute settlement mechanisms are numerous. Article 287, paragraph 1 of the 1982 Law of the Sea Convention is only one of such examples. This article allows States parties to the UNCLOS to submit their disputes concerning the interpretation and application of the Convention to the Law of the Sea Tribunal, the ICJ, arbitral tribunal, and a special arbitral tribunal. United Nations Human Right Committee in its General Comment on Article 2 also stated that:

> The mere fact that a formal interstate mechanism for complaints to the Human Rights Committee exists in respect of States Parties that have made the declaration under article 41 does not mean that this procedure is the only method by which States Parties can assert their interest in the performance of other States Parties. On the contrary, the article 41 procedure should be seen as supplementary to, not diminishing of States Parties' interest in each other's discharge of their obligations.[190]

This logic should be applied to the Torture Convention. Article 30, paragraph 1 of the Torture Convention, simply offers a different forum (i.e. ICJ) for claims which, in essence, have similar objectives, i.e. enforcement of collective interests.

The analysis of the case law prompts a conclusion that the ICJ has been slowly but steadily moving towards recognition of the right of action to protect collective interests before the ICJ in accordance with the terms of the compromissory clauses. Indubitably, central to the Court's decision on admissibility of such claims is the Court's conception of collective obligations under a given treaty instrument as authorizing one State party to invoke responsibility of another State party to the treaty instrument. This conviction informs the ICJ's interpretation of the compromissory clauses of the treaty instrument, more specifically, construction of the "dispute" in such a way as to allow claims to

---

189 Ibid, paras. 19–20, p. 576.

190 Draft General Comment on Article 2: The Nature of the General Legal Obligation Imposed on States Parties to the Covenant, 5 May, 2003, 78th session, Human Rights Committee, CCPR/C/74/CRP.4/Rev.3; http://www.unhchr.ch/tbs/doc.nsf/(Symbol)/f12e2228d384b536c1256d1d003b854f?Opendocument See also Gowlland-Debbas, Judicial Insights into Fundamental Values and Interests of the International Community, in A. Muller, D. Raic, J. Thuranzky (eds.), *The International Court of Justice: Its Future Role After Fifty Years,* (Martinus Nijhoff Publishers, Leiden), pp. 355–356.

protect collective interests. We are therefore observing a process of gradual 'relativization' (adjustment, harmonization) in the ICJ's interpretation of the compromissory clauses and its own rules of standing with the purpose of adjusting them to the nature of substantive norms established to protect collective interests.[191] It seems that 'relativization' of substantive normativity has led to 'relativization' of procedural normativity.

However, the ICJ's case law concerning claims to protect collective interests unrelated to human right obligations opens the door to ambivalence in the court's approach to *actio popularis*. In the recent *Whaling in Antarctic case* which was brought before the ICJ by Australia against Japan by virtue of optional clause declaration pursuant to Article 36, paragraph 2, of the Statute of the Court, Australia claimed that "Japan's continued pursuit of a large-scale program of whaling under the Second Phase of its Japanese Whale Research Program under Special Permit in the Antarctic..., was in breach of obligations assumed by Japan under the International Convention for the Regulation of Whaling..."[192] Australia contended that Japan was in breach of its international obligations in "authorizing and implementing Japanese Whale Research Program under Special Permit in the Antarctic Phase II (JAPRAII) in the Southern Ocean" under Article VIII, paragraph 1 of the Whaling Convention and requested the Court

> to adjudge and declare that Japan violated its obligations under the Convention for the Regulation of Whaling to observe the zero-catch limit in relation to the killing of whales for commercial purposes...; refrain from undertaking commercial whaling of fin whales in the Southern Ocean Sanctuary...; observe the moratorium on taking, killing or treating of whales...[193]

The Applicant (Australia) in both written and oral submissions before the ICJ made references to the collective nature of obligations under the International Convention for the Regulation of Whaling. Collective nature of the Whaling Convention is stated in the preamble of the Convention, which postulates that achieving the "optimum level of whale stock" is "the common interest" of the States parties.[194]

---

191 Generally see A. Nollkaemper, (2012), p. 770.

192 *Australia v Japan, New Zealand Intervening,* Judgment 31 March 2014, p. 226, at p. 234. Application Instituting Proceedings, 31 May 2010, para. 2, p. 4.

193 Ibid. para. 24, p. 238.

194 Australian Memorial, 9 May, 2011, Volume I. para. 2.17, p. 16.

During the oral submissions Australia's legal counsel once again reaffirmed the need for concerted action to "safeguard and manage ... the environment and its constituent elements" which are the common resource.[195] Australia noted:

> It was in fact because of the need to protect the common interest that a specific institutional structure was set up under the 1946 Convention. It was also for the sake of the common interest of the Parties that the Schedule was drawn up to reflect the agreement of the States parties on the levels of conservation to be achieved over the years and in step with scientific findings. The drafters of the 1946 Convention therefore clearly intended that both the Commission and the Schedule should have as their function to guarantee, multilaterally and collectively, the fulfilment of the object and purpose of the 1946 Convention.[196]

Although the commercial/individual interests were also safeguarded by the Whaling Convention by commercial whaling, however, the object and purpose of the Convention extended beyond commercial interests. It was maintained that "the purpose of the Convention was to provide a system through which those individual interests could be managed and resolved in the light of the greater shared interest of the parties in the long-term future of whale stocks".[197]

The nature of Australia's interest in bringing a claim before the Court became clearer after Judge Bhandari's question during the oral proceedings. The question stated as follows:

> What injury, if any, has Australia suffered as a result of Japan's alleged breaches of the ICRW through JARPA II?[198]

195 Year 2013 Public sitting held on Wednesday 26 June 2013, at 10 a.m., at the Peace Palace, in the case concerning *Whaling in the Antarctic* (*Australia v Japan: New Zealand intervening*), para. 7, p. 20 of the pleadings by Agent and Counsel for Australia Mr. Bill Campbell.

196 Ibid. p. 49, para. 59.

197 CR 2013/17, YEAR 2013 Public sitting held on Monday 8 July 2013, at 10 a.m., at the Peace Palace, in the case concerning *Whaling in the Antarctic* (*Australia v Japan: New Zealand intervening*), para. 13, p. 18.

198 CR 2013/13, Public sitting held on Wednesday 3 July 2013, at 10 a.m., at the Peace Palace, President Tomka presiding, in the case concerning Whaling in the Antarctic (Australia *v* Japan: New Zealand intervening), p. 73 (Original).

In her reply to this question Australia noted that it

> does not claim to be an injured State because of the fact that some of the JARPA II take is from waters over which Australia claims sovereign rights and jurisdiction. Every party has the same interest in ensuring compliance by every other party with its obligations under the 1946 Convention. Australia is seeking to uphold its collective interest, an interest it shares with all other parties.[199]

The counsel for Australia proceed to state that:

> [I]n view of their shared values", as set forth in the 1946 Convention, all States parties to that Convention have a common interest in each State complying with its obligations under the Convention and the regime deriving from it. In the words of this Court, "[t]hat common interest implies that the obligations in question are owed by any State party to all the other States parties to the Convention. All the States parties 'have a legal interest' in the protection of the rights involved.[200]

The ICJ also referred to the preambular provisions of the Whaling Convention in its decision to underline the collective nature of the purposes and objectives of the Whaling Convention and "the common interest to achieve the optimum level of whale stocks as rapidly as possible".[201] However, the Court did not make a single reference in its judgment to the Applicant's claim to protect collective interests. The reason for the ICJ's silence on the question of Australia's right to protect collective interests in the absence of express authorization may lie in the fact that Japan itself did not contest the Applicant's standing before the Court on the ground that the claim was *actio popularis*. It has to be noted that Japan did file objections to the Court's jurisdiction.[202] However, these objections did not question Australia's *locus standi* to bring a claim to protect collective interests.[203] Japan's unwillingness to object to the Court's jurisdiction on

---

199 CR 2013/18, Public sitting held on Tuesday 9 July 2013, at 4.30 p.m., at the Peace Palace, President Tomka presiding, in the case concerning Whaling in the Antarctic (Australia *v* Japan: New Zealand intervening), para. 19, p. 28 (Original).

200 Ibid. para. 19, pp. 23–24 (Translation).

201 *Australia v Japan, New Zealand Intervening,* Judgment 31 March 2014, para. 56.

202 Ibid. paras. 31–32, pp. 242–243.

203 Japan's objections to the ICJ's jurisdiction concerned Australia's reservation to the declaration of acceptance of the ICJ's jurisdiction. Australia accepted the ICJ's jurisdiction

the ground of the Applicant's lack of special interest and the Court's silence on the question of the Applicant's right to bring a claim in the absence of any injury (as a state other than injured) may be interpreted as implicit endorsement of *actio popularis* outside the context of human rights protection too both by the Court and the Respondent State.

3.2 *ICJ: the Right of* actio popularis *by Virtue of Express Treaty Provisions*

The cases which, were considered above were brought before the ICJ based on the jurisdictional clauses (either under treaties or optional clause declarations) which did not explicitly vest in states the right to bring a claim before the ICJ. Indeed whether the claimant has *locus standi* depends on the wording of compromissory clauses. The terms of the compromissory clause may define the circle of the potential claimants either very broadly or too narrowly. For instance, nothing precludes the States to define the compromissory clauses in a way that would limit the ICJ's jurisdiction only to disputes arising from a violation of legal obligations, which causes material damage to the claimant. Conversely, the parties may also use in the compromissory clauses such wording as to allow simple 'differences of opinion' to be decided by the Court.[204] Unlike 'classic' compromissory clauses, which vest in the ICJ the power to decide on any dispute concerning interpretation and application of the treaty, the wording of "any difference of opinion" removes the requirement to show any legal interest in the case. The mere difference of opinion suffices to bring a claim before the ICJ. Such wording needs to be viewed as an explicit authorization of *actio popularis* before the Court.

---

except "any dispute concerning or relating to the delimitation of maritime zones, including the territorial sea, the exclusive economic zone and the continental shelf, or arising out of, concerning, or relating to the exploitation of any disputed area of or adjacent to any such maritime zone pending its delimitation". Japan contended that the Court did not have jurisdiction because the dispute was "arising out of, concerning, or relating to the exploitation of any disputed area of or adjacent to any such maritime zone pending its delimitation". *Australia v Japan, New Zealand Intervening,* Judgment 31 March 2014, paras. 31–32, pp. 242–243.

204 An example of such a compromissory clause is Article 23 of the German-Polish Convention which states: "Should differences of opinion respecting the construction and application of Articles 6 to 22 arise between the German and Polish Governments, they shall be submitted to the Permanent Court of International Justice". The ICJ noted that sole purpose of Article 36 in these cases is to ensure that the dispute is 'legal', i.e. 'capable of being settled by the application of principles and rules of international law'. This is how the ICJ defined 'legal dispute' in the *Border and Transborder Armed Actions* (Nicaragua/Honduras), Jurisdiction and Admissibility, ICJ Reports [1998], para. 52, pp. 69, 91.

Article 17 of the Convention of 8 May 1924, concerning Memel Territory exemplifies the point. In the *Interpretation of the Statute of the Memel Territory case* the United Kingdom, France, Japan and Italy brought proceedings before the PCIJ against the Government of the Lithuanian Republic 'in respect of a difference of opinion as to whether certain acts of the latter government are in conformity with the Statute of Memel Territory Annexed to the Convention of 8th May, 1924, concerning Memel".[205] Another example is Article 12 of the Minorities Treaty between the Principal Allied and Associated Powers (The British Empire, France, Italy, Japan and the United States) and Poland of 28 June 1919 which contains a wording similar to the Convention on Memel Territory. This article stipulates:

> Poland further agrees that any difference of opinion as to questions of law or fact arising out of these Articles between Polish Government and any one of the Principal Allied and Associated Powers or any other Power, a Member of the Council of the League of Nations, shall be held to be a dispute of an international character under Article 14 of the Covenant of the League of Nations. The Polish Government hereby consents that any such dispute shall, if the other party thereto demands, be referred to the Permanent Court of International Justice.

Similar wording was employed in the Convention of Geneva concerning protection of Minorities between Germany and Poland. Article 23 of the Convention noted that 'should differences of opinion respecting the construction and application of Articles 6 to 22 arise between the German and Polish Governments, they shall be submitted to the Permanent Court of International Justice".[206] In the *Case Concerning Certain Interests in Polish Upper Silesia,* the Court in reply to Polish preliminary objections to the Court's jurisdiction noted that "... a difference of opinion does exist as soon as one of the Governments

205 Series A./B, *Interpretation of the Statute of the Memel Territory (Preliminary Objections)*, Judgment of June 24th, 1932, pp. 244–245. Article 17 of the Convention which provides for PCIJ's jurisdiction notes: "In the event of any difference of opinion in regard to questions of law or of fact concerning these provisions (provisions of the Convention) between the Lithuanian Government and any of the Principal Allied Powers members of the Council of the League of Nations, such difference shall be regarded as a dispute of an international character under the terms of Article 14 of the Covenant of the League of Nations. The Lithuanian Government hereby consents that any such dispute shall, if the other Party thereto demands, be referred to the Permanent Court of International Arbitration".

206 Quoted in *Case Concerning Certain German Interests in Polish Upper Silesia,* Series A, No. 6, August 25th, 1925, p. 13.

concerned points out that the attitude adopted by the other conflicts with its own views".[207] However, in the 1966 *South West Africa* decision the ICJ brought up a different aspect of these compromissory clauses. The Court noted:

> In this last connection it is of capital importance that the right as conferred in the minorities case was subjected to certain characterizations which were wholly absent in the case of the jurisdictional clause of the mandates. Any *'difference of opinion'* was characterized in advance as being justiciable, because it was to be 'held to be a dispute of an international character' within the meaning of Article 14 of the Covenant (this was the well-known 'deeming' clause), so that no question of any lack of legal right or interest could arise.[208]

In this statement the Court seems to suggest that the wording of the compromissory clause in the *Polish Upper Silesia* case expressly vested in the States parties the right to institute proceedings before the Court in the absence of special interest in the case. The Court's contention is very similar to the arguments of Judges Skotnikov and Xue in the *Extradition Proceedings* case that the right of action before the ICJ to protect collective interests cannot be inferred (implied) from the nature of obligations but must be expressly vested in the States parties to the treaty.[209] The Court's 1966 *South West Africa* decision seems to be based on the same logic. The above passage from the ICJ's 1966 *South West Africa* decision prompts a conclusion that the ICJ did not completely discard the possibility of judicial enforcement of collective interests. However, the passage suggests that such enforcement would have been permissible only in cases of express authorization because as the Court puts it "any difference of opinion was characterized in advance as being justiciable…".

Wimbledon case represents another example of compromissory clauses which can be considered as expressly vesting the right of action before the PCIJ (ICJ) to protect collective interests.[210]

This case was brought before the PCIJ under Articles 380 and 386 of the Treaty of Versailles by Italy, Japan, United Kingdom and France. The Applicants

207 *Case Concerning Certain Interests in Polish Upper Silesia,* Series A, No. 6, August 25th, 1925, p. 14.

208 *South West Africa* case, 1966, para. 70, p. 40. This passage reinforces the argument that whether the Court is competent to adjudicate the case and decide that there arose a dispute between the parties will also depend on the wording of the compromissory clause.

209 Separate Opinion of Judge Skotnikov p. 484, para. 18. Dissenting Opinion of Judge Xue, p. 576, para. 18.

210 For the discussion of the case See C. Tams, (2005), pp. 76–79.

asked the Court to adjudge and declare that "the German authorities … were wrong in refusing free access to the Kiel Canal to the steamship "Wimbledon"".[211] More specifically, that Germany by refusing the access to the Kiel Canal acted in breach of Article 380 of the Treaty of Versailles.[212] Article 380 stated that "the Kiel Canal and its approaches shall be maintained free and open to the vessels of commerce and war of all nations at peace with Germany on terms of entire equality'. The Court noted that the drafters of the Treaty of Versailles intended to "facilitate access to the Baltic by establishing an international regime, and consequently to keep canal open at all times to foreign vessels of every kind…"[213] Article 386, paragraph 1 of the Treaty of Versailles states that:

> in the event of violation of any of the conditions of Articles 380–386, or of disputes as to the interpretation of these articles, *any interested Power* can appeal to the jurisdiction instituted for the purpose by the League of Nations.

In this case the PCIJ found admissible all four complaints of the Applicants against Germany despite only France could claim material/pecuniary damage. France could claim material damage as a State whose national chartered a steamship to transport war materials to Poland through the Kiel Canal. However, the Permanent Court of International Justice stated that 'each of the four Applicant Powers has a clear interest in the execution of the provisions relating to the Kiel Canal, since they all possess fleets and merchant vessels flying their respective flags'.[214] The Court maintained that the Applicants could be characterized as having interest in the case even in the absence of "prejudice to any pecuniary interest".[215]

Despite the Court's statement that each of the four applicants had an interest in the case by virtue of possession of fleet and merchant vessels the legal basis of claims by France was clearly distinguishable from the interests of all other applicants. While France had material/pecuniary interests, other applicants merely sought to ensure compliance by all parties with Article 380 of the Treaty of Versailles. Based on Article 380 of the Treaty the Court declared that the parties intended to allow access to the Kiel Canal to all seafaring nations at peace with Germany and noted that narrow interpretation of the

211 Series A, No. 1, August 17th, 1923, p. 16.
212 Ibid, p. 20.
213 Ibid, p. 23.
214 Ibid, p. 20.
215 Ibid.

relevant provisions of the Treaty contradicted the plain language of the Treaty of Versailles.[216]

The PCIJ's position in the *Wimbledon* is consonant with the ICJ's decision in the *Polish Upper Silesia* case. In both cases the compromissory clauses very loosely defined the standing requirements for potential claimants. The words "in the event of violation of any of the conditions of Articles 380–386" in Article 386, paragraph 1 of the Treaty of Versailles taken together with the entitlement by "any interested Power" to bring a case to the competent court and in light of the international regime of navigation in the Kiel Canal for all seafaring States established under Article 380, the Court had very persuasive evidence to decide that the Treaty of Versailles clearly vested in States parties the right to bring a claim before the Court by way of *actio popularis*. It was beyond any question that all seafaring nations were automatically "interested" Powers and hence could without satisfying further conditions bring proceedings before the PCIJ for any violation of Articles 380 and 386 of the Treaty of Versailles.

3.3 *The Right of* actio popularis *under Optional Clause Declarations: Adjusting Procedural Law to Substantive Obligations*

The ICJ's statement in the 1966 *South West Africa* case that *actio popularis* was alien to international law was strongly criticized and it has been argued that the *South West Africa* decision must now be read in the light of the Court's *obiter dictum* in the *Barcelona Traction* case".[217] In this case the Court stated as follows:

> an essential distinction should be drawn between the obligations of a State towards the international community as a whole, and those arising vis-à-vis another State in the field of diplomatic protection. By their very nature the former are the concern of all States. In view of the importance of the rights involved, all States can be held to *have a legal interest* in their protection; they are obligations *erga omnes*. Such obligations derive, for example, in contemporary international law, from the outlawing of act of aggression, and of genocide, as also from the principles and rules concerning the basic rights of the human person, including protection from slavery and racial discrimination.

216 *Wimbledon* case, pp. 24–25, See on this M S McDougal, H. Lasswell, and J. Miller, *The Interpretation of Agreements and World Public Order: Principles of Content and Procedure*, (Yale University Press, New Haven, 1967), pp. 227–228.

217 Crawford, Third Report, para. 85.

Some of the corresponding rights of protection have entered into the body of general international law (*Reservations to the Convention on the Prevention and Punishment of the Crime of Genocide, Advisory Opinion, ICJ Reports* 1951, p. 23); others are conferred by international instruments of a universal or quasi-universal character.[218]

There is a widely shared view amongst the commentators and the ILC members that paragraphs 33–34 of the *Barcelona Traction* judgment reversed the Court's decision in the *South West Africa* case.[219] For instance, Professor Rodley argued that the ICJ's *obiter dictum* in the *Barcelona Traction* case was an expression of a deep apology for the 1966 *South West Africa* decision.[220] As pointed out by Professor Higgins, paragraphs 33 and 34 of the judgment represent a significant evolution from the 1966 *South West Africa* verdict.[221] While in 1966 the Court had taken the view that Ethiopia and Liberia lacked the necessary legal right or interest to protect collective interests, in 1970 the same Court took the view that an *erga omnes* character of obligations (collective nature of obligations) entitled all states to protect such obligations.[222] It can be argued that the *obiter* of the *Barcelona Traction* case was an attempt to open the door for *actio popularis*. The Court's *obiter* can be construed as a hint that it is willing to construe its rules of standing permissively, i.e. recognize the legal interest of all members of the international community before the Court if such claims arise from obligations which by their nature differ from traditional bilateralizable obligations and are owed *erga omnes*. Although analysed in the context of the Court's denial of *actio popularis* in the *South West Africa* cases which arose from a jurisdictional clause of a treaty, the *obiter* in the *Barcelona Traction* case can be construed as applying to claims brought under optional clause declarations under Article 36, paragraph 2 of the ICJ Statute too. However, for such claims to be admissible the ICJ will have to find sufficient evidence of State practice which establishes the rights owed *erga omnes* and find further

218 Barcelona Traction, (1970), paras. 33–35, p. 32.

219 Fifth Report of Roberto Ago, YbILC, 1976, Volume II, Part I, para. 89, p. 28.

220 N. Rodley, 'Corporate Nationality and the Diplomatic Protection of Multinational Enterprises: The Barcelona Traction Case', 47 No. 11 *Indiana Law Journal* 70 (Fall, 1971), p. 74.

221 R. Higgins, 'Aspects of the Case Concerning the Barcelona Traction, Light and Power Company, Ltd.', 11 *Virginia Journal of International Law* 327 (1971), p. 360. It must be noted that Judge Schwebel, in the Nicaragua case, argued along the same lines. He commented that the Court's earlier decision in the 1966 *South West Africa* case 'was rapidly and decisively replaced' by the Court's dictum in *Barcelona Traction* to the effect that all States have a legal interest in the protection of obligations *erga omnes*. Diss. Op. of Judge Schwebel, *Case Concerning Military and Paramilitary Activities in and against Nicaragua* (Nicaragua v United States of America), (Provisional Measures), ICJ Reports (1984), p. 169, at p. 197.

222 R. Higgins, (1971), p. 360.

evidence in State practice that States are willing to enforce such rules. Caution needs to be applied here because as the ICJ's subsequent statements in the same decision make one hesitate to conclusively argue in favour of enforcement of collective interests at a universal level. In the same decision the ICJ seems to casts doubt on the view that the *obiter* of the *Barcelona Traction* case allows any State to protect victims of human rights violations irrespective of their nationality. The Court stated in paragraph 91 as follows:

> However, on the universal level, the instruments which embody human rights do not confer on States the capacity to protect the victims of infringements of such rights irrespective of their nationality. It is therefore still on the regional level that a solution to this problem has had to be sought; this, within the Council of Europe …, the problem has been resolved by the European Convention on Human Rights, which entitles each State which is a party to the Convention to lodge a complaint against any other contracting State for violation of the Convention, irrespective of the nationality of the victim.[223]

Some argue that it may well be that the Court in this passage implied the right of protection regardless of victim's nationality with regard to the norms that have become part of general international law.[224] Perhaps this conclusion can be supported with reference to the Court's statement that "some of the corresponding rights of protection have entered into the body of general international law…".[225] However, the cogency of this interpretation is highly

223 *Barcelona Traction*, (1970), para. 91, p. 47; The Court noted that the right of protection of human rights irrespective of nationality does not exist at the universal level. Two readings of the Court's statement are possible: a) that the Court simply suggested that not all human rights obligations have *erga omnes* effect; b) that the Court made reference to the 'actual language of the general human rights treaties'. See Crawford, First Report, para. 63. The Government of Singapore in its comments on the Draft Article 40 noted with reference to *Nicaragua* case: "where human rights are protected by international conventions, that protection takes the form of such arrangements for monitoring or ensuring respect for human rights as are provided for in the conventions themselves". para. 267, p. 134. Singapore also referred to *Barcelona Traction* case which stated that in the human rights field the measures available for protection under treaty law are given precedence over the ones available under customary international law. para 3–4 of Singapore's comments on the Draft Article 40 (injured State) Document A/CN.4/488 and Add. 1–3.

224 H. Thirlway, 'The Law and Procedure of the International Court of Justice 1960–1988', *BYIL* 1 (1989), p. 100.

225 With regard to the international instruments not conferring this right, the ICJ might have simply confirmed the reality which existed at the time the decision was made. N. Rodley, 'Human Rights and Humanitarian Intervention: The Case Law of the World

questionable. It is evident from the tone of the statement that the ICJ was not satisfied with the evidence of State practice at the universal level to support the contention that States can sue each other to protect human rights irrespective of victim's state of nationality.[226] In the absence of evidence of such practice at a universal level the ICJ could hardly have pronounced definitively on the right to *actio popularis* before the ICJ, which could be brought under optional clause declarations.

Similarly, the ICJ's decision in the *Nicaragua* case may be interpreted as endorsement of the view that human rights may be enforced in international law irrespective of nationality. The Court in this case stated in relation to US's accusations towards Nicaragua's violation of human rights:

> This particular point requires to be studied independently of the question of the existence of the 'legal commitment' by Nicaragua towards Organization of American States to respect these rights; the absence of such a commitment would not mean that Nicaragua could with impunity violate human rights.[227]

Thus the Court seems to follow the logic of *Barcelona Traction* proposition of *erga omnes,* which any State, could rely upon to invoke responsibility of the delinquent State.[228] Judge Schwebel also argued along the same lines and stated 'the US has, in specific terms of *Barcelona Traction,* 'a legal interest' in the performance by Nicaragua of its fundamental international obligations; to use Ago's words, 'even if it is not immediately and directly affected' by the breaches of international law which it attributes to Nicaragua, the United States 'should

---

Court', 38 *I.C.L.Q* 321 (1989), p. 331, Rodley argues that this was because the Court decided the case before the coming into force of the International Covenant on Civil and Political Rights.

226 Higgins too seems to be sceptical about a right to bring claims before the ICJ to protect *erga omnes* obligations under general international law. She states: "There is surely a general legal interest, in the broadest sense, in the maintenance of legal obligations which admit of diplomatic protection. These are part of the reciprocal fabric of international law, in which there is understandably a collective interest. Is it really correct, as the Court seems to imply, that obligations *erga omnes* entitle any state to claim against the alleged wrongdoer? If in the Court's example, State A engages in racial discrimination against a national of State B, is State C entitled to espouse his claim on the grounds that the obligation of non-discrimination is *erga omnes?* It seems bizarre for the Court to be suggesting this when in 1966 it declined to pronounce on whether racial discrimination was prohibited under general international law". (1971), p. 330.

227 ICJ Reports, 1986, p. 134, para. 267.

228 Thirlway, (1989), p. 100.

therefore be considered justified in invoking the responsibility' of Nicaragua [...] for the internationally wrongful acts which are at issue in this case'.[229] However, the Court further made a statement, which circumscribes possible legal effect of the preceding statement. The Court noted '... where human rights are protected by international conventions, that protection takes the form of such arrangements for monitoring or ensuring respect for human rights as are provided in the conventions themselves'.[230] This holding has been strongly attacked as evidencing a regressive approach by the Court to the questions of standing in the maintenance of human rights akin to the approach taken in the *South West Africa* cases.[231] Thus, if one follows the Court's line of argument a State would be able to bring a claim to the ICJ under Article 36, paragraph 2 of its Statute for the violation of human rights only if the same rights do not form part of the international treaty instrument which contains human rights protection mechanisms. This proposition does not completely discard the possibility of bringing claims for human rights violations irrespective of victim's State of nationality before the ICJ under optional clause declarations. However, the Court seemed to suggest that claims before the ICJ to protect human rights irrespective of victim's nationality should be precluded if the same rights are protected under international treaty instruments with human rights protection mechanisms available to States parties. It follows that States which have accepted the ICJ's jurisdiction in accordance with Article 36, paragraph 2, will not be able to sue one another before the ICJ for violations of human rights irrespective of victim's nationality if they are, for instance, simultaneously parties to the International Covenant on Civil and Political Rights, unless the claim concerns a human right which is not stipulated in the ICCPR.[232]

The passages referred to above from the *Barcelona Traction and Nicaragua* cases are not easy to reconcile. On the one hand, the ICJ in the *Barcelona Traction* case seems to deny the right of protection of human rights violations irrespective of victim's nationality, on the other, the Court in *Nicaragua* case opens the door for such claims, however, on a condition that the claimants are

229 Judge Schwebel, Provisional Measures, (Dissenting Opinion), *Nicaragua case* ICJ Rep. p. 198 with reference to Fifth Report of Roberto Ago, YbILC, 1976, Volume II, Part One, para. 89, pp. 28–29.

230 Nicaragua case (Merits), Judgment, 1986 ICJ Rep. para. 267, p. 134.

231 S. Schwebel, 'Human Rights in the World Court', in R. Pathak & R. Dhokalia (eds.), *International Law in Transition,* (London, Martinus Nijhoff Publishers, 1992), p. 289.

232 Article 41 of the ICCPR provides that a State Party to the Covenant may on a condition that it recognizes the competence of the Human Rights Committee to 'receive and consider communications to the effect that a State Party claims that another State Party is not fulfilling its obligations under the Covenant'.

not parties to international treaty instruments which contain human rights protection mechanisms. The Court is yet to address this indeterminacy. The ICJ's treatment of the right to bring a claim to protect public interests within or outside the context of human rights protection under optional clause declarations raises questions concerning the link between the procedural and substantive character of *actio popularis* claims.

A case in which an attempt to enforce collective obligations under optional clause declaration by bringing *actio popularis* claim outside human rights context was made in the *Nuclear Tests Cases*. Australia brought a claim against France a claim concerning a dispute regarding the holding of atmospheric tests of nuclear weapons by the French Government in the Pacific Ocean and invoked two bases of jurisdiction: "Article 17 of the General Act for the Pacific Settlement of International Disputes done at Geneva on 26 September 1928, read together with Articles 36, paragraph 1, and 37 of the Statute of the Court, and alternatively on Article 36, paragraph 2, of the Statute of the Court".[233] Australia asked the Court to adjudge and declare that "the carrying out of further atmospheric nuclear weapon tests in the South Pacific Ocean is not consistent with applicable rules of international law.[234] France did not appear in these proceedings because it considered that the Court was "manifestly not competent" and "that it (France) cannot accept its jurisdiction".[235] Australia's claim was dismissed. However, it was dismissed on grounds unrelated to the lack of standing.[236]

Despite the case was dismissed the Applicant's claim merits consideration as it sought to protect collective interests. In its submissions Australia noted that "legal interests that can be protected can be 'general' or 'collective', 'particular', 'individual', 'specific' or 'material one'".[237] Australia further contended that "'general' or 'collective' legal interest exist in treaties which had intended to confer rights of enforcement of the treaty on any party; Such 'general' or 'common' legal interests also exist under customary international law".[238] In the *Nuclear Test* cases Australia relied both on the protection of the collective

233 *Nuclear Tests* (*Australia v France*), Judgment, I.C.J. Reports, 1974, p. 253, at p. 254, para. 1.

234 Ibid, p. 256, para. 11.

235 Ibid, p. 257, para. 13.

236 Ibid, p. 253. The Application was dismissed because the ICJ believed that the object and purpose of Australia's claim to prevent further nuclear tests (p. 263, para. 31) was achieved by virtue of French unilateral declarations not to undertake further atmospheric tests (para. 52, p. 270) and because the dispute 'no longer had any object'. para. 62, p. 272.

237 Australian Memorial, Memorial on Jurisdiction and Admissibility, Nuclear Tests cases, 23 November 1973, para. 422, p. 329.

238 Ibid, para. 422, p. 329.

interest suffered by virtue of radioactive fallout as a result of French nuclear tests in the Pacific.[239] Australia stated:

> Is the assertion of what, after all, are the general rights of humanity, of which Australia is a part, always to be thought of in terms such as receiving pecuniary compensation for immediately identifiable damage? Is there not room for recognition of the fact that the community to which we all belong has *both an immediate and a long-term interest* in the identification and prohibition of conduct which cumulatively, over a period of years, is harmful, not only to our generation but harmful to our children and our children's children, if any?[240]

Australia argued to be acting both as an injured State but also in protection of collective interests. Australia first claimed that it suffered material damage as a result of the French nuclear tests which produced radioactive fall out on Australian territory and population in violation of Australian sovereignty and of international law.[241] However, Australia did not claim to have exclusive right of standing before the Court. According to Australia, no matter how far the other States are situated from the centre of explosion the character of 'the exchange of radioactive debris between the stratospheres of the two hemispheres' … will 'essentially affect the whole earth and every person on earth'.[242] Australia maintained that "every State has an enforceable legal interest in asserting the freedom of the seas, especially in relation to nuclear testing".[243] Australia argued that France violated freedom of highs seas by creating a security zone around the area of nuclear testing in the high seas (Mururoa Atoll).[244] Australia's contention was thus based on the *res communis* nature of the high seas, i.e. that high seas formed the common heritage of mankind and any

239 Ibid.

240 *Nuclear Test Cases* (Australia v France), ICJ, Pleadings, Oral Arguments, Documents, Vol. I, Pleadings 1974, at p. 411.

241 See Oral Arguments on Jurisdiction and Admissibility, *Nuclear Tests Cases* (Australia v France), ICJ Pleadings, Oral Arguments, Docs., Vol. I, 1974, p. 409.

242 Oral Arguments on the Request for Indication of Interim Measures of Protection, *Nuclear Tests Cases,* (Australia v France), First Public Sitting, 21 May, 1973, p. 170.

243 Australian Memorial, Memorial on Jurisdiction and Admissibility, *Nuclear Tests cases*, 23 November 1973, para. 461. See also Oral Arguments on Jurisdiction and Admissibility, *Nuclear Tests Cases* (Australia v France), ICJ Pleadings, Oral Arguments, Docs., Vol. I, 1974, p. 338.

244 Oral Arguments on Jurisdiction and Admissibility, *Nuclear Tests Cases* (Australia v France), ICJ Pleadings, Oral Arguments, Docs., Vol. I, 1974, p. 515.

interference with the high seas affected all States and hence entitled them to espouse their claim.[245] Australia therefore noted that "the protection of the freedom of the seas – which constitutes in large part of the Australian interest in the present case and gives to Australia a sufficient *locus standi* to allege a breach of the fundamental freedoms of the sea by the French nuclear activities in the South Pacific area".[246] According to Australia even in the absence of direct interference with Australian ships in the high seas and absence of a material injury, the 'interest in the maintenance of the freedom of high seas' entitled Australia to sue France.[247] Australia argues that despite the length of the distance between the test site and Australia "apart from its general right as a maritime State to assert a right shared by all maritime States, Australia is a Pacific Ocean State with a special interest in matters affecting the Pacific Ocean".[248]

Australia further contended that it became unnecessary to rely on the breach of a right. Australian government noted in this regard: "... suffering or threat of real damage suffices to permit the claim to be propounded, that is to say, a legal interest to propound or to enforce a collective interest arises, *inter alia*, from the threat of or sustaining a real damage by the possessor of that interest".[249]

It follows that Australia's claim was based on two independent causes of action. Firstly, Australia relied on the material injury which it suffered due to the radioactive fall-out, and secondly, the collective interest, which it claimed to have in the high seas by virtue of their *res communis* nature.[250] If one puts Australia's claims in the context of Articles on State Responsibility, Australia could be considered both as an injured State under Article 42 of the Articles on State Responsibility and a State other than an injured State under Article 48. The damage, which Australia claimed to have suffered as a result of radioactive fall-out, qualifies Australia as an injured State. On the other hand, Australia's

245 Australian Memorial, Memorial on Jurisdiction and Admissibility, Nuclear Tests cases, 23 November 1973, para. 462, p. 338.

246 See para. 485 of the Australian Memorial, p. 342. Australia based its arguments to support its *locus standi* before the Court on the *obiter dictum* of the *Barcelona Traction case*. See Australian Memorial, paras. 488–489, p. 343.

247 French navy, however, interfered with American and Canadian vessels. See Pleadings 1974, p. 517.

248 Australian Memorial, Memorial on Jurisdiction and Admissibility, Nuclear Tests cases, 23 November 1973, para. 460. pp. 337–338. See also Austalia's Pleadings, Tenth Public Sitting, July 9, 1974, p. 518.

249 Oral Arguments on Jurisdiction and Admissibility, *Nuclear Tests Cases* (Australia v France), ICJ Pleadings, Oral Arguments, Docs., Vol. I, 1974, p. 473.

250 Oral Arguments on Jurisdiction and Admissibility, *Nuclear Tests Cases* (Australia v France), ICJ Pleadings, Oral Arguments, Docs., Vol. I, Tenth Public Sitting, July 9, 1974, p. 518.

claim aimed at protection of interest of the international community derives from French interference with high seas.

Although the ICJ in this case did not pronounce on the claimant's right to enforce the collective interests, the opinions of some of the judges provide useful guidance on the legality of *actio popularis*. Judges noted that:

> If the materials adduced by Australia were to convince the Court of the existence of a general rule of international law, prohibiting atmospheric nuclear tests, the Court would at the same time have to determine what is the precise character and content of that rule and, in particular, whether it confers a right on every State individually to prosecute a claim to secure respect for the rule. In short, the question of "legal interest" cannot be separated from the substantive legal issue of the existence and scope of the alleged rule of customary international law. Although we recognize that the existence of a so-called *actio popularis* in international law is a matter of controversy, the observations of this Court in the *Barcelona Traction, Light and Power Company, Limited* case suffice to show that the question is one that may be considered as capable of rational legal argument and proper subject of litigation before this Court.[251]

This passage once again underlines the link between the procedural rule and substantive obligation. It postulates that the right to bring a claim before the ICJ to protect collective interests depends on the nature of the substantive right. In cases of applications brought before the Court to protect collective interests under optional clause declarations with reference to the dispute settlement in accordance with Article 36, paragraph 2 of the ICJ Statute the Court will interpret the requirement to have a "legal dispute (legal interest)" in line with the collective nature of substantive obligations.

The foregoing analysis of the ICJ/PCIJ's case prompts a conclusion that the methodology of deciding on admissibility of *actio popularis* under optional clause declarations or jurisdictional clauses of treaty instruments does not differ. In both cases, the ICJ will have to look into the background rule, to see whether the background substantive norm allows to invoke the responsibility to protect collective interests and then proceed to adjust its interpretation of a "dispute/legal dispute" to the nature of the background norm. The minor difference lies in the material sources based on which the ICJ makes its decision

---

251 Joint Dissenting Opinion of Judges Onyeama, Dillard, Jiménez de Aréchaga and Sir Humphrey Waldock, *Nuclear Test cases, Nuclear Tests (Australia v France), Judgment,* I.C.J. Rep. 1974, para. 52, p. 521.

on the claimant's *locus standi*. Whereas the evidence for existence of a background substantive norm established to protect collective interests to bring *actio popularis* claims under optional clause is found in general practice of States, the treaty law right of *actio popularis* will be based on the practice confined to the international treaty instrument. However, the above conclusion is without prejudice to the argument that *actio popularis* should be treated as a question of jurisdictional *jus standi* decided by each and every international court and tribunal independently, including the International Court of Justice. The reason to treat *actio popularis* as a question pertaining to the ICJ's jurisdiction lies in the existence of an inextricable link between the claimant's assertion of *locus standi* (interest to sue before the ICJ) and the question of interpretation of a "dispute/legal dispute".

3.4 *Procedural Bar to Judicial Enforcement of Collective Obligations before International Court of Justice:* actio popularis *and Indispensable Third-Party Rule: Insignificance of Erga Omnes (Collective) Nature of Obligations*

That the ICJ's jurisdiction is consent based does not require extensive discussion.[252] However, attempts have been made to circumvent the requirement of consent by relying on the community (collective) nature of the obligations violated. The question whether the rule of consent to the Court's jurisdiction can be withheld when the obligations of collective nature are involved was addressed by the ICJ in the *East Timor* case.[253]

In this case Portugal asked the Court to decide that by negotiating, concluding and initiating performance of the Agreement of 11 December 1989 with Indonesia which lead to delimitation of the Timor Gap and its prospective exploration and exploitation Australia violated *inter alia* the right of the people of East Timor "to self-determination, territorial integrity and unity and its permanent sovereignty over its natural wealth and resources…" as well as "infringed the powers of Portugal as administering Power of the Territory of East Timor", and "impends the fulfilment of its duties to the people of East Timor and to the international community".[254] Portugal submitted to the Court *inter alia* that, as an administering Power of East Timor, it was entitled to act on behalf of East Timor to ensure the right to self-determination to the people of East Timor.[255] Portugal maintained that the right to self-determination

252 Article 36 of the ICJ Statute.

253 *East Timor case,* (Portugal v Australia) (Merits), [1995] ICJ Rep 90.

254 Portugal's Memorial, p. 123. *East Timor* case, p. 94.

255 Application, para 34(1), p. 17.

was opposable *erga omnes* including against Australia, which was under international obligation to respect this right independently of Indonesia and that Portugal was entitled to enforce this right as against Australia.[256] Portugal further contended that by bringing a claim on behalf of the people of *East Timor* it was doing what it called *"service public international"* in public interest of the members of the community of the UN, but first and foremost, of the people of the Territory.[257] It follows that Portugal asserted standing to institute proceedings against Australia and represent people of East Timor on two grounds. Firstly, in the capacity of the administering Power which is entrusted with the 'sacred duty' to ensure the self-determination of the people of East Timor[258] and secondly, to represent the people as a guardian of the interests of the people of East Timor where people of East Timor are viewed as independent subjects of international law as one of the UN members. Portugal argued that the latter right belonged to all States members of the United Nations.[259] By invoking powers of administration of the territory of East Timor, Portugal sought to establish a link between itself and East Timor and thus make its claim of *locus standi* stronger. In the absence of such a link (which Australia claimed not to exist) the application of Portugal would be identical to those of the Applicants in the *South West Africa* cases.[260] Australia objected to the Court's jurisdiction first because it claimed that the Applicants lacked interest in the case and hence the *locus standi* before the ICJ. Second, Australia questioned the Court's jurisdiction because Portugal's claim required the Court to decide on the rights of a third State (Indonesia), which did not consent to the ICJ's jurisdiction.[261] As far as the issue of the Applicant's interest is concerned

256 Application, para 34(1). See also para. 4.71, p. 123 of Portugal's Memorial on the *erga omnes* nature of the peoples' right to self-determination. The Applicant maintained that Australia violated its obligations towards Portugal by concluding a Timor Gap Treaty which delimited the continental shelf of East Timor (including the resources) between Indonesia (which at the time occupied the Territory of East Timor and controlled it) and Australia.

257 See Memorial of the Government of Portugal, para. 5.42, pp. 149–150.

258 Ibid, para. 8.03, pp. 204–205.

259 Reply of Portugal, para. 8.15., p. 246.

260 However, Judge Weeramantry maintained in his dissenting opinion that despite the link with the people of East Timor Portugal's claim was similar to the applications of Ethiopia and Liberia in that they all brought claims "based solely on their membership of the community of nations and their right as such to take legal action in vindication of public interest". Diss. Op., ICJ Rep. p. 182.

261 Furthermore, Australia noted in this regard that even if the jurisdictional link between Portugal and Indonesia had existed Australia would still have been absolved from being sued before the Court based on the violation of right to self-determination of the people of East Timor. Australian Counter-Memorial, *East Timor case*, 1 June 1992. para. 197, p. 96.

Australia maintained that Portugal did not have a right of its own to defend nor had it been authorized either by people of East Timor or the United Nations to act as a guardian of the interests of East Timorese people and represent them before the Court.[262] According to Australia, the scope of the Mandate granted by the UN to Portugal did not authorize Portugal to represent *East Timor* before the Court.[263] In the absence of individual legal interest in the subject-matter of the claim general international law does not entitle Portugal to bring a claim before the Court.[264] Australia relied on *Barcelona Traction and South West Africa* cases to support its proposition that, in the absence of specific authorization, a State cannot institute proceedings before the Court without first demonstrating a legal interest in the subject matter.[265] Neither UN, let alone the international community, authorized Portugal to represent people of East Timor before the Court.[266] According to Australia, only in the event of direct authorization by the international community could the action of Portugal be permitted.[267] Conversely, Australia noted: "To allow States to proceed – assuming a *locus standi* – in the absence of a collective decision would lead to action of a highly subjective character, and such action might not always take the form of initiating proceedings before the International Court".[268] Failure to meet above conditions would transform Portugal's claim into *actio popularis*, a claim which Australia maintained, Portugal was not entitled to bring against Australia "unless it can show that an entitlement to do so arises from the *erga omnes* character of the obligations which it asserts".[269] However, Australia argued that such entitlement did not derive from Article 36(2) and the Applicants could not institute proceedings before the ICJ on any

---

262 Australian Counter-Memorial, para. 236, p. 109. Australia's noted: "The Court should, in the present case, refrain from deciding on the substance of the Portuguese claims since the application of Portugal is clearly admissible. The claimant is engaged in an attempt to misuse the Court's process. There are no rights of its own in issue, and it has no rights which by virtue of their close identification with rights of the people of East Timor would support these proceedings". para. 20, pp. 8–9 of the Counter-Memorial.

263 Ibid, para. 243, p. 112. Australia contrasted the scope of authorization granted to Portugal with the UN SC's authorization to the UK with respect to Southern Rhodesia. The scope of the former was much narrower, i.e. limited only to cooperation "with the United Nations in the consultation and negotiation process. para. 251, pp. 115–116 of the Australian Counter-Memorial, *East Timor case*.

264 Ibid, para. 259, p. 118.

265 Ibid.

266 Ibid.

267 Ibid. para, 263, p. 119.

268 Ibid. para. 263, p. 119.

269 Ibid. para. 261, p. 118.

matter of international law, which does not affect their individual interests.[270] With reference to the *South West Africa* cases, Australia contended that *actio popularis* did not exist under general international law. Australia further maintained that *Barcelona Traction* case recognized the rights of protection of *erga omnes* obligations under customary international law, but not for all obligations. Only those obligations *erga omnes* the protection of which was envisaged by 'international instruments of universal or quasi-universal character' could be subject to protection by way of *actio popularis*.[271]

Portugal also submitted that the *erga omnes* nature of obligations precluded the requirement of consent to the ICJ's jurisdiction. Portugal maintained that the Monetary Gold rule was inapplicable because the *Monetary Gold case* involved the right *erga singulum,* exclusively as between Italy and Albania but not the rights *erga omnes*.[272]

270 Ibid. para. 259, p. 118. In support of its proposition Australia relied on the 1966 *South West Africa* case.

271 Ibid. para. 262, p. 119. Australia's conclusion is consonant with the arguments of Judges Skotnikov and Xue in their Opinions in the *Questions Concerning Extradition* case that the right of action before the ICJ under optional clause declarations will have to be established with reference to State practice which is reflected in the customary rule of international law.

272 Reply of Portugal, para.7.12–7.15, pp. 206–209. See also Separate Opinion of Judge Ranjeva who supports the view that the *Monetary Gold* principle must be revisited in light of the objective nature of the obligations which Portugal sought to protect. See pp. 131–132 of the Opinion. In arguing this proposition Weeramantry maintained that unlike the *Monetary Gold* case where the rights of Albania (i.e. gold which belonged to Albania) formed the subject-matter of the dispute, the rights of Indonesia do not form the subject-matter of the dispute in *East Timor* case, ICJ Rep. p. 156. Weeremantry noted that the Court should apply the third party rule (consent to the court's jurisdiction by third parties) less restrictively and construe Article 36 teleologically. Judge Skubiszevski draws a line between the *East Timor* case and the *Monetary Gold* rule maintaining that the Monetary Gold rule does not apply to East Timor case because the "rights and duties of Indonesia and Australia are not mutually interdependent". para. 82, p. 249 of the Opinion. According to Skubiszevski the obligations owed to East Timor are owed by all States independently of each other and hence the responsibility of each State can be invoked independently, i.e. without affecting the interests of other States. This feature, he argues, distinguishes the *East Timor* case from the *Monetary Gold* rule which was prompted by the fact that in the latter case Italy could only claim Albanian property subject to the finding that Albania violated its international obligations towards Italy. para. 84, p. 250 of the Opinion. Skubiszevski notes: "The present case does not involve direct harm to the legal rights of the plaintiff State in a context of delict", but it is one in which the claim is grounded "either in a broad concept of legal interest or in special conditions which give the individual State *locus standi* in respect of legal interests of other entities. East Timor is such an entity", para. 100, p. 255 of the Opinion.

The *Monetary Gold* rule postulates that the Court may not proceed to consider the merits of the case if the rights (legal interests) of third States which have not consented to the Court's jurisdiction form the 'very subject matter of the decision'.[273] According to Australia, by accepting Portuguese claim and by deciding on the validity of the Timor Gap Treaty the ICJ would have acted in contravention to the well-established Monetary Gold principle because the Court would first have to pronounce on Indonesia's capacity to conclude such a treaty with Australia.[274] Given Portugal's claim that Australia violated international law by concluding the Timor Gap Treaty with Indonesia, any decision from the Court would first have to assess the legality of Indonesia's act (i.e. conclusion of the treaty with Australia) and only 'consequentially' the legality of the conclusion of the Treaty by Australia.[275] In such a case, the Court's consideration of the legality of Indonesia's conduct would form subject-matter of the claim brought by Portugal against Australia. Therefore, absence of Indonesia's consent to the Court's jurisdiction precludes the Court from proceeding to the merits of the claim despite the *erga omnes* nature of the right claimed.[276] Australia noted as follows:

> Portugal contends that as the right to self-determination of the people of East Timor gives rise to an obligation *erga omnes* to promote that right,

---

273 *Monetary Gold Removed from Rome in 1943* (Italy v France, United Kingdom and United States), ICJ Reports, June 15th (1954), p. 19, at pp. 32–33. See also *Nauru case* in which the ICJ refused to decline jurisdiction in a case brought before the Court by Nauru against Australia. The Court found that interests of New Zealand and United Kingdom did not constitute the very subject-matter of Nauru's claim and hence the Court's prospective judgment. Therefore the Court noted that it did not have to rule on the responsibility of New Zealand and UK in order to hold Australia responsible. *Case Concerning Certain Phosphate Lands in Nauru (Nauru v Australia), Preliminary Objections,* ICJ Reports, Judgment of 26 June, 1992. p. 240, at para. 55. p. 261. On the issue of applicability of Monetary Gold rule in the *East Timor case* Judge Skubiszevski states: "Portugal may be said not to have any interest of its own in the narrow sense of the term, i.e. a national interest, one of a myriad of interests which States have as individual members of the international community. However, Portugal received a "sacred trust" under Chapter XI of the Charter. It is taking care of interests which, it is true, are also its own, but primarily they are shared by all United Nations Members: the Members wish the tasks set down in Chapter XI to be accomplished". para. 103, p. 256 of the Opinion. Skubiszevski notes: "At any rate, it is clear that an actual controversy exists. What doubt could there be regarding the *locus standi?*" para. 103, p. 256 of the Opinion.

274 See Australian Counter-Memorial, paras. 202–204 and para. 221, pp. 98–99, 103–104.

275 Ibid.

276 Ibid. paras. 178–182, pp. 88–89 and para. 194. In refusing to adjudicate on the rights of third States the Court invoked as authority the Monetary Gold principle.

> its claim is opposable to Australia, irrespective of the position of other States. This fails to take account of the fact that the direct violation of the right to self-determination which Portugal's claim against Australia assumes must, on the facts relied on by Portugal, be attributable solely to Indonesia. Any other (indirect) violation can only be consequential on Indonesia's wrongdoing. Even if there is an obligation *erga omnes* to promote the right of the East Timorese to self-determination, the alleged violation of that right by Australia lies in Australia's treaty relations with Indonesia.[277]

This view is cogent given that the nature of the rights should be separated from the question of consent to the Court's jurisdiction.[278] The Court in the *East Timor* case found that the declarations which parties made under Article 36, paragraph 2 of the ICJ's Statute did not serve as a basis to exercise jurisdiction. The Court noted that the decision on the merits would compel the Court to first rule on the "lawfulness of Indonesia's conduct in the absence of that State's consent", hence, the refusal by the Court to proceed to the merits of the case.[279]

The preceding analysis prompts a conclusion that the question of legality of *actio popularis* depends on the ICJ's interpretation of its standing rules, more specifically of the concept of a "legal dispute". The analysis of the case law suggests that the ICJ considers the interpretation of the "legal dispute" as a question which falls within its exclusive competence, however, which it carries out with due regard to the State practice under a relevant treaty instrument as well as state practice in general if the case is brought before the ICJ under optional clause declarations. It is submitted that the ICJ's permissive interpretation of the standing rules has become possible with the recognition of the obligations established to protect collective interests and willingness of States to enforce such obligations. This development suggests that relativization of international substantive normativity has led to relativization of procedural normativity too thus opening the door for *actio popularis* before the ICJ.

---

277 para. 194, p. 94 of the Australian Counter-Memorial, *East Timor* case, 1 June 1992.

278 The Court noted in this regard: "… the Court finds that it is not required to consider Australia's other objections and that it cannot rule on Portugal's claims on the merits, whatever the importance of the questions raised by those claims and of the rules of international law which they bring into play". *East Timor case*, para. 35, p. 105.

279 Ibid. para. 105, pp. 105–106. But as judge Weeremantry pointed out, 'had the present case passed the jurisdictional stage, it would have been just such a case where the doctrine's (*erga omnes*) practical effect would have been considered'. Weeremantry, Sep. Op., p. 565.

CHAPTER 6

Actio popularis: Other International Courts and Tribunals

1 ITLOS

1.1 Actio popularis *in Cases of Protection of the Area*

The idea that States can invoke responsibility for polluting the high seas in the absence of a special injury is not novel.[1] There is very little State practice to support the view that customary international law entitles States to protect the high seas, deep-seabed or Antarctica from environmental damage or any other unlawful use by way of *actio popularis*. Philippe Sands notes that in certain exceptional cases of significant environmental damage to commons *actio popularis* could be permissible.[2] Although Sands may be right to say that massive environmental damage may justify invoking responsibility to protect collective interests, bringing such claims before a competent international court or tribunal is subject to different conditions.[3] As noted above, while the right to invoke responsibility to protect collective interests under customary international law depends on the evidence of State practice and *opinio juris* an *actio popularis* before a relevant tribunal will additionally be subject to the claimant's ability to satisfy the rules of standing of the relevant international court or tribunal. Hence, an *actio popularis* before a judicial forum necessitates looking into the terms of the rules of standing. In light of this necessity, the following analysis will focus on the legality of *actio popularis* before ITLOS.

It has already been noted that an attempt to protect marine environment (the high seas) from damage by *actio popularis* was made in the *Nuclear Tests* cases before the ICJ.[4] In these cases Australia and New Zealand relied on the

1 L. Teclaff, *International Law and the Protection of the Oceans from Pollution,* 40 Fordham L. Rev. 529 1971–1972, at p. 542. L. Caflisch, International Law and Ocean Pollution: The Present and the Future. *Revue belge de droit international,* (1972), p. 33. K. Leigh, *Liability for Damage to Global Commons,* (1993), 14 *Australian Yearbook of International Law*, pp. 150–151. J. Cameron, J. Werksman & P. Roderick, *Improving Compliance with International Environmental Law,* (Routledge, 1990), p. 61.

2 P. Sands, J. Peel, A. Fabra & R. MacKenzie, *Principles of International Environmental Law,* (CUP, New York, 2012), p. 150.

3 Articles on State Responsibility, paragraph 1 of the commentary on Article 33.

4 See discussions on pp. 143–146 of the book.

 | DOI:10.1163/9789004380981_008

freedom of high seas to claim the right to institute proceedings against France to protect the high seas from the environmental damage caused by the French nuclear testing in the Pacific Ocean.[5] Australia claimed a general kind of *locus standi* which stemmed from its interest to maintain the freedom of high seas for all States.[6] Unfortunately, the ICJ in this case did not opine on the legality and validity of Australia's claim to enforce collective interests in the high seas and dismissed Australia's claim on grounds unrelated to standing. The only supporting evidence in favour of *actio popularis* can be found in the separate opinions of some of the judges who contended that existence of *actio popularis* depended on the nature of the obligation in question.[7]

The question of third party actions to enforce the collective interests in the context of preservation of marine environment also featured in Behring's Sea Arbitration.[8] The decision was based on the Treaty concluded between the USA and UK of February 29, 1892 which entitled the parties to submit to the Tribunal of Arbitration "questions concerning the jurisdictional rights of the United States in the Behring's Sea and concerning also the preservation of the fur-seal in or habitually resorting to the said sea, and the rights of the citizens and subjects of either Country as regards the taking of fur-seals in or habitually resorting to the said waters".[9] Among the five points put before the Tribunal under Article VI of the Treaty point number five is most relevant to our analysis. The question (point) was as follows: "Has the United States any right, and if so, what right of protection or property in the fur-seals frequenting the islands of the United States in Behring Sea when such seals are found outside the ordinary three-mile limit?"[10] The Tribunal noted in this regard:

---

5 Australian Memorial, Memorial on Jurisdiction and Admissibility, *Nuclear Tests cases,* 23 November 1973, para. 461, p. 338.

6 French navy, however, interfered with American and Canadian vessels. See *Nuclear Tests cases* (Australia v France), Pleadings 1974, p. 517.

7 "In short, the question of "legal interest" cannot be separated from the substantive legal issue of the existence and scope of the alleged rule of customary international law. Although we recognize that the existence of a so-called *actio popularis* in international law is a matter of controversy, the observations of this Court in the *Barcelona Traction, Light and Power Company, Limited* case suffice to show that the question is one that may be considered as capable of rational legal argument and a proper subject of litigation before this Court". Joint Dissenting Opinion of Judges Onyeama, Dillard, Jiménez de Aréchaga and Sir Humphrey Waldock, *Nuclear Test cases,* (Australia v France), Judgment, I.C.J. Reports, [1974], para. 117, p. 370.

8 Award between the United States and the United Kingdom relating to the rights of jurisdiction of United States in the Bering's sea and the preservation of fur seals, *Recueil des Sentences Arbitrales,* 15 August 1993, Volume XXVIII pp. 263–276.

9 Award between the United States and the United Kingdom, p. 266.

10 Ibid. p. 267.

> As to the fifth of the said five points, We, the said Baron de Courcel, Lord Hannen, Sir John Thompson, Marquis Visconti Venosta and Mr. Gregers Gram, being a majority of the said arbitrators, do decide and determine that the United States has not any right of protection or property in the fur-seals frequenting the islands of the United States in Behring Sea, when such seals are found outside the ordinary three-mile limit.[11]

The Tribunal's conclusion seems to reject the US claim that it could protect fur-seals beyond the limits of its national jurisdiction without express authorization from other States or an international organization.[12] Though no explicit reference is made to *actio popularis* in the award the Tribunal's rejection of the US claim should be viewed as its rejection.[13]

But even if the above decisions were in favour of applicants' right to protect collective interests can they be considered as conclusive for ITLOS? Previous chapters already addressed this question by stating that proliferation of international courts and tribunals with most international courts and tribunals having their own independent sources of substantive law and distinct procedural rules precludes a conclusion that the ICJ's or any other international court's decision in favour of *actio popularis* will be conclusive for other international courts and tribunals. This means that the answer to the question concerning the legality of *actio popularis* before ITLOS can only be given by probing into substantive norms which ITLOS applies (i.e. the UNCLOS) as well as the applicable rules of standing.

It has to be noted that UNCLOS does not expressly entitle States to bring *actio popularis* claims.[14] Therefore the question is whether such a right can be inferred from substantive and procedural (jurisdictional) clauses of the UNCLOS.

UNCLOS contains substantive provisions, which do not operate in the purely contractual manner of reciprocal rights and obligations. The collective interests can be found in the preambular and other provisions of the UNCLOS. The preamble mentions amongst the objectives of the Convention "the equitable and efficient utilization" of the resources of the seas as well as "the conservation of their living resources, and the study, protection and preservation of

11 Ibid. p. 269.

12 T. Kuokkanen, *International Law and the Environment: Variations on the Theme.* (Kluwer Law International, The Hague, 2002), p. 55.

13 V. Lowe, *International Law,* Clarendon Law Series, (OUP, Oxford 2007), pp. 235–239. P. Sands, J. Peel, A. Fabra & R. MacKenzie, (2012), pp. 399–340.

14 B. Magnusson, *The Continental Shelf Beyond 200 Nautical Miles: Delineation, Delimitation, and Dispute Settlement,* (Brill, Nijhoff, 2015), p. 243.

the marine environment". The preamble further states that the "achievement of these goals will contribute to the realization of a just and equitable international economic order which takes into account the interests and needs of mankind as a whole and, in particular, the special interests and needs of developing countries, whether coastal or land-locked". UNCLOS also contains operative provisions, which are established to protect collective interests of the States parties. For instance, provisions of the UNCLOS relating to the freedom of the high seas,[15] conservation of the living resources of the high seas[16] and the Area exemplify the norms, which are established to protect collective interests of the international community as a whole.

Part XI of the UNCLOS establishes the status and the relevant rules related to the use of the Area. Article 136 (Part XI, Section 2) of the UNCLOS states that the "Area and its resources are the common heritage of mankind".[17] The Area is not subject to the jurisdiction of any State.[18] It belongs to all.[19] Moreover, Article 137(2) of the UNCLOS stipulates: "All rights in the resources of the Area are vested in mankind as a whole, on whose behalf the Authority shall act". The legal status of the Area suggests that no State has special interest in the Area. The interests of all States are equal and no State's interest in the Area enjoys a priority over the interests of any other State. All States are equally interested in the use of the Area. The wording of Article 137(2) implicitly suggests that the Authority is the organ entitled to act as a guardian of the Area or as *parens patriae*. Furthermore, Article 139(1) of the UNCLOS provides that "States Parties shall have the responsibility to ensure that activities in the Area, whether carried out by States Parties, or State enterprises or natural or juridical persons which possess the nationality of States Parties or are effectively controlled by them or their nationals, shall be carried out in conformity with this Part".

UNCLOS contains other provisions, which are established to protect collective interests of the States parties. Article 192 of the UNCLOS states that "States have the obligation to protect and preserve the marine environment". Article 194 of the UNLCOS imposes on States parties to the Convention an obligation to "take all measures ... that are necessary to prevent, reduce and control

15 Article 87 of the UNCLOS.

16 Article 119 of the UNCLOS. This includes the high seas freedoms of navigation, overflight, laying of submarine cables and pipelines, freedom to construct artificial islands and other installations, fishing, and scientific research. See Article 87, UNCLOS.

17 Article 140(1) states: "Activities in the Area shall, as specifically provided for in this Part, be carried out for the benefit of mankind as a whole".

18 "Area" means the seabed and ocean floor and subsoil thereof, beyond the limits of national jurisdiction; Article 1, para. 1(1) of the UNCLOS.

19 Article 137(1) of the UNCLOS.

pollution of the marine environment from any source…". This obligation applies both to instances of environmental damage inflicted on the coastal States but also instances of polluting the high seas. In the former case States act as injured whereas in the latter they act to protect collective interests.[20]

Status of the high seas also concerns interests of all. Article 87 of the UNCLOS provides that "the high seas are open to all States, whether coastal or land-locked. The freedoms[21] which States are entitled to exercise on the high seas should be exercised "with due regard for the interests of other States in their exercise of the freedom of the high seas, and also with due regard for the rights under this Convention with respect to activities in the Area".[22]

There is no doubt that inclusion of these provisions into UNCLOS was aimed to protect the interests beyond individual (special) interests of States parties. The purpose of these provisions is to protect collective interests which States have in the protection and preservation of the marine environment, exploitation of the resources of the Area or exercising the rights on the high seas. However, the very existence of norms aimed to protect collective interests does not automatically resolve the question of enforcement of such interests. It is important to reiterate that the means of enforcement of such norms may vary. Such norms can be enforced either in accordance with customary norms[23] concerning responsibility of States or pursuant to rules of the relevant treaty instruments.

UNCLOS contains dispute settlement provisions, which are aimed at resolving disputes between the States parties. Whether dispute settlement provisions of UNCLOS can be invoked to enforce substantive norms of the UNCLOS established to protect collective interests will be considered below. It has already been noted that UNCLOS does not expressly authorize *actio popularis* claims. Therefore, the existence of such a right need to be inferred from the dispute settlement provisions of the UNCLOS.

According to Article 288(1) (Part XV of the Convention) the jurisdiction of the International Tribunal for the Law of the Sea comprises disputes over

---

20 See para. 12 of the Commentary to Article 42 of the Articles on State Responsibility.

21 (a) freedom of navigation; (b) freedom of over flight; (c) freedom to lay submarine cables and pipelines, subject to Part VI; (d) freedom to construct artificial islands and other installations permitted under international law, subject to Part VI; (e) freedom of fishing, subject to the conditions laid down in Section 2; (f) freedom of scientific research, subject to Parts VI and XIII.

22 Article 87(2).

23 Oppenheim and Lauterpacht were amongst the scholars who supported the third-party actions in cases when the freedom of high seas was infringed. L. Oppenheim and H. Lauterpacht, *International Law,* (Longmans, Green & Co., London, Vol. I, 8th ed. 1955), p. 308.

interpretation and application of the Law of the Sea Convention referred to the Tribunal by the States parties. Unfortunately, Tribunal's case law does not provide any guidance on the meaning of the 'dispute' and whether the ITLOS is prepared to adjudicate claims intended to protect collective interests.

A missed opportunity for the ITLOS to deal with the question of enforcement of collective interests under the UNCLOS arose in the *Case Concerning the Conservation and Sustainable Exploitation of Swordfish Stocks in the South-Eastern Pacific Ocean*.[24] In this case Chile requested the Chamber to decide:

> (a) whether the European Community has complied with its obligations under the Convention, especially articles 116 to 119 thereof, to ensure conservation of swordfish, in the fishing activities undertaken by vessels flying the flag of any of its member States in the high seas adjacent to Chile's exclusive economic zone; (b) whether the European Community has complied with its obligations under the Convention, in particular article 64 thereof, to cooperate directly with Chile as a coastal State for the conservation of swordfish in the high seas adjacent to Chile's exclusive economic zone as also to report its catches and other information relevant to this fishery to the competent international organization and to the coastal State.[25]

The Tribunal did not decide the case on its merits because the Chamber of the Tribunal ordered discontinuance of the case due to the parties' agreement to conclude an "Understanding concerning the conservation of swordfish stocks in the South Eastern Pacific Ocean".[26]

Although one could argue that Chile had special interests in the preservation of the swordfish as a coastal State, this nevertheless does not deprive Chile's claim of its *actio popularis* nature. Chile expressly asked the Tribunal to decide that European Community violated its obligations under Articles 116–119 (Part VII, Section 2) of the UNCLOS. It has to be emphasized that conservation and management of environment of the high seas sits at the heart of Part VII of UNCLOS as the title of this part suggests. It can therefore be presumed that had the parties not discontinued the case the Tribunal could have found the Chile's claim as admissible. Although this presumption has little support in the practice of States parties to the UNCLOS, nevertheless the collective nature of the obligations in question and the need to ensure their effectiveness justifies

24 Chile/European Community, 20 December 2000, List of Cases No. 7.
25 Ibid. para. 3.
26 Ibid., para. 12.

a conclusion in favour of introducing mechanisms to enforce such obligations. *Actio popularis* claims can indubitably serve as one of the possible means of such enforcement.

The Seabed Disputes Chamber in the advisory opinion on the Responsibilities and Obligation of States Sponsoring Persons and Entities with Respect to Activities in the Area addressed the question concerning permissibility of *actio popularis* before ITLOS.[27] However, two caveats have to be made regarding this Opinion. Firstly, the opinion was given in a very specific and limited context as applicable to the regime of the Area. Secondly, the Chamber addressed the question of *actio popularis* in the context of non-binding advisory proceedings. Both issues raise serious concerns about the legal importance of the Chamber's findings as regards the general status of *actio popularis* before ITLOS. These caveats notwithstanding, the Chamber's decision may be illuminating in understanding the Chamber's thinking in giving practical effect to the concept of common heritage of mankind.

The Council of the International Seabed Authority asked the Court to decide on "legal responsibilities and obligations of States Parties to the Convention with respect to the sponsorship of activities in the Area…" as well as on the extent of liability of a State Party for any failure to comply with the provisions of the Convention, in particular Part XI, and the 1994 Agreement, by an entity whom it has sponsored under Article 153, paragraph 2 (b), of the Convention. However, the Court went beyond the questions posed and attempted to address further three points concerning the 'obligation to ensure', the precautionary approach and the enforcement of collective interests. The Chamber's analysis of these issues prompts a conclusion in support of existence of *actio popularis* before ITLOS.[28] The Chamber noted with reference to the Pulp Mills case that States have a customary law obligation to carry out an Environmental Impact Assessment related to activities beyond the limits of national jurisdiction.[29] The Chamber stated: "The Court's reasoning in a transboundary context may also apply to activities with an impact on the environment in an area beyond the limits of national jurisdiction; and the Court's references to 'shared resources' may also apply to resources that are the common heritage of mankind".[30] The Chamber's position on the question of EIA in the Area is informed by significance it attributes to the Area as a common heritage of mankind and the view of the Chamber that "the role of the sponsoring State is

27 List of cases: No. 17, Advisory Opinion of 1 February 2011, ITLOS Reports 2011, p. 10.
28 D. French, *The International Journal of Coastal and Maritime Law, 26* (2011), p. 534.
29 Ad. Opinion, para. 148. See also D. French, (2011), p. 543.
30 Ad. Opinion, para. 148.

to contribute to the common interest of all States in the proper implementation of the principle of the common heritage of mankind".[31] D. French poses a question as to who has the standing to sue the sponsoring State for failure to act in accordance with its obligations under the regime.[32] The Chamber's view on this question was that the damage to the Area and the marine environment could be compensated upon a claim made by coastal States (this entitlement arises from general international law for injured States) and "entities engaged in deep-seabed mining".[33] Chamber took a very progressive view, first of all, when it decided that the Authority could make claims as part of its power to act "on behalf of" the mankind under Article 137. The Chamber made this decision in the absence of any express conventional stipulation concerning the power of Authority to make such claims.[34] The Chamber's decision was based on the role UNCLOS assigned to the Authority as a guardian of the Area to act "on behalf" of the mankind. It follows that the Authority's power to act was implied in the nature of obligations concerning the Area.[35] However, the Chamber's position extended as far as recognizing the right of each State party to claim compensation from the sponsoring state for failure to comply with its obligations.[36] According to the Chamber subjects entitled to claim compensation may include the Authority, entities engaged in deep seabed mining, other users of the sea, and coastal States.[37] The Chamber's conclusion amounts to recognition of *actio popularis* claims submitted by States to protect the

31 Ibid, para. 226. The Chamber noted in this regard: "In the sphere of the obligation to assist the Authority acting on behalf of mankind as a whole, while deciding what measures are reasonably appropriate, the sponsoring State must take into account, objectively, the relevant options in a manner that is reasonable, relevant and conducive to the benefit of mankind as a whole. It must act in good faith, especially when its action is likely to affect prejudicially the interests of mankind as a whole". para. 230 of the Opinion.

32 D. French, (2011), p. 544.

33 Ibid., p. 545. The Chamber noted in this regard: "No provision of the Convention can be read as explicitly entitling the Authority to make such a claim. It may, however, be argued that such entitlement is implicit in article 137, paragraph 2, of the Convention, which states that the Authority shall act "on behalf" of mankind". para. 180 of the Opinion.

34 D. French, (2011), p. 545.

35 D. French, (2011), p. 545.

36 The Chamber notes: Neither the Convention nor the relevant Regulations (regulation 30 of the Nodules Regulations and regulation 32 of the Sulphides Regulations) specifies what constitutes compensable damage, or which subjects may be entitled to claim compensation. It may be envisaged that the damage in question would include damage to the Area and its resources constituting the common heritage of mankind, and damage to the marine environment. para. 179.

37 para. 179.

environment of the Area.[38] The Chamber justified its view with reference to the *erga omnes* character of the obligations relating to the Area.[39]

Similarly, the right of action by third States before ITLOS can be justified in the claims to extend the continental shelf into the international deep seabed. The 1982 Law of the Sea Convention provides for the right by coastal States to extend the limits of the continental shelf beyond 200 nautical miles in accordance with Article 76 of the UNCLOS. The deep seabed, an Area which stretches beyond the limits of the coastal State's continental shelf constitutes a common heritage of mankind.[40]

States parties to the UNCLOS may submit data and other material to the Commission on the Limits of the Continental Shelf in order to extend the limits of their continental shelf beyond 200 nautical miles.[41] The Commission makes recommendations as to the limits and this recommendation serves as a basis for States to determine the limits of the continental shelf, which shall be final and binding.[42] In case a dispute arises regarding the limits so established (i.e. by following the procedure in the convention) courts have little to say about such disputes because the continental shelf established by recommendation of the Commission becomes final and binding.[43] However, when a State extends its continental shelf without a recommendation from the Commission its claim of extension may be disputed by third States "whose rights and interests are affected by such a claim" as well as third States parties to the UNCLOS whose rights and interests are not specially affected by determination of the outer limits of the continental shelf.[44] The latter's action to challenge the claimed limits of the outer continental shelf will amount to *actio popularis* because a State party will not act in its own interests but in the interest of securing the international seabed which forms part of the common heritage of mankind.[45] According to Karagiannis a claim concerning the Area (delimitation of the

38 D. French, (2011), p. 546.

39 The Chamber noted: "Each State Party may also be entitled to claim compensation in light of the *erga omnes* character of the obligations relating to preservation of the environment of the high seas and in the Area". Para. 180 of the Opinion.

40 See Part XI of the UNCLOS.

41 Article 76(8) of the UNCLOS.

42 Ibid.

43 Ibid. See also L. Nelson, The Settlement of Disputes Arising from Conflicting Outer Continental Shelf Claims, *The International Journal of Maritime and Coastal law*, 24 (2009), p. 418.

44 Ibid.

45 Ibid., pp. 419–420. J. Noyes, 'Judicial and Arbitral Proceedings and the Outer Limits of the Continental Shelf' (2009) 42 *Vanderbilt Journal of Transnational Law*, p. 1126.

shelf) under Part XV of the Law of the Sea Convention resulting in a binding decision would amount to *actio popularis* which, Karagiannis argues, is not a permissible right of action under Law of the Sea Convention.[46]

However, Karagiannis is right to say that no express stipulation of *actio popularis* concerning the outer limits of the continental shelf exists under UNCLOS. Wolfrum also adheres to this view.[47] Wolfrum contends that unlike provisions of UNCLOS which expressly entitle States parties for instance to delimit the territorial sea between States with opposite or adjacent coasts,[48] delimit the EEZ between States with opposite or adjacent coasts[49] or delimit the continental shelf between States with opposite or adjacent coasts UNCLOS does not expressly allow States parties to bring claims concerning extension of the outer limits of the continental shelf.[50] Wolfrum raises a more fundamental question whether claims against the States, which extend their continental shelves into the Area amount to *actio popularis* or a simple *actio*.[51] In support of his view that claims over the excessive delimitation of the outer limits of the continental shelf do not amount to *actio popularis* Wolfrum invokes Articles 140, para. 2 and 153, para. 2(b) together with Article 4, Annex III to the UNCLOS.[52] He maintains that because Article 153, para. 2(b) entitles States parties and persons of the States parties to engage in activities in the Area excessive delimitation of the continental shelf may affect the States' individual potential interests in maintaining the mining sites in the Area rather than collective interests as one of the members of the international community.[53] He further contends that Article 140, para. 2 also provides basis to object against extension of the outer limits of the continental shelf because it may affect the '... equitable sharing of financial and other economic benefits derived from activities in the Area...".[54] Wolfrum contends that claims under these articles will not

46 S. Karagiannis "Observations sur la Commission des Limites du Plateau Continental" (1994) 8 *Espaces et Ressources Maritimes*, p. 189.

47 R. Wolfrum, The Outer Continental Shelf: Some Considerations Concerning Applications and the Potential Role of the International Tribunal for the Law of the Sea Statement at the 73rd Biennial Conference of the International Law Association, Rio de Janeiro, Brazil, 21 August 2008, pp. 9–10.

48 Article 298, paragraph 1(a), UNCLOS.

49 Article 74, UNCLOS.

50 Article 83, UNCLOS.

51 S. Suarez, *The Outer Limits of the Continental Shelf: Legal Aspects of their Establishment*, (Springer, Berlin, 2008), p. 250.

52 R. Wolfrum (2008), pp. 13–14.

53 Ibid. p. 13.

54 Ibid. p. 14.

amount to *actio popularis* given the specific interest of the States in the resources of the Area. This interest, he argues, constitutes a legal interest for the purposes of Article 287 of the UNCLOS.[55] Nevertheless, he does not completely rule out the possibility of *actio popularis* under the UNCLOS. On the contrary, Wolfrum contends that Article 288 of the UNCLOS provides sound basis for *actio popularis* because it does not contain an express requirement to show a legal interest and that a mere disagreement on application or interpretation suffices for the dispute to exist under Article 288 of the UNCLOS.[56]

Perhaps one must agree with Wolfrum that the term "dispute" is open to interpretation by the relevant court or tribunal. Furthermore, in the absence of a requirement to show a special (legal) interest nothing precludes bringing an *actio popularis* claim by way of liberal interpretation of the term dispute and of substantive rules in the Convention.[57]

It has to be noted that the wording of the jurisdictional clause in Article 288(1) of the UNCLOS is similar to the wording in most compromissory clauses of international treaties.[58] The ICJ's slow but steady departure from the strict interpretation of the term "dispute" in the *South West Africa* cases to a more liberal interpretation of the term in the *Questions relating to the Obligation to Prosecute or Extradite* case suggests that, in cases concerning collective interests, the ICJ is prepared to decide cases which involve interests beyond the claimant's special interests. This approach can also be adopted by ITLOS.

Another important issue relates to the nature of the interests protected under the UNCLOS. Wolfrum argues that interests in the Area are not collective and indeed special because every State party has special interest in the resources of the Area. Indeed, every collective interest can be viewed as an aggregate

55 Ibid.

56 Ibid.

57 However, under some treaties this requirement is expressly stated in the jurisdictional clauses of the international treaty instruments which serve as a basis of the claim. For instance Article 2 of the Hispano-Belgian Treaty of Conciliation, Judicial Settlement and Arbitration of 19 July 1927 which formed the basis of the ICJ's jurisdiction in the *Barcelona Traction* case states that "disputes of every kind between the High Contracting Parties with regard to which the Parties are in conflict *as to their respective rights,* and which it may not have been possible to settle amicably by the normal methods of diplomacy, shall be submitted for decision to an arbitral tribunal or to the Permanent Court of International Justice".

58 Majority of compromissory clauses in treaty instruments refer to "disputes" concerning "interpretation" or "application" of treaties. See J. Charney, Compromissory Clauses and the Jurisdiction of the International Court of Justice, 81 *AJIL*, 1987, p. 856.

of individual interests and if this logic is followed the divide between general and special (individual) interests becomes redundant. Broadly speaking States acting to protect collective interests can also invoke individual interest as a basis of their claim. Even in the most vivid example of enforcement of collective interests, e.g. willingness to protect global environment, such protection can arguably be based on special interests of States because apart from collective interest of all States to protect environment that interest can also be perceived as aggregate of special interests of every State. Therefore, potentially dual character of collective interests involved in the protection of the resources of the Area does not preclude *actio popularis*.

It also has to be stressed that Karagiannis's contention that UNCLOS does not expressly provide for *actio popularis* does not completely rule out the possibility of bringing *actio popularis* as means of enforcement of collective obligations under UNCLOS. It has already been noted that provisions of the UNLCOS, which are established to protect collective interests, taken in conjunction with Article 288 of the UNCLOS, may be taken as a legal basis to assert *actio popularis* claims before ITLOS by inference. For instance, in cases before the ICJ to which reference has been made, treaty instruments, which did not expressly vest in the States parties the right to bring an *actio popularis* claim could be interpreted by the Court to envision such a right by inference. In all of the cases before the ICJ the right of *actio popularis* had been inferred from the nature of the substantive norm coupled with the ICJ's liberal interpretation of the terms of the compromissory clause (i.e. of the rules of standing). Therefore nothing precludes ITLOS to adopt (or mirror) the ICJ's approach and interpret Article 288 of UNCLOS (compromissory clause) together with its substantive norms established to protect collective interests as vesting in States parties to the UNCLOS to bring *actio popularis* claims.

The foregoing analysis suggests that the admissibility of *actio popularis* before ITLOS will depend on whether the primary norm is established to protect collective interests and the Court's willingness to construe its standing provisions in light of the nature of the obligations. This reinforces the central argument in the book between the interdependence of the primary norms (i.e. whether they are established to protect collective interests) and secondary rules devised to enforce such primary norms. Although the following section applies the same test to address the question of legality of *actio popularis*, however the difference in the institutional character in which CJEU operates reveal challenges of applicability of *actio popularis* that are specific to the European Union's *sui generis* nature.

2 CJEU

2.1 *Conception of Causes of Action: Cautious Approach to Relaxing the Direct and Individual Interest Test*

Article 258 of the Treaty on the Functioning of the European Union (hereinafter TFEU)[59] entitles the Commission to bring before the Court of Justice of the European Union cases of failure by member States to comply with their obligations under Treaties. The Commission acts as *parens patriae*, i.e. the "guardian of the Treaties".[60] This procedure is similar to relator actions in UK administrative law or actions taken to enforce criminal laws by the law enforcement authorities in municipal laws of some countries. Actions of this kind aim to protect interests of objective character such as the interest in compliance with the law and basically amount, as Anthony Arnul puts it, to "abolition of any requirement of standing".[61] In this sense actions brought by the Commission are in the nature of *actio popularis*. This express stipulation in the Treaty text raises no controversy as to the entitlement by the Commission to bring claims before the CJEU. The same is true for privileged applicants, which bring actions for annulment under Article 263(2) as well as semi-privileged applicants under Article 263(3) of the TFEU.[62] Interests of these institutions are automatically presumed. However, legality of *actio popularis* in cases of private parties under Article 263(4) has been the source of heated debate due to the strictness of the standing requirements envisaged thereunder. In fact, it is argued that the requirement of direct and individual concern envisaged in Article 263 was introduced to preclude the possibility of *actio popularis*.[63]

Article 263, paragraph 4 of the Treaty on the Functioning of the European Union (TFEU) stipulates:

> Any natural or legal person may, under the conditions laid down in the first and second paragraphs, institute proceedings against an act addressed to that person or which is of direct and individual concern to

59 OJC 326, 26.10.2012, pp. 47–390.

60 A. Kaczorowska, *European Union Law*, 3rd ed., Routledge, London, 2013, p. 377. On the notion of *parens patriae* claims before the CJEU see D. Hare, 'Blue Jeans, Chewing Gum and Climate Change Litigation: American Exports to Europe', *Utrecht Journal of International and European Law*, 2013, Vol. 29/76, pp. 65–87.

61 A. Arnull, Challenging Community Acts – an Introduction, in H. Micklitz & N. Reich (eds.), *European Public Interest Litigation*, (Nomos, Baden-Baden), 1996, p. 40.

62 The privileged applicants are: The Council, the EP, the Commission and the Member States. The semi-privileged applicants include CoA, the ECB and the CoR and they have *locus standi* in order to protect their prerogatives (Article 263(3)).

63 L. Gormley, *Public Interest Litigation and State Subsidies* in H. Miclitz (1996), p. 159.

> them, and against a regulatory act which is of direct concern to them and does not entail implementing measures.

Despite the conditions to bring private action before the EU judicature is clearly spelled out in the Treaty, the main difficulty, however, lies in determining the precise meaning of "direct and individual concern".

The EU courts have produced extensive case law on the construction of the term "direct and individual concern". The Court's case law suggests that the CJEU has applied the "individual concern" requirement very strictly even for claims seeking to protect such diffuse interests as environment. Kramer notes in this regard: "The barrier of 'direct and individual concern in Article 173 is a barrier which individuals or environmental organizations are not able to overcome. That barrier remains as insurmountable as ever".[64] Despite suggestions to liberalize the individual concern test[65] the Court remained loyal to the narrow and rigid construction of the concept as articulated in the *Plauman & Co v Commission*.[66] The Court noted:

> Persons other than those to whom a decision is addressed may only claim to be individually concerned if that decision affects them by reason of certain attributes which are peculiar to them or by reason of circumstances in which they are differentiated from all other persons and by virtue of these factors distinguishes them individually just as in the case of the person addressed. In the present case the applicant is affected by the disputed Decision as an importer of Clementines, that is to say, by reason of a commercial activity which may at any time be practiced by any person and is not therefore such as to distinguish the applicant in relation to the contested Decision as in the case of the addressee.[67]

It follows from the foregoing passage that belonging to the open rather than closed group serves as a decisive factor in dismissing the application.[68] Thus,

---

64 L. Kramer, Public Interest Litigation in Environmental Matters Before European Courts, in H. Miclitz, (2013), p. 315.

65 Advocate-General's Opinion in Case C-50/00 *Union de Pequeños Agricultores v Council* (UPA) [2002] ECR I-6677.

66 See S. Peers & M. Costa, Court of Justice of the European Union (General Chamber), Judicial review of EU Acts after the Treaty of Lisbon, p. 1, available at http://openaccess.city.ac.uk/5846/1/; Case T-262/10 *Microban v Commission*, (2012) 8 European Constitutional Law Review, pp. 82–104, p. 85.

67 Case 25/62, *Plaumann & Co v Commission* [1963] E.C.R. 95.

68 A. Albors-Llorens, The Standing of Private Parties to Challenge Community Measures: Has the European Court missed the boat, *Cambridge Law Journal*, 2003, p. 77. See also, K. Davis, Understanding European Union Law, (Routledge, Oxford, 2011, 4th ed.), p. 104.

Plaumann decision sets a very restrictive test of individual concern which is extremely hard to satisfy because all areas of business are normally open to everyone.[69]

The requirement of individual concern and its construction by the Court have been subjected to harsh criticism amongst the commentators as excessively limiting access for the private parties to the Court and leading to a denial of justice.[70] On the other hand, arguments were made the preliminary reference procedure available for courts of EU member states provided for effective judicial protection capable of compensating the rigid standing rules limiting the rights of private parties to access CJEU.[71] This explains the CJEU's consistency and uniformity in applying the *Plaumann test*, unwilling to reverse or loosen the strict, generally known as "closed class test" of admissibility before the Court.[72] As noted above, the need to apply the condition of individual and direct concern as strictly as possible aimed to preclude *actio popularis* claims.[73] Despite its general unwillingness to liberalize the standing requirements, the CJEU singled out particular areas of EU law in which it was prepared to depart from the *Plaumann test* and to interpret Article 263 more permissively and thus to expand the scope of potential applicants. These included anti-dumping,[74]

69 P. Craig, *Legality, Standing and Substantive Review in Community Law, Oxford Journal of Legal Studies*, vol. 14, No. 4, pp. 509–510.

70 M. Eliantonio and H. Roer-Eide, Regional Courts and *locus standi* for Private Parties: Can the CJEU Learn Something from the Others? *The Law and Practice of International Courts and Tribunals* 13 (2014), p. 29. R. Kovar, Chronique de la jurisprudence de la Cour de Justice des Communautés européennes, *Journal de Droit International*, 93, 1966, No. 1, p. 710. On the point that restrictive rules of standing constitute a bar to effective judicial protection see J. Haynes, Revisiting the *locus standi* of private applicants in judicial review proceedings under CARICOM and EU law: a comparative perspective, Commonwealth Law Bulletin, 2015 Vol. 41, No. 1, p. 59. Some even argue that restricted access to the CJEU to challenge EU measures violates article 6(1) of the European Convention on Human Rights.

71 See Case 294/83 Parti écologiste "Les Verts" v European Parliament [1986] ECR 1339, para. 23. A. Ward, Locus Standi under Article 230 (4) of the EC Treaty: Crafting a Coherent Test for a 'Wobbly Polity', *Yearbook of European Law*, 2003, Vol. 22, Issue 1, pp. 52–53. For the view that the CJEU should interpret standing provisions teleologically when effective protection of the rights of citizens is at stake, see A. Arnull, 'The Action for Annulment: A Case of Double Standards?' in D. O'Keefe and A. Bavasso (eds.), *Judicial Review in European Union Law*, (Liber Amicorum in honour of Lord Slynn of Hadley, Volume I (The Hague, 2000), p. 188.

72 See the line of cases Kik case (Case T-107/94) 2 CMLR 857; *Producteurs de fruits* case (Case 16+17/62, (1962) ECR 517).

73 See G. Berg, *Development of Judicial Control in the European Communities*, (The Hague, 1981), p. 21.

74 Joined Cases 239 and 275/82 *Allied Corporation v Commission* [1984] E.C.R. 1005, para. 11; Case C-358/89 *Extramet v Council* [1991] E.C.R. I-2501, para. 14; E. Vermulst, D. Rovetta, "Judicial Review of Anti-dumping Determinations in the EU" (2012) 7 *Global Trade and*

state aid,[75] competition,[76] agriculture[77] cases. However, even in these cases the Court's willingness to liberalize the "individual concern" requirement was nothing but a move from a very strict *Plaumann* test to simply strict test of standing, falling short of introducing *actio popularis*. What is more, the CJEU's case law of past few years does not provide a glimpse of hope that the *Plaumann* test will be revisited.[78]

The Court was unwilling to lax the standing requirements even in cases which extended beyond individual rights/interests of applicants and involved diffuse interests such as the interest in environmental protection. Greenpeace case is a good case in point where the Court refused to depart from the *Plaumann* test.[79] The case involved applications filed to the Court, seeking to annul the EU Directive to allocate to the Spanish government funds to "reimburse the expenses incurred in the construction of the two power stations in Canary Islands".[80] The applicants proposed that the CFI and the Court grant standing based on the fact that "third-party applicants had suffered or would potentially suffer loss or detriment from the harmful environmental effects arising out of unlawful conduct on the part of Community institutions".[81] For CFI and the Court position of the applicants, i.e. "fisherman", "local resident", or "farmer" "or of persons concerned by the impact which the building of two power

---

Customs Journal, Issue 5, pp. 240–247; A. Arnull, Private Applicants and the Action for Annulment since Codorniu, CMLR, 38, 2001, pp. 7–8.

75 Parti écologiste "Les Verts" v European Parliament, Judgment of the Court of 23 April 1986, Case 294/83, (Grounds). T. Tridimas, The Court of Justice and Judicial Activism. *Eur. L. Rev*, 1996, p. 208. A. Albors-Llorens, (2003), p. 79. This decision departs from the *Plaumann* test by ignoring the "closed group" test and according standing to the unidentifiable group. The decision is portrayed by some commentators as exemplifying judicial activism by the European Court owing to the importance of the issues involving public interests served as a basis for the Court to depart from the straightjacket of standing requirements under Article 230(4) of the Treaty.

76 N. Reich, *Public Interest Litigation before European Jurisdictions*, in H. Micklitz (1996), p. 11. Competition case involving liberal interpretation of the standing provisions is Case 26/76, *Metro-SB-Großmärkte GmbH & Co KG v Commission* [1977] ECR, p. 1875.

77 *Codorniu v Council*, Case C-308/89 [1994] E.C.R. I-1853, para. 19.

78 S. Weatherill, *Cases and Materials on EU Law* (OUP, Oxford, 2014), p. 200.

79 For a criticism of the CFI's interpretation of the standing requirements in Greenpeace case see P. Sands, *Rethinking Environmental Rights – Climate Change, Conservation and the ECJ* (2008), *ELM*, 17, pp. 120–126.

80 *Stichting Greenpeace Council (Greenpeace International) and Others v Commission*, Judgment of the Court, 2 April 1998, CASE C-321/95, para. 3, p. I–1707. Applications were brought by NGOs, people who lived in the neighbourhood and in the immediate vicinity of the construction site. See also *Marie-Thérèse Danielsson, Pierre Largenteau, Ewin Haoa v Commission of the European Communities* case (T-219/95 R, 22 December 1995, [1995] ECR:II 3051) where the Court applied the same standing standards as in Greenpeace case.

81 *Greenpeace*, para. 8, p. I–1708.

stations might have on local tourism, on the health of Canary Island residents and on the environment, relied on by the applicants, did not differ from that of all the people living or pursuing an activity in the areas concerned".[82] Applicants maintained that *Plaumann* test does not compel application of the closed class test to all situations.[83] They further contend that effective protection of environment warrants less restrictive construction of standing rules.[84] The Court rejected the applicants' argument that the claims brought to protect environment justify differential treatment of the standing requirements envisaged under Article 173(4).[85]

The foregoing analysis suggests that the CJEU is unwilling to depart from its rigid construction of the "individual concern" requirement to allow for *actio popularis* even in cases involving protection of collective interests.[86] The reasons for such a conservative stance are analysed in great detail in the final chapter of the book. However, as a preliminary point it is important to note that the CJEU has considered the issue of standing by private parties as a question of policy which involves variety of concerns ranging from increase in the Court's case load to the relations of the Court with other EU organs and States parties to the Lisbon Treaty. For CJEU, like for other international courts and tribunals, the question of interpretation of the rules of standing has been an act of balancing between competing interests of exercising judicial discretion and providing better access for private parties to the Court on the one hand, and the demands of deferring the issue of standing to other EU organs or the States on the other.[87] These issues as applicable to CJEU will be dealt with in

82 Ibid, para. 12, p. I–1709.

83 Ibid, para. 26, p. I–1714.

84 *Greenpeace,* para. 26, p. I–1714, See E. Valencia-Ospina, who also argues in favour of revision of rules of standing in favour of laxing them in cases of environmental protection before the ICJ. International Court of Justice and International Environmental Law, *Asian Yearbook of International Law,* 1992, Volume 2, p. 5.

85 *Greenpeace,* para. 30, p. I–1715; See P. Sands who maintains that because environmental harm cannot be caused to one particular person it is even hypothetically impossible to apply the "closed group" test to such applications. P. Sands (2008), p. 121.

86 General analysis of the reasons for CJEU's conservative stance on the question of standing in environmental matters see S. Bogojević, "Judicial Protection of Individual Applicants Revisited: Access to Justice through the Prism of Judicial Subsidiarity," *Yearbook of European Law,* 33 (2015), pp. 5–25.

87 The CJEU noted in this regard: "While it is, admittedly, possible to envisage a system of judicial review of the legality of Community measures of general application different from that established by the founding Treaty and never amended as to its principles, *it is for the Member States, if necessary, in accordance with Article 48 EU, to reform the system currently in force*". *UPA v Council,* Judgment of the Court, paras. 44–45; See also Christopher Harding who notes that the Court is not favourable to step into what it thinks to be the realm

greater detail in Chapter VI as part of the broader question of judicial policy concerns which international courts and tribunals face when interpreting the rules of standing.

The analysis of the CJEU's case law reflects a restrictive view of the standing rules and unwillingness by the judicature to interpret the standing provisions permissively. The reasons, which underlie such an approach, are discussed in the final Chapter of the book dealing with judicial policy concerns, which affected strict interpretation of standing rules. The next section addresses *actio popularis* before the European Court on Human Rights.

3 ECtHR

The ECtHR's approach to the admissibility of claims has remained unchanged since its inception. Victim requirement stated in Article 34 refers to "the person directly affected by the act or omission in issue, the existence of a violation being conceivable even in the absence of detriment; detriment is relevant only in the context of Article 50 (art. 50)".[88] The Court assesses the admissibility of individual applications under Article 34 against two main conditions. First "an applicant must fall into one of the categories of petitioners mentioned in Article 34", second "he or she must be able to make out a case that he or she is the victim of a violation of the Convention".[89]

According to the ECtHR's case law Article 34 precludes filing *actio popularis* claims, challenging the law *in abstracto*, or prior to the violation has actually taken place.[90] The ECtHR repeatedly rejected admissibility of *actio popularis* claims. It noted:

---

of member States' legislative power. *The Private Interest in Challenging Community Action,* 1980, 5 *European Law Review,* p. 354.

88 Case of Van Der Sluijs, Zuiderveld and Klappe v the Netherlands, (Application no. 9362/81; 9363/81; 9387/81), Judgment, 22 May 1984, para. 37, *Amuur v France,* judgment of 25 June 1996, Reports of Judgments and Decisions 1996 III, para. 36.

89 See, among other authorities, *Tauira and Others v France,* no. 28204/95, Commission decision of 4 December 1995, Decisions and Reports (DR) 83-B, p. 112; *Association des amis de Saint-Raphaël et de Fréjus and Others v France,* no. 38192/97, Commission decision of 1 July 1998, DR 94-B, p. 124; *Comité des médecins à diplômes étrangers v France and Others v France* (dec.), nos. 39527/98 and 39531/98, 30 March 1999).

90 Most recently, *Ouardiri v Switzerland* in which the Court dismissed the application in which the applicant contended that the Swiss constitutional prohibition to build minarets violated Article 9 of the European Convention. The Court found that because the applicants did not plan to build the minarets they were not victims under Article 34, hence their claim amounted to *actio popularis.* No. 65840/09 (2011)DA. The Christian Federation of Jehovah's Witnesses in France v France, (Translation) 06.11.2001, 53430/99, available at

> that Article 34 of the Convention requires that an individual applicant should claim to have been actually affected by the violation he alleges. That Article does not institute for individuals a kind of *actio popularis* for the interpretation of the Convention; it does not permit individuals to complain against a law *in abstracto* simply because they feel that it contravenes the Convention. In principle, it does not suffice for an individual applicant to claim that the mere existence of a law violates his rights under the Convention; it is necessary that the law should have been applied to his detriment.[91]

As far as the victim requirement under Article 34 is concerned, it serves as a guardian of the Court's "admissibility gates". The conventional wisdom, as far as admissibility of the claim is concerned, states that only those, who suffer direct damage in the form of impairment of their convention rights, can claim to be a "victim" under Article 34 of the Convention. However, the Court interpreted the victim requirement in variety of ways depending on the circumstances of each case. Although the ECtHR requires that the applicant is directly affected by the violation, under some circumstances the Court has been willing to construe the standing requirements not in a "rigid, mechanical and inflexible way…"[92] The Court tried to shed light on this problem in the case of *Leigh and Others v the United Kingdom.* According to the Court, "the form of detriment required must be of a less indirect and remote nature". For instance, in cases when the "direct victim dies before the application is lodged with the Court" the Court was prepared to construe the victim requirement more liberally to allow the relative of the deceased to bring a claim before the Court "when the complaints raised an issue of general interest pertaining to "respect for human rights".[93]

For ECtHR a victim is not only a person who is directly affected by the breach but also anyone who can "produce reasonable and convincing evidence of the likelihood that a violation affecting them personally will occur;

---

http://hudoc.echr.coe.int/sites/eng/pages/search.aspx?i=001-23238"itemid":["001-23238"] para. 35. *Klass and Others v Germany*, 6 September 1978, § 33, Series A no. 28; *The Georgian Labour Party v Georgia* (dec.), no. 9103/04, 22 May 2007; Matija OČIĆ v Croatia, Application no. 46306/99, 25 November 1999.

91 *Klass and Others v Germany*, 6 September 1978, Series A no. 28, para. 33. The Christian Federation of Jehovah's Witnesses in France v France, (Translation) 06.11.2001, 53430/99.

92 *Case of Karner v Austria*, (Application no. 40016/98), 24 July 2003, para. 25, and *Fairfield and Others v the United Kingdom*, No. 24790/04, ECHR 2005-VI).

93 *Case of Centre for Legal Resources on behalf of Valentin Câmpeanu v Romania*, Grand Chamber, (Application no. 47848/08), Grand Chamber, 17 July 2014, para. 98.

mere suspicion or conjecture is insufficient in this respect".[94] However, it should be noted that the criteria, which the Court developed, are open ended. The open-ended nature of these criteria has raised legitimate concerns that they may open the door for *actio popularis* claims. For instance, the open-ended nature of the criteria has allowed the Court to introduce the concept of a potential victim and thus broaden the scope of applicants to the Court. *Klass and others v Germany* case exemplifies the former. In this case the claimants challenged the Act of 13 August 1968 on Restrictions on the Secrecy of the Mail, Post and Telecommunications as being contrary to the European Convention in that "it permits those measures without obliging the authorities in every case to notify the persons concerned after the event …", hence depriving persons of the opportunity to challenge the surveillance measures in violation of Articles 6, 8 and 13 of the Convention.[95] Because the German Government never applied the Law against the applicants, it maintained in the course of the proceedings before the Commission and the Court, that the applicants did not qualify as "victims" under Article 25 (former) of the Convention. According to German government, the applicants were neither actual nor even potential victims and that they sought from the Court simply a hypothetical review of the legislation.[96] The Court stated as follows:

> Article 25 (art. 25) does not institute for individuals a kind of *actio popularis* for the interpretation of the Convention; it does not permit individuals to complain against a law *in abstracto* simply because they feel that it contravenes the Convention. In principle, it does not suffice for an individual applicant to claim that the mere existence of a law violates his rights under the Convention; it is necessary that the law should have been applied to his detriment. Nevertheless, as both the Government and the Commission pointed out, a law may by itself violate the rights of an individual if the individual is directly affected by the law in the absence of any specific measure of implementation.[97]

The Court furthermore noted: "A right of recourse to the Commission for persons potentially affected by secret surveillance is to be derived from Article

94 *Tauira and 18 Others v France*, application no. 28204/95, Commission decision of 4 December 1995, Decisions and Reports (DR) 83-B, p. 131, and *Monnat v Switzerland*, no.73604/01, paras. 31–32, ECHR 2006-X)- Quoted at para. 101 of the *Valentin Câmpeanu v Romania* case.

95 *Klass v Germany*, para. 10.

96 Ibid. para. 30.

97 Ibid. para. 33.

25 (art. 25), since otherwise Article 8 (art. 8) runs the risk of being nullified".[98] The Court also pointed out that the facts of the case suggested that the surveillance system established by the relevant law put all persons in Germany under the risk of having their mail and other means of communication monitored.[99] Although the measure was not applied to the applicants specifically, all persons in Germany could have been potentially subjected to this measure.[100] Based on the foregoing the Court concluded that "... the disputed legislation directly affects all users or potential users of the postal and telecommunication services in the Federal Republic of Germany.[101] The foregoing prompts a conclusion that where the law of a country is likely to have immediate effect on persons and where the risk that the law will be applied is 'real and effective, but not hypothetical' individuals shall have a right to challenge such law before the ECHR.[102] The Court applied the same reasoning in the *Campbell and Cosans v UK* case[103] in which the applicants complained of the school disciplinary system, which allowed to apply corporal punishment to children in schools to enforce discipline. The applicants in this case maintained, with reference to the *Klass v Germany* case, that their children could claim to be victims of the violation for the purposes of Article 25 of the Convention despite they were not actually punished.[104] By describing the school as a 'closed society' the claimants submitted that the risk of children being punished by the age of sixteen was too serious (high) to satisfy the victim requirement under Article 25 of the Convention.[105] Contrary to the Government submission that the claims amounted to *actio popularis* because the applicants suffered no real punishment, the Commission found that the Government's interpretation of the victim requirement under Article 25 was too 'rigid and run counter to the object and purpose of the Convention in general and Article 25 in particular.[106] However, the Court's case law suggests that the interpretation and application of the victim requirement has not been consistent with the Court's commitment to exclude *actio popularis* claims. An argument can be made that the

98 Ibid. para. 36.
99 Ibid.
100 Ibid.
101 Ibid.
102 D. Harris, O'Boyle & Warbrick, *Law of the European Convention on Human Rights,* (OUP, Oxford, 2nd ed., 2009), p. 792.
103 A 48(1982).
104 *Campbell and Cosans v UK,* Report of the Commission, 16 May 1980, Applications Nos. 7511/76 and 77 3/76, para. 36.
105 Ibid. para. 37.
106 Ibid. para. 116.

Court, intentionally or not, introduced *actio popularis* by liberally interpreting the victim requirement. The *Open Door Well* case exemplifies the point.[107]

The case concerned multiple applications brought before the Commission by two Irish companies, Open Door Counselling Ltd and Dublin Well Woman Centre Ltd, one US citizen, Ms. Bonnie Maher, and three Irish citizens, Ms. Ann Downes, Mrs. X and Ms. Maeve Geraghty.[108] All applicants challenged the injunction issued by Irish courts, which banned Open Door and Dublin Well to provide abortion-related counselling to pregnant women, who wanted to have abortion outside Ireland.[109] All applicants claimed that the injunction interfered with the right under Article 10 of the ECHR to "impart or receive" information, while Open Door, Mrs. X and Ms. Geraghty further complained of interference with "their right to respect for private life" in violation of Article 8 of the Convention.[110] The Respondent, government of Ireland, objected to the Court's jurisdiction as far as the applications of Ms. Maher, Ms. Downes, Mrs. X and Ms. Geraghty who were not pregnant and neither did they take part in the proceedings before the courts in Ireland.[111] According to Irish government, this circumstance disqualified Ms. Maher, Ms. Downes, Mrs. X and Ms. Geraghty from being "victims" and their claims amounted to *actio popularis*.[112] This was especially the case so as far as the claims Mrs. X and Ms. Geraghty were concerned.[113]

In the course of the proceedings before the Commission the Irish Government accepted that Mrs. Maher and Downes were victims of the violation by virtue of the direct application of the Supreme Court's injunction to these applicants.[114] As far as Mrs. X and Ms. Geraghty were concerned the Court stated as follows:

> In the present case the Supreme Court injunction restrained the corporate applicants and their servants and agents from providing certain information to pregnant women. Although it has not been asserted that Mrs. X and Ms. Geraghty are pregnant, it is not disputed that they belong to a class of women of child-bearing age which may be adversely affected by the restrictions imposed by the injunction. They are not seeking to

107 Application no. 14234/88; 14235/88).
108 *Dublin Well*, para. 1.
109 Ibid. para. 9.
110 Ibid. para. 36.
111 Ibid. para. 41.
112 Ibid.
113 Ibid.
114 Ibid. paras. 42–43.

> challenge *in abstracto* the compatibility of Irish law with the Convention since they run a risk of being directly prejudiced by the measure complained of. They can thus claim to be "victims" within the meaning of Article 25 para. 1 (art. 25–1).[115]

The main criterion which the Court relied on to consider Mrs. X and Ms. Geraghty as "victims" was the fact that they "belonged to a class of women of child-bearing age" and therefore ran the risk of being directly affected by the injunction.[116] Although this test seemingly confines the circle of potential claimants to the women of child-bearing age, what constitutes a child-bearing age for women, especially in the age of medical progress is not certain. The test applied by the Court is too loose having the effect of broadening the circle of potential female applicants almost unrestrictedly. The Court did this by interpreting the term "victim" permissively and finding admissible the claim of Mrs. X and Geraghty, persons who had in no way claimed that they wished to seek information of the type the disclosure of which the contested injunction restrained.[117] The reasoning is implausible given that there is hardly any objective test that can be applied to determine the potentiality of the detriment as far as the category of "women of child-bearing age" is concerned. The circle of women of child-bearing age is too broad a category of persons as it includes both women who may wish to have children and those who may not. Besides, a "child-baring" age is also hard to define. It may range (depending on a society, health of a woman and quality of the healthcare system) from fifteen to above sixty. Hence, the "child-baring" age applies almost to all women excluding only very limited age group. Stretching the scope of the victim requirement this far does not preclude stretching it even further to apply it to husbands of those women who are equally as interested in the fate of the baby and health of their partners. In general, all members of the society are interested in issues of population control and may thus be qualified as victims of the violation as members of the society.[118]

By adopting such a broad interpretation, the Court run the risk of blurring the distinction between simple *actio* by an actual victim and claims brought by way of *actio popularis*.[119] The domestic judicial decisions applied restrictions

115 Ibid. para. 44.

116 Ibid.

117 *Dublin Well* case, Partly Dissenting Opinion of Judge Matscher, para. 1.

118 *Dublin Well* case, Partly Dissenting Opinion of Judge Baka, para. 5.

119 *Dublin Well case,* Partly Dissenting Opinion of Judge Matscher, para. 1. See also joint dissenting opinions of Judges Pettiti, Russo, Lopes Rocha, Bigi who shared the same view with judge Matscher on the question of Mrs. X and Geraghty's lack of standing before the Court. para. 1 of the opinion.

only to the activities of Open Door and Dublin Well Woman and their clients, which received counselling on pregnancy outside Ireland. Mrs. X and Geraghty, though clients of the two companies, nevertheless, were not pregnant to be immediately and directly affected by the measures or to run a 'possible risk of a direct, immediate interference' with their individual rights.[120]

The Court's recent case law suggests that the Court is revisiting its rigid interpretation of the victim requirement to give effect to the main purpose of the European Convention, protection of human rights. In the line of decisions involving claims brought by persons other than the actual victim the Court applied the victim requirement very liberally, potentially introducing *actio popularis* through the Court's back door. The Court's decisions in *Karner v Austria* and *Câmpeanu v Romania* illustrate the point. In *Karner v Austria* the claimant who brought the case before the Court under Article 14 in conjunction with Article 8 of the Convention died in the course of proceedings.[121] However, the Court, despite no individual interest was involved in the case due to the claimant's passing found the case admissible refusing to strike it out of the list. While reiterating that the applicant must be a victim of the violation under Article 34 of the Convention the Court stressed the need to interpret the victim requirement in light of the object and purpose of the Convention.[122] The Court noted with reference to the *Ireland v UK* decision:

> although the primary purpose of the Convention system is to provide individual relief, its mission is also to determine issues on public-policy grounds in the common interest, thereby raising the general standards of protection of human rights and extending human rights jurisprudence throughout the community of Convention States.[123]

In this case the Court considered the issue of differential treatment between homosexual and heterosexual partners concerning "succession to tenancies under Austrian law" as a question of collective interest shared by "all States parties to the Convention" and consideration of the case on the merits 'would contribute to elucidate, safeguard and develop the standards of protection under the Convention".[124] The Court's statements are indicative of the shift,

120 *Dublin Well case*, Partly Dissenting Opinion of Judge Baka, p. 5.

121 Judgment, 24 July, 2003, (Application no. 40016/98), para. 3.

122 *Karner v Austria*, paras. 23–24.

123 It has to be noted that the *Ireland v UK* decision epitomizes the Court's belief that the human rights protection system under the Convention transcends individual interests and that the protection of the collective interests is one of its objectives. *Ireland v UK*, (18 January, 1978, Judgment, application number: 5310/71, para. 239).

124 *Karner v Austria*, para. 27.

which the Court has made towards finding admissible claims which fall short of satisfying the victim requirement as confined to applicants, which are direct victims of the violation. The Court's teleological interpretation of the Convention rights to attain the collective interests protected by the Convention has prompted the Court to revisit the strict requirement to be a victim of the violation.[125] Although the Court did not discard the victim requirement as a precondition to file applications, it has interpreted it so broadly as to allow claims of disseized persons whose individual interests are not and cannot be affected.[126] This approach makes the victim requirement devoid of purpose. The Court unequivocally states that the only purpose to proceed with the case was to ensure the public collective interest envisaged under the Convention. Whatever the language the Court is cloaking its actions the Court runs the risk of potentially opening the door for *actio popularis*.

The Court's case law concerning protection of the rights of disabled and children under the European Court of Human Rights also reveals that in certain exceptional cases the Court is prepared to liberalize the standing requirements seeking to achieve the object and purpose of the European Convention on Human Rights, i.e. protection of human rights.[127] The Grand Chamber decision in the *Valentin Câmpeanu v Romania* case exemplifies the point.[128] The applicant in this case, a non-governmental organization, the Centre for Legal Resources (CLR), which acted on behalf of Mr. Câmpeanu. The applicant claimed that Romania violated articles 2, 3, 5, 8, 13 and 14 of the European Convention. The Romanian Government challenged the admissibility of the claim on the basis that CLR was neither a direct, indirect nor potential victim of the violation as required by Article 34 of the European Convention and the Court's case law on the victim requirement. According to the Romanian Government the application did not involve any of the rights of CLR. Neither was CLR a potential or indirect victim because it could not demonstrate "with sufficient evidence, either the existence of a risk of a violation, or the effect that a violation of a third party's rights had had on him or her, as a consequence of

125 On the question of the Court's power to interpret the convention provisions as a living instrument see A Mowbrai, *The Creativity of the European Court of Human Rights, Human Rights Law Review*, 5 (1), 2005, pp. 57–79.

126 D. Harris also found the Court's decision as "unusual". *Law of the European Convention on Human Rights,* (2009). p. 800.

127 C. Cojocariu, Handicapping Rules: The Overly Restrictive Application of Admissibility Criteria by the European Court of Human Rights to Complaints concerning Disabled People, E.H.R.L.R., Issue 6, 2011, Sweet and Maxwell, p. 687.

128 *Case of Centre for Legal Resources on behalf of Valentin Câmpeanu v Romania,* Grand Chamber, Application No. 47848/08, Judgment, 17 July 2014.

a pre-existing close link, whether natural (for example, in the case of a family member) or legal (for example, as a result of custody arrangements)".[129] The Government rejected the contention that a victim's vulnerability as a disabled person was sufficient to consider the CLR as a potential or indirect victim.[130] The Romanian Government maintained that CLR's application amounted to *actio popularis,* an action which is impermissible under the European Convention on Human Rights.[131] On the other hand, CLR claimed *inter alia* that the *"utile effectif"* (the need to protect human rights more effectively) principle imposed an obligation on the Court to interpret the rules of standing more permissively in order to provide to the victims better access to the Court and ensure effective protection of the rights under the ECHR.[132]

According to the facts of the case the CLR neither "had a significant contact" with the applicant while he was ill nor did CLR or having received any authority or instructions from him or any other competent person" to act on his behalf before the Court.[133] Therefore the Court did not find any basis to consider the CLR as an indirect victim of the violation or as someone who has "personal interest" or "sufficiently close link with the direct victim".[134] However, the Court found the case admissible by relying on the fact that CLR's standing to act on behalf of Mr. Câmpeanu was not challenged before domestic courts and therefore the ECtHR considered CLR as a *de facto* representative.[135] Such a decision of the Court raises a question as to the relevance of the CLR's status under domestic law for the purposes of the CLR's *jus standi* before the ECtHR. The Court previously pointed out that it develops its autonomous interpretation of the standing rules independently of the meaning attached to them under do mestic legislation of States parties to the Convention.[136] It needs to be stressed that the Court itself acknowledged the fact that CLR was neither an indirect victim nor did it have any other link to the direct victim. This notwithstanding,

129 Ibid. para. 82.

130 Ibid. It has to be noted that the CLR was neither a legal guardian nor did it act as a victim's authorized representative.

131 Ibid. para. 84.

132 Ibid. para. 87. Note that the victim requirement applies to NGOs in the same way as it applies to any other applicant. See L. Mayer, NGO Standing and Influence in Regional Human Rights Courts and Commissions, 36 *Brook. J. Int'l L.*, p. 917.

133 *Case of Centre for Legal Resources,* para. 104.

134 Ibid. para. 107.

135 Ibid. paras. 110–114.

136 *Hoffman Karlskov v Denmark,* No 62560/00 (2003); available at http://caselaw.echr.globe24h.com/0/0/denmark/2003/03/20/hoffman-karlskov-v-denmark-23118-62560-00.shtml.

the Court considered CLR as the applicant's *de facto* representative and found the application as admissible. In doing so the Court sought to achieve two main objectives, namely, that the rights of the most vulnerable people are not left without protection and not to allow "the respondent State to escape accountability".[137] The Court noted in this regard that finding CLR's claim inadmissible would be contrary to the "general spirit of the Convention" and the obligation under Article 34 of the Convention not to hinder in any way the effective exercise of the right to bring an application before the Court".[138]

It is beyond any doubt that in *Valentin Câmpeanu v Romania* the ECtHR departed from its well-established jurisprudence and allowed standing to an NGO which was not a victim of the violation *per se*. This was a "novelty" and an "open approach" given the Court's established case law limiting the right of claim only to applicants acting to protect their individual interests.[139] Indeed, the novelty, which the Court introduced, was the notion of *de facto* representation. According to the rules of the Court the right to represent must be clearly vested by a written and signed document.[140] Applicants acting upon such authority are considered victims for the purposes of Article 34 of the ECHR. In this case because no such authority was vested in CLR the Court devised a new technique named *de facto* representation to fill the gap in the system of human rights protection. By introducing the notion of *de facto* representation, the Court sought to attain the objective of ensuring effectiveness of human rights protection without reversing its established case law on inadmissibility of *actio popularis*.

The Court's decision therefore can be characterized as a shift towards relaxation of the victim requirement and "broadening the concept of legal standing" within a limited context of protection of persons unable to do so on their own.[141] Such a move by the Court sought to achieve a much broader interest that is of "guaranteeing the interests of justice".[142] Commentators agree that

---

137 *Case of Centre for Legal Resources*, para. 112.

138 Ibid.

139 I. Motoc & C. Caufman, Romania and the European Convention on Human Rights: A Dialogue with Judges, in I. Motoc & I. Ziemele (eds.) *The Impact of the ECHR on Democratic Change in Central and Eastern Europe*, (CUP, Cambridge, 2016), pp. 336–337.

140 Rule 45, para. 3 and 36, para. 1. See also *Aliev v Georgia*, 13/01/2009, Application No. 522/04, paras. 44–49.

141 E. Pirjatanniemi, Greening Human Rights Law: A Focus on the European Convention on Human Rights, in G. Bos & M. Düwell, (eds.), *Human Rights and Sustainability: Moral Responsibilities for the Future*, (Routledge, New York, 2016), p. 18.

142 Ibid.

the Court departed from its previous case law on standing and relaxed the test applicable to the victim requirement.[143] The Court's departure from the established case law was justified by the "unique" circumstances of the case.[144] However, the Court's relaxation of the standing requirements may raise a question as to whether the Court is willing to open the door for *actio popularis*. The reason to beg such a question lies in the fact that on the face of it the claim brought by CLR resembles elements of *actio popularis*. Indeed, traditionally *actio popularis* claims are brought to protect most vulnerable people and such claims seek to ensure that the transgressor does not evade accountability. Both objectives constitute community interests.[145] Given the frequent references by the Court to the need to protect vulnerable persons and ensuring that the respondent State does not evade accountability the application brought by CLR creates an impression of an *actio popularis* claim.

However, commentators are hesitant to argue that the relaxation of victim test went as far as introducing *actio popularis*. For instance, Iulia Motoc and Crina Kaufman note that "despite the open approach in that case, the judgment was all but a door open to an *actio popularis* reasoning".[146] Indeed the Court considered the fact that the Romanian Government did not "question or challenge" CLR's representation of Mr. Câmpeanu in the domestic proceedings and failed to "appoint a legal guardian or other representative" as "exceptional circumstances" that justified CLR to "act as a representative of Mr. Câmpeanu, notwithstanding the fact that it had no power of attorney".[147] Perhaps, this fact makes it difficult to argue in favour of *actio popularis* nature of the claim because the Court simply considered absence of power of attorney as irrelevant

143 D. Shelton, *Remedies in International Human Rights Law,* (OUP, Oxford, 3rd ed., 2015), p. 244. I. Motoc & C. Caufman, (2016), pp. 336–337. C. Cojocariu, Hit and Miss: Procedural Accommodations Ensuring the Effective Access of People with Mental Disabilities to the European Court of Human Rights, in P. Blanck & E. Flynn (eds.), *Routledge Handbook of Disability Law and Human Rights,* (Routledge, London, 2017), pp. 107–109. See also H. Hembach, Admissibility of an Application Lodged by an NGO on Behalf of deceased victim – Centre for Legal Resources on Behalf of Valentin Câmpeanu v Romania, 2014, available at http://echr-online.info.

144 C. Cojocariu, (2017), pp. 107–109.

145 In India courts liberalized standing rules and allowed for *actio popularis* to protect the human rights of most vulnerable groups whose rights were otherwise denied. *SP Gupta v Union of India*, p. 126. See also H. Hershkoff who argues that one of the objectives of *actio popularis* was to protect vulnerable groups. Public Law Litigation: Lessons and Questions, (2009)10 *Human Rights Review,* pp. 157–181.

146 I. Motoc, (2016), p. 337.

147 Judgment, paras. 110–112.

given the victim's factual representation by CLR in the domestic proceedings. This notwithstanding, the judgment raises a question regarding the extent to which NGOs can represent vulnerable people in the absence of any formal link.[148] For instance, Judge Pinto in his concurring opinion argues that the denial of protection, including representation at the domestic level justifies construction of admissibility requirements "in the broadest possible way in order to ensure that the victim's right of access to the European human rights protection system is effective".[149] On the face of it, Judge Pinto's approach may be interpreted as an attempt to introduce *actio popularis*. This is particularly so given his definition of "vulnerable persons" as a "broad concept" that "should include people of tender age, or elderly, gravely sick or disabled people, people belonging to minorities, or groups subject to discrimination based on race, ethnicity, sex, sexual orientation or any other ground".[150] However, he preconditions such liberal interpretation of standing requirements to the cumulative presence of two conditions, i.e. "the extreme vulnerability of the alleged victim and the absence of any relatives, legal guardians or representatives" which provide safeguards against *actio popularis*.[151]

It is apparent that the Court, as it did in the *Open Door, Karner, and Valentin Câmpeanu* cases, invokes the effectiveness of human rights protection in general, but more specifically the "effective exercise of the right to bring an application before the Court" under Article 34 as a justification to consider as "victims" the applicants which are not affected in any way in their own personal interest and act as a *parens patriae* to protect the general interest. Despite the Court in these decisions does not refer to *actio popularis* it is apparent that the Court's relaxation of the victim requirement was informed by its desire to achieve the collective interest of ensuring the effectiveness of human rights protection.

Preceding analysis very well illustrates how the need to fill the lacunas in the human rights protection system compels the ECtHR to 'silently' reconsider its case law on standing and allow for more permissive interpretation of the "victim" requirement. In construing the "victim requirement" permissively the ECtHR was driven by its aspiration to live up to the main purposes of the European Convention on Human Rights, i.e. ensuring effectiveness in human rights protection.

---

148 Joint Partly Dissenting Opinion of Judges Spielmann, Bianku and Nussberger, p. 75.

149 Judge Pinto, Sep. Op. para. 9.

150 Ibid. para. 11.

151 Judge Pinto, Sep. Op. para. 11.

4 WTO DSB

The preceding section focused on the legality of *actio popularis* within a very specific context of the human rights instrument – ECHR. The following section addresses the question of legality of *actio popularis* in the framework of international trade law, an area of law to which protection of collective interests has traditionally been alien.

The successive analysis conceptualizes *actio popularis* claims in two contexts. It first examines *actio popularis* in light of the nature of WTO obligations and conceptualizes the notion of *actio popularis* in the context of WTO rules of standing which are distinct from the classical standing rules. *Actio popularis* is then considered in a very narrow context of GATT Article XXIII which allows WTO member States to bring a suit when "attainment of any objective of the Agreement is being impeded".

4.1 *Determining the Nature of WTO Obligations and Their Legal Consequences: the Problem of a Legal Interest*

The question about the nature of the WTO obligations is generally linked to the legal consequences that flow from the breach of obligations.[152] Traditionally, WTO obligations are perceived as bilateralizable and reciprocal obligations. However, occasionally some commentators voiced opinions that WTO obligations are established not only to protect individual interests but also to achieve a "common interest" which consists of "defending the system itself".[153] It is argued that in such a case "the applicant plays a dual role and the complainant has effect of its action on behalf of the international community.[154] Such a conception of WTO obligations allows for WTO member to act by way of *actio popularis*.[155] For instance, Chios Carmody also highlights a collective aspect of the WTO obligations. He argues that "… WTO obligations are not about trade *per se*, but rather about expectations concerning the trade-related behaviour of governments. These are unquantifiable and indivisible, and therefore fundamentally unitary in nature. They cannot be conceived of as bilateral. Rather,

152 C. Tietje & A. Lang, Community Interests in World Trade Law, Beiträge zum Transnationalen Wirtschaftsrecht, Issue 141, December 2016, p. 5, forthcoming in A. Benvinisti & G. Nolte (eds.), *Community Obligations in Contemporary International Law*.

153 H. Fabri, Is There a Case – Legally and Politically – for Direct Effect of WTO Obligations? *EJIL*, 2014, vol. 25, no. 1, p. 170. Y. Iwasawa, WTO Dispute Settlement as a Judicial Supervision, *JIEL* (2002), p. 295.

154 Y. Iwasawa, p. 295.

155 H. Fabri (2014), p. 170.

they should be thought of as collective".[156] He argues this based on the proposition that the WTO law serves to achieve interdependence by safeguarding and furthering "interaction among the consumers in different countries … to spin an indissoluble web of economic relations".[157] This aspect of relations governed by WTO law manifests itself primarily in the MFN and NT clauses, which guarantee that WTO members "enjoy the same expectation within a given Member country".[158] It is submitted that ensuring such mutual expectations extends beyond individual interests of member States and forms a "common interest" of States parties.[159] Professor Dan Sarooshi considers these principles as "a reflection of the application of the value of equality – that governments should ensure that like cases are treated equally".[160] He also categorizes interests into those possessed by individual WTO members and institutional interest of WTO, which he calls a "systemic interest" which consists of trade liberalization "by seeking the reduction and gradual abolition of governmental barriers to trade".[161] These systemic interests are underpinned by a "common set of underlying values embodied in a common agreement" and as such help developing the law by the WTO bodies (judicial bodies) to achieve the general objective reflected in the systemic institutional interests.[162] However, one of the arguments against the communitarian character of WTO obligations is that the multilateral trading system is intrinsically unfair towards "unprivileged members of the trade community".[163] Hence, intrinsic unfairness of the system precludes its communitarian nature because the system does not aim to protect interests of all community members.[164] This notwithstanding, attributing WTO obligations the character of either exclusively bilateral or community norms is methodologically erroneous. The best way to proceed is to approach the WTO obligations individually and identify legal instruments (norms), which are potentially established to protect and promote community interests.[165] Indeed, the prevailing view is that unlike human rights or other

156 WTO Obligations as Collective, *EJIL* (2006), Vol. 17 No. 2, p. 421.

157 Ibid. p. 422.

158 Ibid. p. 427.

159 Ibid.

160 D. Sarooshi, The Move from Institutions: The Case of the World Trade Organization, 100 *Am. Soc'y Int'l L. Proc.* 2006, p. 299.

161 'Investment Treaty Arbitration and the World Trade Organization: What Role for Systemic Values in the Resolution of International Economic Disputes', 49(3) *Texas International Law Journal*, 445 (2014), p. 448.

162 Ibid, p. 466.

163 C. Tietje & A. Lang, (2016), p. 13.

164 Ibid.

165 J. Baeumler, The Legal Nature of WTO Obligations: Bilateral or Collective, LLM Thesis, University of Western Cape, pp. 47–48.

treaties, which are established to protect collective interests, obligations in the field of trade, including GATT, consist of bilateralizable obligations to which reciprocity and protection of individual interests is central.[166] WTO members first and foremost seek to secure their individual economic (trade) interests.[167] Pauwelyn argues that GATT obligations are neither integral nor interdependent.[168] He posits that they are primarily in the nature of bundle of bilateral obligations.[169] In fact it is argued that the very notion of nullification and impairment of the benefits of any of the contracting party supports the argument in favour of bilateralizable nature of the GATT obligations which distinguishes them from obligations in the field of human rights or environmental law.[170] The notion of nullification or impairment of benefits is spelled out in Article XXIII of GATT. Article XXIII GATT states as follows:

> 1. If any contracting party should consider that any benefit accruing to it directly or indirectly under this Agreement is being nullified or impaired or that the attainment of any objective of the Agreement is being impeded as the result of
> (a) the failure of another contracting party to carry out its obligations under this Agreement, or (b) the application by another contracting party of any measure, whether or not it conflicts with the provisions of this Agreement, or...

166 Y. Fukunaga notes: "free and open trade cannot be placed on the same footing as environment and human rights that obviously possess an intrinsic universal value that cannot be said to satisfy the individual interest of each State". Securing Compliance Through the WTO Dispute Settlement: Implementation of the DSB Recommendations. *Journal of International Economic Law,* 9(2), p. 387. Bruno Simma notes in this regard: "It is crucial to distinguish between reciprocity as a formal characteristic of a norm on the one hand, and reciprocity as a substantive *do-ut-des* relationship on the other. Human rights treaties do not involve such a substantive exchange, since their ultimate beneficiaries are individuals under the jurisdiction of the State undertaking the obligation. However, since human rights remain 'mutual, bilateral undertakings' owed to the other State parties to the respective convention, there is no compelling systematic reason why States should be precluded from bilateral enforcement of human rights". B. Simma, Of Planets and the Universe: Self-contained Regimes in International Law, *EJIL* (2006), Vol. 17 No. 3, p. 527.

167 C. Carmody, (2006), p. 419.

168 J. Pauwelyn, A Typology of Multilateral Treaty Obligations: Are WTO Obligations Bilateral or Collective in Nature? *EJIL,* 2003, (14), pp. 907–951, p. 928.

169 Ibid. p. 930. See also T. Gazzini, 'The Legal Nature of WTO Obligations and The Consequences of Their Violation', (2006), 17(4) *EJIL*, pp. 727–728.

170 US statement at the DSB meeting of 7 May 2003 (posted at http://www.us-mission.ch/press2003/0507DSB.html) reacting to the Decision by the Arbitrators in United States – Tax Treatment for 'Foreign Sales Corporations' – Recourse to Arbitration by the United States under Article 22.6 of the DSU, WT/DS108/ARB, 30 August 2002, para. 6.10 in J Pauwelyn, (2003), p. 930. See also Y. Fukunaga, (2006), p. 387.

However, this article should not be interpreted as granting standing only in cases of nullification or impairment. Mavroidis notes in this regard: "WTO members do not have to show trade effects as a condition for bringing forward a violation complaint"[171] which means that it is unnecessary in such a case to establish nullification or impairment to have standing.

It has to be noted that some WTO treaties allow for *actio popularis* irrespective of the nature of obligations. Under these treaties the nature of the obligations is decoupled from the consequences of their violation. Pauwelyn argues that bilateralist nature of WTO obligations does not preclude a possibility for WTO members to invoke responsibility by way of *actio popularis* because GATT provisions may provide for such a right in the form of *lex specialis*. This is true of all other bilateralizable treaties. This view questions the necessary link between *actio popularis* and collective nature of WTO obligations, i.e. it decouples the legal consequences from the nature of the obligations.[172] Gazzini holds the same view and refers to Article 4 of the Agreement on Subsidies and Countervailing Measures (SCM) and obligations deriving from the General Agreement on Trade in Services (GATS) as examples of treaties of bilateralizable nature but which provide for collective enforcement.[173] However, the panel noted concerning the obligations under Article 3 of the SCM that "it is an *erga omnes* obligation owed in its entirety to each and every Member. It cannot be considered to be "allocatable" across the Membership. Otherwise, the Member concerned would be only partially obliged in respect of each and every Member, which is manifestly inconsistent with an *erga omnes per se* obligation".[174] Whether provisions of SCM are of *erga omnes* or bilateralizable nature can be debated infinitely. What matters is that States parties to SCM expressly stipulate in Article 4 a general interest of all parties to enforce obligations under Article 3 of SCM.

Another stipulation in WTO law in favour of enforcement of a general interest is in GATS, Article XXIII(1) reads as follows: If any Member should consider that any other Member fails to carry out its obligations or specific commitments under this Agreement, it may with a view to reaching a mutually satisfactory resolution of the matter have recourse to the DSU. Article 4.4 of the

171 See also P. Mavroidis, Remedies in WTO Legal Systems: Between a Rock and a Hard Place. *EJIL, 2000,* vol.11, pp. 777–778 with reference to EC – *Regime for the Importation, Sale and Distribution of Bananas,* WT/DS27/AB/R, 9 September 1997, at para. 132. A. Lowenfeld, *International Economic Law,* (OUP, Oxford, 2008). p. 149. C. Carmody, (2006), p. 419.

172 J. Pauwelyn, (2003), p. 926. See also J. Pauwelyn, (2003), p. 55.

173 T Gazzini, (2006), p. 730.

174 WTO, *US – FSC* (*Article 22.6 Arbitration*), WT/DS108/AB/R, Report of the Panel of 30 August 2002, para. 6.10.

SCM also provides for cause of action to any Member to "refer the matter to the Dispute Settlement Body".

Although SCM and GATS do not *per se* establish collective obligations, and such obligations do not form *raison d'être* (core) of these treaties they nevertheless provide for enforcement of general systemic interest. The interest in such circumstance lies in the enforcement, albeit of bilateralizable obligations.[175]

For those who claim that WTO obligations are established to protect common interests, absence of a requirement to show a legal/individual interest in the GATT and the Dispute Settlement Understanding (DSU) to bring a case before DSB is presented as further evidence of recognition of *actio popularis*.[176] However, the cogency of this argument is highly questionable and further analysis tests this proposition.

It has to be noted that the case law of the WTO dispute settlement organs is illuminating in a sense that it reveals the fundamental distinction in the way the ICJ and other international courts and tribunals and WTO perceive the notion of the individual legal interest and the need to demonstrate such interest in order to bring a case before a relevant dispute settlement body. The reason lies in the *lex specialis* nature of the WTO obligations.[177]

In fact such influential authors as Matsushita, Schoenbaum and Mavroidis interpret GATT and DSU provisions, which do not require a member State to show a legal interest as recognition of *actio popularis*.[178] The *South West Africa* cases are often invoked as a basis to argue that an action before the court in the absence of a legal interest amounts to *actio popularis*. The question whether the same condition applies to the complaints brought before the WTO DSB was raised in the *European Communities – Regime for the Importation, Sale and Distribution of Bananas* case.[179] According to the EC the legal interest or interest constitutes a cause of action under any legal system, i.e. no interest no

175 Gazzini argues that obligations concerning under SCM are not established to protect collective interests of all. T Gazzini, (2006), p. 729.

176 R. Fabri, (2014), p. 170.

177 See also J. Pauwelyn, Jean Monnet Working Paper 1/02, *The Nature of WTO Obligations*, 2002, p. 1.

178 See M. Matsushita, T. Schoenbaum, and P. Mavroidis who argue that all WTO members have an interest in any material breach of the covered agreements. This in principle amounts to recognition of *actio popularis*. *The World Trade Organization: Law, Practice, and Policy*, (OUP, Oxford, 2nd ed., 2006), p. 26. See also Y. Iwasawa, (2002), p. 298.

179 Panel Report, European Communities – Regime for the Importation, Sale and Distribution of Bananas, 22 May 1997, WT/DS27/R/ECU). For a detailed analysis of the case see R. Bustamante, The Need For GATT Doctrine of Locus Standi: Why the United States Cannot Stand The European Community's Import Regime, 6 *Minn. J. Global Trade*, 1997, p. 533

action.[180] Under many legal systems the legal interest is set as a condition to bring a claim in order to avoid *in abstracto* claims and thus reduce courts' caseload.[181] In this case, the USA, along with four other WTO member States,[182] and following the unsuccessful consultations with the European Communities under Article 4 of the DSU requested the panel regarding "the EC regime for the importation, sale and distribution of bananas established by Council Regulation (EEC) 404/931, and the subsequent EC legislation, regulations and administrative measures, including those reflecting the provisions of the Framework Agreement on Bananas, which implemented, supplemented and amended that regime".[183] The panel had to consider the issue in light of the GATT, the Agreement on Import Licensing Procedures, the Agreement on Agriculture, the General Agreement on Trade in Services ("GATS") and the Agreement on Trade-Related Investment Measures.[184]

EC maintained that the US's claim was devoid of any practical significance because the Panel Report would only be declaratory failing to award any compensation due to a minimal banana production in the US and absence of banana trade with EC.[185] It followed from the EC's arguments that US's and others' claims amount to *actio popularis* for two reasons: (a) that complainant States are not affected, i.e. no benefit accruing to them under WTO Agreement is nullified or impaired (Article 3.3 of the DSU); (b) they have no interest in the outcome of the proceedings because the proceedings are devoid of any practical significance for the claimants in the absence of the concept of advisory opinions and declaratory judgments (Article 22 of the DSU).[186] It worth noting that EC's construction of the conditions set out in GATT Article XXIII was more in line with the classical view of standing dependent on the claimant's ability to show a legal interest. EC maintained with reference to the ICJ's decision in the *South West Africa* cases that showing a legal interest was required "in any system of law, including international law" and that it was required

180 See Panel Report, European Communities – Regime for the Importation, Sale and Distribution of Bananas, 22 May 1997, WT/DS27/R/ECU, para. II.21. For discussion see J. Hu, *The Role of International Law in Development of WTO Law,* Journal of International Economic Law 7(1), p. 159.

181 See Panel Report, European Communities – Regime for the Importation, Sale and Distribution of Bananas, 22 May 1997, WT/DS27/R/ECU, Para. II.21.

182 Ecuador, Guatemala, Mexico, Honduras.

183 Panel Report, European Communities – Regime for the Importation, Sale and Distribution of Bananas, 22 May 1997, WT/DS27/R/USA, para. 1.1.

184 Ibid. para. 1.2.

185 See Panel Report, European Communities – Regime for the Importation, Sale and Distribution of Bananas, 22 May 1997, WT/DS27/R/ECU, Para. II. 21.

186 Ibid. para. 7.47.

under customary international law.[187] EC noted that unlike countries like Ecuador and Brazil, the US did not have any "legal right, or legal or material interest in the case…".[188] Although EC acknowledged Mexico's and Ecuador's legal interest owing to its potential in exporting bananas to EC, it nevertheless denied existence of US's legal interest because the latter, in EC's judgment, had neither real nor potential capacity to export bananas to EC.[189] EC further maintained that in the absence of individual interest the US was acting "as private attorney-general" and its suit was in the nature of *actio popularis* to protect public interest a concept which was alien to GATT/WTO system.[190] Conversely, the complaining parties claimed that they were affected by EC measures and hence they brought claims in their own interest, an interest, which ensued from the impairment and nullification of the benefit accruing to them. Hence, according to the claimants, they "were not standing in the place of others, in *actio popularis*, as the EC suggested".[191] More specifically, the US argued that its material interest was affected because the measures taken by EC affected the US companies which had extensive experience in marketing bananas and thus contributed significantly to the growth of European banana market.[192] The US rejected EC's contention that under WTO Agreement States had to demonstrate a legal interest to be able to sue other States parties to WTO Agreement.[193] Article XXIII of the WTO Agreement did not require a legal interest as a precondition to file a complaint.[194] According to Article XXIII any

187 Panel Report, European Communities – Regime for the Importation, Sale and Distribution of Bananas, 22 May 1997, WT/DS27/R/USA, para. 2.21. The EC relied on the *South West Africa, Mavrommatis Palestine Concessions* and *Barcelona Traction* cases to support its contention and argued that a claim instituted without a legal interest amounts to *actio popularis,* a claim which is alien to international law. See para. 15 of the Appellate Body Report. Given the *lex specialis* nature of the WTO Agreement, EC maintained that unless the WTO Agreement had made a clear exception to what EC claimed was a customary rule of international law, requiring that the claimant demonstrate a legal interest the claim could not have been found admissible by the Panel. para. 16 of the Appellate Body Report, p. 8 of the same Report. According to EC, rejection of the requirement of a legal interest amounts to acceptance of the concept of *actio popularis.* para. 16, p. 8 of the Appellate Body Report.

188 (1997), para. 2.21.

189 Ibid.

190 Ibid.

191 Ibid. para. 2.32.

192 See Panel Report, European Communities – Regime for the Importation, Sale and Distribution of Bananas, 22 May 1997, WT/DS27/R/ECU Para. II.23. For the view that US did not have interest in the case see R. Bustamante, (1997), p. 575.

193 Ibid. para. II.25.

194 Ibid.

WTO member can institute proceedings if it believes that a benefit accruing to it under any WTO Agreement has been nullified or impaired.[195] The US's interest to sue is therefore dependent on US's ability to show that it had a potential benefit and the benefit was nullified and impaired by the EC's measure, whether consistent or inconsistent with WTO Agreements.[196]

The Panel accepted the complainants' arguments. The Panel noted that neither Article XXIII of GATT nor Articles 3.3 or 3.7 requires showing of a legal interest to bring a claim before the WTO DSP and "nullification and impairment" is not a "procedural requirement".[197] The Appellate Body noted in this regard:

> "We do not read any of these judgments as establishing a general rule that in all international litigation, a complaining party must have a "legal interest" in order to bring a case. Nor do these judgments deny the need to consider the question of standing under the dispute settlement provisions of any multilateral treaty, by referring to the terms of that treaty".[198] The Appellate Body rejected all claims advanced by EC and upheld Panel's Report that US had a right to bring a case before the DSP because its potential benefit as a potential exporter of bananas could be nullified or impaired".[199]

The AB's finding clarifies two points. Firstly, the requirement to show legal interest does not form part of general international law. Even assuming that such rule was part of custom WTO dispute settlement organs were still exempt from applying it by virtue of *lex specilis* nature of WTO rules of standing. Secondly, AB's findings prompts a conclusion that WTO members may institute proceedings when measures adopted by any member do not directly affect any other WTO member. As Lamy puts it: "In other words, any State may initiate dispute settlement procedures on the basis of a claim that another Member is not complying with its obligations under WTO law".[200]

The above analysis suggests that WTO agreements, including GATT, do not completely rule out a possibility of action to protect interests, extending beyond individual interests.

---

195 Ibid.

196 Ibid.

197 (1997), para. 7.49.

198 para. 133, p. 61 of the WTO Appellate Body Report, WT/DS27/AB/R (1997).

199 Ibid, para. 136, p. 62.

200 P. Lamy, The Place of WTO and its Law in the International Legal Order. *EJIL* (2006), Vol. 17 No. 5, 969–984, at pp. 976–978.

On some other issues, e.g. preservation of marine environment the AB has been inclined to recognize the interest of WTO member States to protect resources outside their jurisdiction. In the *Unites States – Import Prohibition of Certain Shrimp and Shrimp Products* where the US by virtue of domestic legislation imposed embargo on the import of shrimps, which were caught in breach of the requirements of US Section 609 as applicable to shrimp catch resulting in deaths of dolphins.[201] Philippe Sands argues that by recognizing a link between the US and the migratory and endangered marine populations[202] the AB effectively recognized US's "legitimate interest" in their protection by way of *actio popularis*.[203] However, Sands himself notes that the turtles were from time to time located in the US waters and the recognition of a link between the US and turtles could be based on a US's individual rather than a collective interest in protection of these animals.[204]

Some commentators rely on the wording of Article XXIII which allows the State parties to invoke responsibility of WTO member States "If any contracting party should consider that ... the attainment of any objective of the Agreement is being impeded ..." and argue that GATT also seeks to protect collective interests alongside the individual interests of member States. Entitlement to invoke responsibility in such a way is interpreted as explicit recognition of *actio popularis*.[205] This avenue of invoking responsibility has been rarely utilized and in all of these cases the complainants did not rely solely on impediment to the attainment of an objective under the Agreement.[206]

---

201 See interesting discussion by D. Sarooshi, (2014), pp. 450–454.

202 para. 133 of the AB Report in the Shrimps/Turtles case.

203 P. Sands, J. Peel, A. Fabra & R. MacKenzie, (2012), pp. 150–151.

204 Ibid. This notwithstanding some WTO member States which were parties to the case recognized the common interest in preservation of the marine environment. For instance Malasia stated: "the concept of permanent sovereignty had not prevented international law from treating conservation issues within a state's territory as a question of common concern in which the international community possesses a legitimate interest", para. 300, Report of the Panel, United States-Import Prohibition of Certain Shrimp and Shrimp Products, WT/DS58/R, 15 May, 1998.

205 Y. Iwasawa, (2002), p. 294. See also M. Matsushita, T. Schoenbaum & P. Mavroidis, (2006), p. 114. They note with reference to Article XXIII: "These provisions seem to suggest that a contracting party can bring a case before WTO Dispute Settlement Body with regard to a measure of another party in order to maintain the soundness of the WTO system even if there is no immediate trade effect on the claiming party". p. 114.

206 E. Petersmann, *The GATT/WTO System of Dispute Settlement*, (Kluwer Law International, Boston, 1996), p. 74. A total of three complaints were brought before the DSB invoking the impediment of attainment of the objectives of the Agreement. The first case was brought by Australia, which claimed that "that the system of sugar export subsidies granted or maintained by the European Communities had impeded the attainment of the objectives

Assessment of the WTO law suggests that *actio popularis* is limited to the instances of express treaty stipulation under SCM and GATS and also GATT Article XXIII (attainment of the objectives). The latter is most vivid example of how the dispute settlement provisions serve to protect both individual and general/systemic interests of the WTO member States.

However, outside the context of above stated treaty norms *actio popularis* in WTO law can only be instituted by inference from substantive WTO norms, which are established to protect a particular collective interest. Preservation of marine environment seems to be one of such norms. Although the law in this field is still in the process of development, the Shrimps/Turtle case can, subject to reservations stated above, be viewed as implicit recognition of *actio popularis*.

---

of the General Agreement". However, it has to be noted that the claim was not solely based on the "impediment of objectives" argument. Australia also relied on "nullification and impairment of benefits accruing to it" and other more direct interests. *L/4833 – 26S/290*, Report of the Panel, 6 November, 1979, EC-Refunds on Exports of Sugar. Other two complaints include EC's complaint regarding Japan's nullification and impairment of the benefits and impediment to the attainment of the GATT objectives due to the "persistent trade imbalance between Japan and EC" (*Japan – Nullification and Impairment of Benefits and Impediment to the Attainment of GATT Objectives*, L/5479, C/M/167, 6 May, 1983), as well as complaint by Australia concerning EC's beef and veal regime which it claimed to have nullified the benefits and impeded the attainment of the objectives. L/5734, C/M/183, 20 November, 1984.

CHAPTER 7

Actio popularis as a Question of Judicial Policy

Preceding Chapters of the book argued that *actio popularis* can be validated either by express normative stipulation (e.g. statute, treaty provision) or judicial interpretation of standing rules.[1] In the latter case, *actio popularis* is a result of judicial activism,[2] which manifests itself in liberal construction of the standing rules.[3]

Courts, including those at international level, have exclusive competence to interpret their rules of standing and decide on their own jurisdiction.[4] When an action is brought before a judicial body, it becomes subject to procedural scrutiny and compliance of the claim with the rules of standing of a given court or a tribunal. International tribunals are free to adopt and interpret their rules of procedure or inherently exercise the power to decide which cases are admissible in order to avoid abuse of process.[5] Some courts may interpret the standing rules restrictively, others may be liberal in their construction of the rules of standing.

Previous chapters extensively analysed the question of legality of *actio popularis* before different international courts and tribunals. The analysis revealed

---

* Dupuy defines judicial policy as follows: "The term "judicial policy" of the ICJ should be interpreted as the general orientations which underlie the jurisprudence of the Court with regard to some basic legal issues connected with the way the Court understands its judicial function. Alternatively, and in a broader exception, the term "judicial policy" could be interpreted as pointing to "the way by which the Court tends to apply international law, in order to adapt the interpretation and contents of the applicable rules to the necessities which it considers to be implied by the general evolution of the international legal order". See P. Dupuy, (1999), p. 801.

1 R. Uitz, "May Less be More? Public Interest Standing and the Protection of Constitutional Rights. Lessons from Hungary's Actio Popularis" in *La giustizia costituzionale ed i suoi untenti: Atti del convegno internationale in onore del Prof. Valerio Onida, Milano, 15 aprile 2005*, Pasquale Pasquino and Barbara Randazzo (eds.), 2006, p. 93.

2 P. McHugh, New Dawn to Cold Lights: Courts and Common Law Aboriginal Rights, in *Public Interest Litigation:* New Zealand Experience in International Perspective (by Rick Bigwood, Wellington, *Lexis Nexis NZ Limited,* 2006), p. 27. See also R. Uitz, p. 93.

3 However, there are also dangers in relaxing the criteria of standing because courts may turn "into the place to market every single idea of public concern". R. Uitz, (2006), p. 94.

4 See Article 36(6) of the ICJ Statute.

5 C. Brown, *The Inherent Powers of International Courts and Tribunals*, 2005, *BYIL,* 76(1) p. 205. See also T. Tridimas who justifies judicial activism as far as procedural questions are concerned, but not questions pertaining to substantive law. *European Law Review,* 1996, 21(3), p. 209.

DOI:10.1163/9789004380981_009

that some courts and tribunals allowed for *actio popularis* by permissively interpreting the standing requirements (activist courts),[6] yet others rejected *actio popularis* by imposing self-restraint and deferring the matter for ultimate decision of States or non-judicial organs of the organization of which an international court is an organ. The analysis further revealed that the question of legality of *actio popularis* could only be answered in a fragmented manner by each and every international court or tribunal independently based on the court's standing rules and policy concerns.[7]

The following analysis aims to identify policy concerns, which international courts take into account in interpreting standing rules and making decision on the legality and admissibility of *actio popularis*. To avoid repetition and by way of example, the analysis will focus only on three international tribunals: the ICJ, CJEU and ECtHR out of five tribunals examined in the book.

1 *Actio popularis* as a Result of Judicial Law Making

Courts often employ interpretative tools and act as 'activist' courts in order to fill the gaps which the lawmakers have left open. It is by engaging in judicial activism that some lacunae in law are filled. However, judicial activism is a "slippery term" which has multiple meanings[8] and deconstructing the concept of

6 "For example, activism might be found in the mere interpretation of statutes. A Justice might interpret a statute in a manner contrary to what the legislature meant or wrote as its text". F. Cross & S. Lindquist, The Scientific Study of Judicial Activism, *91 Min.L.Rev.* 2006–2007, p. 1763.

7 "... unlike domestic judges, international judges operate within specialized and often self-contained legal regimes and structures. Judicial preferences are therefore likely to vary according to the regime to which the international court or tribunal belongs. Preferences held by CJEU judges about the proper scope of EU trade regulation may not have much salience for ECHR judges dealing with human rights issues". S. Jodoin, Understanding the Behaviour of International Courts: An Examination of Decision-Making at the *ad hoc* International Criminal Tribunals, 6 *J. Int'l Law & Int'l Rel.* 1, (2010), p. 8.

8 K. Kmiec, The Origin and Current Meanings of "Judicial Activism", *California Law Review*, 2004, Vol. 92, p. 1442. C. Green, An Intellectual History of Judicial Activism, *Emory Law Journal*, Vol. 58, No. 5, p. 1195. However, one could summarize the elements of judicial activism under domestic law as follows: "overruling actions by other federal branches or state governments, failing to follow textual meaning, departing from history or tradition, issuing maximalist and not minimalist holdings, using broad remedial powers, basing decisions upon partisan preferences, failing to follow an originalist view of the Constitution, issuing an opinion inconsistent with prior precedent, exercising power beyond a court's jurisdiction, creating new rights or theories, altering prior doctrines or interpretations, establishing substantive policy, and failing to use an accepted interpretative methodology". C. Rayburn Yung,

judicial activism falls beyond the scope of this Chapter.[9] Rather the purpose is to understand why some international courts and tribunals are inclined to interpret their rules of standing more permissively to allow *actio popularis* while others impose self-restraint and defer the matter to States or other organs if the action is brought within a self-contained regime.[10]

Judicial activism becomes relevant when the law is not clear, i.e. when the law does not expressly prohibit or allow a conduct. In such a case the law may require clarification via judicial interpretation.[11] As applied to *actio popularis*, vagueness of such concepts as interest, legal interest, dispute, individual concern, attainment of the objectives etc. open the door for judicial intrusion to "give meaning to uncertain words and phrases, rules and principles…".[12] As

---

Flexing the Judicial Muscle: An Empirical Study of Judicial Activism in the Federal Courts, *Northwestern University Law Review*, 2011, Vol. 105, No. 1, p. 10.

9 Extensive literature exists on the topic all of which seem to underline the difficulties in providing a conclusive definition of judicial activism. E. Segall, Conceptualizing the Judicial Activism Debate as Judicial Responsibility: The Tales of Two Justice Kennedys, *Arizona State Law Journal*, Vol. 41, 2009, pp. 1–45. K. Kmiec, 'The Origin', *California Law Review*, 2004, Vol. 92, p. 1460.

10 F. Cross & S. Lindquist, The Scientific Study of Judicial Activism, *91 Min.L.Rev.* 2006–2007, p. 1753. Some judge-made augmentations of authority may engender political controversies and thus call a court's legitimacy into question. We define such expansive lawmaking as occurring when international courts or tribunals "identify new legal obligations or constraints not found in treaty texts or supported by the intentions of their drafters, and when these obligations or constraints narrow States' discretion". K. Alter & L. Helfer, Nature or Nurture? Judicial Law-Making in the European Court of Justice and the Andean Tribunal of Justice, 64 *Int'l Org.* (2010), p. 566 (Two types of expansionist lawmaking are especially likely to raise legitimacy concerns – the use of aggressively teleological or purposive methods of treaty interpretation, and the expansion of an international court's mandate to encompass subject areas that States have not expressly delegated to it. L. Helfer, J. Karen, Legitimacy and Lawmaking: A Tale of Three International Courts, Theoretical Inquiries in Law, 2013(14), p. 487.

11 However, in international law judicial activism should be assessed in a contextualized manner because each international court and tribunal operates within an independent political and institutional framework. F. Zarbiyev, Judicial Activism in International Law – A Conceptual Framework for Analysis, *Journal of International Dispute Settlement*, Vol. 3, No. 2 (2012), p. 251. I. Scobbie, The Theorist as a Judge: Hersch Lauterpacht's Concept of International Judicial Function, 8 *EJIL*, 1997, p. 269. C. Ford, (1994–1995), p. 59.

12 D. Popovic, 'Prevailing of Judicial Activism over Self-restraint in the Jurisprudence of the European Court of Human Rights', *Greighton Law Review*, vol. 42, 2009, p. 365. Similarly, in the context of the ICC the elements of crime were left open ended for the ICC to engage in interpretation of the elements and thus contribute to the gap-filling in law and addressing the vagueness in law. W. Lietzau, Checks and Balances and Elements of Proof: Structural Pillars for the International Criminal Court. *Cornell International Law Journal*, (1999) 32, pp. 481–482. See also L. Helfer, J. Karen who notes: "many treaties are the international equivalent of incomplete contracts, and judges often cannot avoid clarifying ambiguities

Judge Posner put it: "Some statutes, indeed, are so general that they merely provide an initial impetus to the creation of frankly judge-made law…".[13]

In fact, it is a well-established fact that because statutes are not perfect legal instruments without gaps or vague notions it becomes part of judicial function to engage in a certain amount of judicial lawmaking for further clarification of the standing provisions.[14] In international law each international court or tribunal independently determines the limits of such lawmaking.[15] The power to interpret the standing rules falls within the exclusive competence of the relevant international court or tribunal.[16] Interpreted rigidly the rules of standing serve as a bar for claims brought by anyone other than the injured State.[17] Conversely, a liberal interpretation of the standing rules may open the door for *actio popularis* claims by entities other than the injured State.

However, the exercise of the inherent function of interpretation of standing rules by international courts and tribunals becomes subject to extraneous policy constraints which are dealt with in greater detail below.

2 The Problem of Non-Liquet and Limits of Judicial Law Making

It has to be stressed that in the context of standing rules an international court's willingness to interpret such rules either permissively or restrictively,

---

or filling gaps in their texts" in Legitimacy and Lawmaking, (2013) p. 484. Letsas argues along similar lines and contends that most ECHR provisions allow for divergent interpretations. G. Letsas, The Truth in Autonomous Concepts: How to Interpret the ECHR, *EJIL* (2004), Vol. 15 No. 2, p. 280.

13 R. Posner, The Meaning of Judicial Self-Restraint, 59 *Indiana Law Journal,* 1 (1984), pp. 5–6. However, historically, most international courts and tribunals have been loyal to Montesquieu's conception of the role of judiciary as being simply the "…the mouth (*la bouche de la loi*) that pronounces the words of law, mere passive beings, incapable of moderating either its force or rigour". Montesquieu, 1980, book XI, Ch. 6. Quoted in E. Pattaro, H. Rottleuthner, A. Shiner, '*A Treatise of Legal Philosophy and General Jurisprudence*': *Vol. I* (*The Law and the Right*), (Springer, Berlin, 2012), p. 233. For the view that judges can't fill the gaps in the law and that this task should be vested with States see also H. Kelsen, *Principles of International Law,* (The LawBook Exchange, Ltd. Clark, New Jersey), 2003, pp. 305–306.

14 F. Zarbiyev, (2012), p. 269.

15 As the Special Tribunal for Lebanon recently stated, in international law 'each tribunal constitutes a self-contained unit'. Decision on Appeal of pre-trial Judge's Order Regarding Jurisdiction and Standing, Special Tribunal for Lebanon, Appeals Chamber, 10 November 2010, para 41.

16 C. Brown, (2005), p. 203.

17 S. Freedman, '*Human Rights Transformed*,' (OUP, Oxford, 2008), p. 126.

will depend both on the role a court is prescribed within a given institutional framework (international organization), whether it is the ICJ within the UN or the CJEU within the EU or any other tribunal and also on individual perceptions of judicial policy concerns.[18] Helfer and Slaughter note in this regard:

> In the narrowest case, ... independent tribunals would do no more than hold states to the precisely defined international obligations to which they had initially agreed. International law is rarely so clear, however. In practice, giving a tribunal a mandate to resolve the parties' dispute in accordance with pre-existing rules also includes an implicit mandate to complete the parties' contract by filling gaps and clarifying ambiguities. Such interpretative ventures often require the tribunal to engage in some type of minimal law-making. Some tribunals have a more capacious mandate: to achieve a treaty's overall objectives or to read its specific rules in the light of those objectives. At the outer margins, a tribunal may interpret its mandate even more expansively, advancing particular substantive goals during periods of political impasse among the member states. These are different degrees of judicial expansiveness, and governments respond to them in different ways, using one or a combination of the structural/formal and political-control mechanisms...[19]

Helfer and Slaughter identifies two issues. The first issue is that international courts and tribunals are inevitably involved in law making at some level in case of *non-liquet*[20] and second is that such law making, if extends beyond certain limits, may trigger reactions from States. It should be added that if an international court or tribunal operates within an institutional framework (self-contained regime) extensive law-making might trigger negative reactions of non-judicial (political) organs too. The concept of *non-liquet* is closely

18 S. Jodoin, 'Understanding the Behaviour', 6 *J. Int'l Law & Int'l Rel.* 1, Summer, 2010, p. 7.

19 L. Helfer & A. Slaughter, 'Why States Create International Tribunals', 93 *Cal. L. Rev.* 2005, p. 937. Ginsburg argues along similar lines. He contends that international courts and tribunals have no choice but engage in law-making because laws are not always clear and courts act to fill the existing gaps. He maintains that although courts engage in "explicit" or "implicit" law-making they are not inclined to accept this fact. See T. Ginsburg, 'Bounded Discretion', 45 *Va. J. Int'l L.*, 2004–2005, pp. 635–640. See also R. Jennings, *The Role of the International Court of Justice*, BYIL, 1997, 68(1), p. 40. L. Gross, '*The International Court of Justice*' 65 *AJIL*.,1971, p. 265. Leo Gross makes this point with reference to the ICJ's unwillingness to engage in law-making in the *North See Continental Shelf* cases.

20 Refers to situation when "any of the judges after hearing a cause, were not satisfied that the case was made clear enough for them to pronounce a verdict...". *Black's Law Dictionary.* 6th ed., 1990, West Group.

intertwined with the idea of law-making function of international tribunals.[21] Recognition of *non-liquet* in international law compels international tribunals to acknowledge gaps in the law and sometimes leave it to the discretion of States to fill such gaps.[22] Rejection of *non-liquet* coupled with normative vagueness shifts the task of law-making to international courts and tribunals which are to fill the gaps.[23] However, it has to be noted that courts are not under an obligation to declare *non-liquet*, yet they are free to do so if they find that there is no rule of international law applicable to a given set of facts. The *Nuclear Weapons* advisory opinion, which failed to explicitly opine on the legality of use of nuclear weapons in an extreme circumstance of self-defence exemplifies a declaration of *non-liquet*.[24] The ICJ in the Fisheries Jurisdiction case noted: "In the circumstances, the Court, as a court of law, cannot render

---

21 J. Stone, *Non-Liquet and the Function of Law in the International Community,* 35 *BYBIL*, 1959, p. 131.

22 Ibid. 132. For similar arguments in the context of international criminal tribunals see L. Grover, A Call to Arms: Fundamental Dilemmas Confronting the Interpretation of Crimes in the Rome Statute of the International Criminal Court. 21 *EJIL*, 2010 p, 549. C. Ford, (n104), p. 59. Ford argues that historically the exclusive dominance of States in international law-making made the concept of *non liquet* welcomed and relied upon by international courts and tribunals. p. 59. Nowadays, this attitude of courts and scholars has profoundly changed and *non-liquet* is widely discarded. pp. 59–60. Rejection of *non-liquet* had, as a logical outcome, given judges more room for manoeuvre in terms of exercising their discretion to develop law through judicial interpretation. pp. 60–61. Ford suggests that the general principles of law as prescribed under Article 38(1)(C) of the ICJ Statute may be employed to fill the gaps in international law and thus dispose of the *non-liquet* problem. p. 64. The *Barcelona Traction* case exemplifies the point where the ICJ referred to the domestic law principle of legal personality of the corporation.

23 J. Stone, (1959), p. 132. C. Greenwood argued that the ICJ's pronouncement on the illegality of use of nuclear weapons would have gone beyond ICJ's judicial function as the Court would engage in legislating. 'The *Advisory Opinion on Nuclear Weapons* and the Contribution of the International Court to International Humanitarian Law' (1997) 316 *International Review of the Red Cross,* p. 74. The role of the ICJ, however, is to impose restraint on itself and allow it for the States to decide on whether they wish to fill the gaps which the Court had identified. A. Coleman, The ICJ and Highly Political Matters, *Melb. Journal of Int. Law,* 29, 2003, p. 56. I. Scobbie, (1997), p. 269.

24 L. Bartels, The Separation of Powers in the WTO: How to Avoid Judicial Activism, *I.C.L.Q.* 2004, 53(4), p. 874. The ICJ noted: "The anti-nuclear forces in the world are immensely influential, but that circumstance does not swerve the Court from its duty of pronouncing the use of the weapons legal if that indeed be the law. A second alternative conclusion is that the law gives no definite indication one way or the other. If so, that neutral fact needs to be declared, and a new stimulus may then emerge for the development of the law. Thirdly, if legal rules or principles dictate that the nuclear weapon is illegal, the Court will so pronounce, undeterred again by the immense forces ranged on the side of the legality of the weapon". *Nuclear Weapons Opinion* [1996] 1 ICJ Rep. 226, at p. 440.

judgment *sub specie legis ferendae,* or anticipate the law before the legislator has laid it down".[25] This statement is informed by the ICJ's philosophy of imposing self-restraint and acting deferentially when it comes to areas of law where it considers that gaps have to be filled by States.[26] Marc Weller is right to say that the ICJ "does not see itself as an agency dedicated to advancing the law or its scholarly discussion".[27] Nor is the ICJ willing to create law when States themselves are uncertain about the status of law in a given area. As has been noted the ICJ's unwillingness to intrude into the realm of law-making is observable from its early decisions in the *Nicaragua, Nuclear Weapons, Kosovo Advisory Opinion* and other cases.[28] Fuad Zarbiyev rightly points out "that the areas in which the judicial courage of international judges is most pronounced are not those where 'vital interests' of states come into play ..."[29]

25 *Fisheries Jurisdiction case* (UK v Iceland), 1974 I.C.J. 3, 23 (Judgment of July 25).

26 D. Partan, Introduction: Increasing the Effectiveness of the International Court. *Harvard International Law Journal,* Vol. 18, No. 3, 1977, p. 561. See also, P. Kooijmans, The ICJ in the 21st Century: Judicial Restraint, Judicial Activism, or Proactive Judicial Policy, *ICLQ,* vol. 56, October 2007, pp. 741–757. Kooijmans maintains that the Court's non-admissibility decisions in the *East Timor and Armed Activities on the Territory of Congo case* reflects this approach. p. 745. See also J. Jackson, who maintains that the DSU precludes the possibility of reports aimed at modifying the rights and duties of the WTO members. Fragmentation or Unification Among International Institutions: The World Trade Organization. 31 *N.Y.U.J. Int'l L. & Pol.*, 1998–1999, p. 830.

27 M. Weller, Modesty Can be a Virtue: Judicial Economy in the ICJ Kosovo Opinion, *Leiden Journal of International Law,* 24 (2011), p. 132. See M. Bothe, who notes with reference to ICJ's statement that "general international law contains no applicable prohibition of declarations of independence" that it amounts to a statement of *non-liquet.* See Kosovo – So What? The Holding of the International Court of Justice is not the Last Word on Kosovo's Independence, *German Law Journal,* Vol. 11, No. 08, 2010, p. 837.

28 M. Weller, (2011), pp. 130–133. For criticism of the Court's silence on the question of secession see A. Peters, Does Kosovo Lie in the *Lotus*-Land of Freedom? *Leiden Journal of International Law,* 24(2011), p. 99. See also *Legal Consequences of the Construction of a Wall in the Occupied Palestinian Territory,* ICJ Reports 2004, 136, at p. 194. Some commentators note that International Courts (with reference to the ICJ and ITLOS specifically) are unwilling to decide cases which States are most likely will be unwilling to execute. See F. Palombino, Judicial Economy and Limitation of the Scope of the Decision in International Adjudication, *Leiden Journal of International Law,* 2010, 23(4), p. 928.

29 F. Zarbiyev, (2012), p. 263. See also R. Falk who agrees with this conclusion, Realistic Horizons for International Adjudication, 11 *Virginia Journal of International Law,* 1970–71, p. 317. Charney also notes that ICJ's exceeding intrusion into the areas where the law is unsettled may lead to countermeasures by States. Such countermeasures may take the form of withdrawal of consent to the ICJ' jurisdiction or cutting down the Court's budget. See J. Charney, The Impact on the International Legal System of the Growth of the International Courts and Tribunals. 31 *N.Y.U.J. Int'l L. & Pol.*,1998–1999, p. 703.

Concepts such as judicial deference and non-justiciability were seen as limitations imposed on the judicial "intrusiveness". Self-restraint imposed by international courts and tribunals is usually caused by the caution that they are acting contrary to the intent of the drafters which otherwise might eventually lead to revision of the judge-made law by States.[30] Therefore, when international courts and tribunals interpret the law they will assess the possibility of subsequent endorsement of the judge made law by States.[31] Judicial activism of international courts and tribunals is often perceived as transgression of the permissible limits of adjudication and as being against values and interests of States.[32] These perceptions shape the States' attitudes towards international adjudication as a means of peaceful settlement of international disputes and the more States think that an international court transgresses the limits of what States think as permissible the more likely it is that the States (or 'mandate givers', using the words of Yuval Shany) will refuse recourse to international adjudication.[33]

This is particularly true of international courts and tribunals, which are more dependent on States in terms of consent to jurisdiction and compliance with the decisions. It would be plausible to argue that the ICJ's decision in the *South West Africa* cases to reject *actio popularis* was informed by three main policy concerns. First was the ICJ's concern about the possible reaction of States. A second factor was the ICJ's concern about an increase in the Court's case law. A third consideration was the ICJ's perception of its role vis-à-vis other, political organs of the UN. It has to be noted that the first two factors

30 W. Schabas, Prosecutorial Discretion v Judicial Activism at the International Criminal Court, *Journal of International Criminal Justice* 6 (2008), pp. 755–756. In line with the preceding observations about the ICJ's function it is important to note that the purposes (the central functions) of courts (including ICJ) may change. This change in the purposes and hence of court's self-perception are caused by changes in the attitudes of the States. However, the inability, for instance, in the case of ICJ, of the UN members to reformulate the purposes of the ICJ by amending the UN Charter (ICJ Statute) has led the courts to identify and set such objectives without the participation of the UN members. Y. Shany, (n25), p. 235.

31 See C. Tams, A. Tzanakopoulos, (2010) 20(4), *Leiden Journal of International Law*, pp. 784–786. For the view that ICJ makes law see T. Buergenthal, *Law Making by the ICJ and other International Courts*, Proceedings of the Annual Meeting (American Society of International Law), Vol. 103 (March 25–28, 2009), pp. 403–406.

32 R. Bork, Coercing Virtue: The Worldwide Rule of Judges, (AIE Press, 2003), p. 10. As a consequence of such an approach by the ICJ States may even withdraw their consent to ICJ's jurisdiction. E. Posner and J. Yoo, Judicial Independence in International Tribunals, *California Law Review*, Vol. 93, No. 1, 2005, pp. 7 and 36.

33 See R. Steinberg, Judicial Law-Making at the WTO: Discursive, Constitutional, and Political Constraints, 98 *AJIL*, 247 (2004) pp. 263–267.

are taken into account by all international courts and tribunals, which choose to impose self-restraint and construe the standing rules restrictively rejecting any claim of *actio popularis*. The third factor only applies to those international courts and tribunals, which operate within self-contained regimes where the functions are divided between various judicial and political organs.

The following analysis examines in more detail the policy concerns which underlie the ICJ's, ECtHR's and CJEU's decisions on *actio popularis*.

3 *Actio popularis* and Judicial Policy Concerns

The starting point of analysis is the ICJ's seminal decision in the *South West Africa* cases which marks the first step in the judicial treatment of *actio popularis*. The differences in judges' perception of adjudication and law should be pointed out as the main reason for the ICJ's two conflicting decisions in the *South West Africa* cases.[34] Friedman explains that the ICJ's decision in the 1966 *South West Africa* case reflects a profound conflict of jurisprudential thought relating to the role of the judiciary. The problem feeds from fundamental difference between perceptions of adjudication, on the one hand, as a purely interpretative exercise, and on the other, as a means of revising, changing or creating law.[35]

It has been maintained that the ICJ's 1966 decision in the SWA case can be described as "judicial conservatism" reflected in the 'very narrow conception of judicial function', involving 'a sharp separation of law and morals and of law and politics', 'deference to the nation state and to the doctrine of national sovereignty'.[36]

Indeed, the diametrically opposing views held by the ICJ in the 1962 and 1966 decisions show the fundamentally divergent perceptions of the ICJ's role.[37]

34 W. Friedmann, *The Jurisprudential Implications of the South West Africa Case*, 6 *Columbia Journal of Transnational Law*, 1, 1967, p. 3.

35 Ibid. pp. 5–6. The view is that by giving purposive meaning to the Mandate Agreement and Article 22 of the Covenant of the League of Nations and by doing so the Court could remain within permissible limits of judicial interpretation without 'establishing law independently of an existing legal system, institution or norm'. See Dissenting opinion of Judge Tanaka, *South West Africa* case 1966, ICJ Rep. pp. 277–278.

36 R. Falk, The South West Africa Cases: An Appraisal, *International Organization*, Vol. 21, No. 1 (Winter, 1967), p. 7.

37 Some writers argued in favour of a more dominant role of the ICJ in providing for "supremacy of law". It was submitted that this objective could be more easily attained through the judicial rather than the legislative function. The latter needs an unlikely revision of the UN Charter. Therefore, a proposition was made to view ICJ as "...the central judiciary body of the international community". F. Vicunia and C. Pinto, *The Peaceful*

The 1962 decision reflects the internationalist view of the legal enforcement of the rights of the Mandated Territories and the role which the ICJ is given as a 'judicial arm of the organized international community'.[38] Conversely, the ICJ's 1966 decision mirrors the Court which performs a minimalist judicial function of applying the law as it stands and to settle the dispute between the parties in a bilateralist context.[39] The ICJ's 1966 SWA decision that the right to *actio popularis* was unknown to international law as it stood at the time of the Court's decision prompts a conclusion that the Court considered the question of the legality of *actio popularis* as one that could be held by States either by a rule of customary international law or general principles of law. This notwithstanding the 1966 decision conspicuously demonstrates the ICJ's deferential attitude towards States and unwillingness to interpret the standing rules permissively to allow for *actio popularis*.[40] However, the ICJ would have acted much more resolutely had it found sufficient support in State practice for a right to vindicate public interests. The Court's deferential attitude in the 1966 SWA case reflects the Court's perception as a judicial body whose main function is simply to decide 'in accordance with international law' disputes referred to it by the States.[41] This is also in line with Bruno Simma's characterization of the most of the ICJ's decisions as having 'transactional' rather than law-developing nature.[42]

Settlement of Disputes: Prospects for the Twenty-First Century, Preliminary Report Prepared for the 1999 Centennial of the First International Peace Conference, C.E. Doc. CAHDI (98), paras. 103 and 110.

38 R. Falk, (1967), p. 14. See also Y. Shany, No Longer a Weak Department of Power? Reflections on the Emergence of a New International Judiciary. *EJIL,* Vol. 20, No. 1, 2009, pp. 74–75.

39 R. Falk, (1967), p. 14.

40 It has been argued throughout the book that ICJ went beyond the Applicants' request. The ICJ had to examine the legality (admissibility) of Applicants' claim simply under Article 7 of the Mandate Agreement taken together with Article 22 of the Covenant of the League of Nations.

41 A. Pellet, Commentary to Article 38 in A. Zimmermann, Ch. Tomuschat, Karin Oellers-Frahm (eds.), *The Statute of the International Court of Justice: A Commentary.* (OUP, Oxford, 2006), p. 693.

42 See B. Simma, Universality of International Law from a Perspective of a Practitioner, *EJIL,* 2009, Vol. 20, No. 2, p. 288. Amongst the opponents of allocating any role to the ICJ in developing the rules of international law was Judge Oda who argued against the ICJ acting as a legislator. Oda saw in the ICJ the organ performing a dispute settlement role when there is an inter-state dispute. Separate Opinion of Judge Oda in *Legality of the Use by a State of Nuclear Weapons in Armed Conflict,* Ad. Opinion of 8 July, 1996, ICJ Rep. at p. 88. For the opposite view see Armin von Bogdandy and Ingo Venzke, who contend that the role of international courts nowadays extends beyond dispute settlement between particular parties to the case and has general normative value. *Beyond Dispute: International Judicial Institutions as Lawmakers,* (2011) 12(5) *German Law Journal,* pp. 980–983; Vicufia

However, while acknowledging ICJ's potentially dualist role as a dispute settler on the one hand, and a law developer on the other, the ICJ's critics are inclined to argue that the role of the ICJ needs to be expanded in the light of the creation of norms of an *erga omnes* and *jus cogens* nature. Dupuy notes that the "... international community needs a judge to identify these norms and show their implications to the States".[43] According to Higgins, a more liberal stance on the question of standing which favours the interests of the international community is inherent in the ICJ's judicial function.[44] In fact the ICJ's recent case law demonstrates a gradual endorsement of this position. In its two recent decisions in the *Whaling in Antarctic*[45] and *Questions relating to the Obligation to Prosecute or Extradite* case[46] the ICJ accepted claims which were brought to vindicate public (collective) rather than applicant's special interests. The ICJ's gradual transition to recognition of claims to vindicate public (collective) interests and its more activist position in interpreting the rules of standing could be explained with reference to the changes in State practice in favour of recognition of the right to enforce collective interests.[47]

ICJ's unwillingness to step into the area, which falls within the competence of the political organs of the United Nations, can be mentioned as a second reason for rejection of claims in protection of collective interests. *South West Africa* cases once again exemplify the point.[48]

Article 7 of the UN Charter allocates to the ICJ the role of the "principal judicial organ of the United Nation". The drafters intended to delineate the role of the ICJ from that of the administrative and political organs of the United Nations.[49] There are issues, which cannot be resolved by means of judicial

and Pinto push the view of the ICJ as an organ whose function is not limited to settlement of disputes between the parties but which aims at making contribution "to the development of the principles of international law governing the international society generally". (1998), para. 110.

43 See P. Dupuy, (1999), pp. 803–806.

44 R. Higgins, Policy Considerations and the International Judicial Process, *ICLQ*, January, Vol. 17, No.1, Jan., 1968, p. 62.

45 *Australia vs Japan, New Zealand Intervening,* Judgment 31 March 2014, General List No. 148, p. 18.

46 *Questions relating to the Obligation to Prosecute or Extradite* (Belgium v Senegal), Judgment, I.C.J. Reports 2012, p. 422.

47 See Article 48 of the Articles on State Responsibility.

48 See Higgins, (1968), p. 73. Jessup, on the other hand noted that the Court's decision would not have been 'an attack on the validity of the Council's decision as if such decision were *ultra vires*.' Dissenting Opinion, *South West Africa* case, 1966, pp. 385–386.

49 Hon. Justice J. Evensen, 'The International Court of Justice: Main Characteristics and Its Contribution to the Development of the Modern Law of Nations', 57 *Nordic J. Int'l L.*, 1988, p. 10.

process. This is because judicial process tends to be time consuming and where prompt action needs to be taken other UN organs may be more suitable to take action rather than the ICJ.[50]

It has been noted that the 1966 *South West Africa* decision was strongly influenced by the Court's understanding of the limits of the competences of various UN organs.[51] The Court by putting special emphasis on the extra-legal character of Mandate provisions and Article 22 of the Covenant of League of Nations (well-being of the inhabitants of the Mandated territory) sought to argue that the questions brought before the Court had to be addressed in the political rather than legal realm, i.e. by political organs of the UN and not legal. Thus the Court deferred the matter to the assessment by UN's political bodies because, in the Court's view, consideration of the question raised before the Court would preclude the Court from exercising its judicial function.[52] What forms part of the Court's judicial function is determined by the Court itself.[53] The Court in the 1966 *South West Africa* case juxtaposed judicial functions with political ones and noted that the Court for reasons of judicial propriety could not exercise the former.[54] As has been noted, concerns about an increase in the case load also affect decisions of international courts and tribunals to reject *actio popularis*, and the ICJ is no exception. Concern about increased case load

50 R. Jennings, (1997), p. 51.

51 However, Higgins notes that where the line between the competences of various organs is blurred nothing precludes the Court from stepping into the realm of what may be perceived competence of political organs, provided that the Court may authoritatively resolve the legal aspects of the problem. See R. Higgins (1968), pp. 82–83.

52 E. Gordon, '*Old Orthodoxies*,' 1 *Denver Journal of International Law and Policy,* 65, 1971), p. 71 and 84. See also, B. Kingsbury, Foreword: Is Proliferation of International Courts and Tribunals a Systemic Problem? 31 *N.Y.U. J. Int'l L. & Pol.* 679 1998–1999, at pp. 693–694. Judge Spender also reflects on the question of division of political and judicial functions and maintains that the question of Administering Authority's compliance with the Trusteeship Agreement was one which fell in the domain of political assessment rather than judicial. *Northern Cameroons case,* pp. 79–80 of Judge Spender's Opinion.

53 In the Lockerbie case Judge Weeramantry noted: "As a judicial organ, it will be the Court's duty from time to time to examine and determine from a strictly legal point of view matters which may at the same time be the subject of determination from an executive or political point of view by another principal organ of the United Nations. The Court by virtue of its nature and constitution applies to the matter before it the concepts, the criteria and the methodology of the judicial process which other organs of the United Nations are naturally not obliged to do. The concepts it uses are juridical concepts, its criteria are standards of legality, its method is that of legal proof. Its tests of validity and the bases of its decisions are naturally not the same as they would be before a political executive organ of the United Nations". *Lockerbie Case* (Provisional Measures) [1992] ICJ Rep 3, p. 56.

54 E. Gordon, (1971), p. 77.

also played a role in the ICJ's refusal to allow for a more liberal construction of the standing requirements.[55]

The issue of a deferential attitude towards States, and as a result, a more restrictive interpretation of the standing rules also features in the case law of CJEU. The question of the limits of interpretation applicable to the standing provisions under Article 263(4) of TFEU has been one of the salient issues for the CJEU. It has been most conservative in its interpretation of the standing requirements under the TFEU. Fearing accusations of judicial activism the Court refused to take the lead and to provide a liberal interpretation of the requirement to show "direct and individual concern" to allow for *actio popularis*.[56] The CJEU preferred to defer the matter to States by asking them to loosen the standing requirements by enacting amendments to the TFEU.[57] The CJEU noted in this regard:

> While it is, admittedly, possible to envisage a system of judicial review of the legality of Community measures of general application different from that established by the founding Treaty and never amended as to its principles, *it is for the Member States, if necessary, in accordance with Article 48 EU, to reform the system currently in force.*[58]

55 Leo Gross noted in this regard: "Clearly the Court (in the Northern Cameroons case) was faced with a policy issue of first magnitude. Had the Court rejected the United Kingdom's preliminary objections as unfounded and in its own finding that a dispute existed at the time of Cameroon's application and its broad interpretation of the adjudication clause in the *South West Africa* cases as comprising disputes relating to the general administration of the Mandate, there may have been no convincing or convenient way to do so – the Court might well have opened the sluice gates to a flood of litigation. If policy considerations, including the requirements of sound administration of justice, made it desirable to discourage cases such as this from being steered in the direction of the Court, some other and more restricted ground might have been found". *Essays on International Law and Organization,* Vol. 1, (Springer, Berlin, 1984), pp. 827–828.

56 R. Caranta, Judicial Protection against Member States: The Indirect Effects of Art. 173, 175, and 177 in Micklitz (1996), p. 109. Notwithstanding the CJEU's conservative stance on the question of standing the Court occasionally construed the Treaty beyond its textual meaning, especially on such issues as direct effect, supremacy of Union law etc. A. Faeh, Judicial Activism, the Biotech Directive and its Institutional Implications: Is the Court Acting as a Legislator or a Court when Defining the "Human Embryo"? *E Rev.* 2015, 40(4), 613–627, at p. 618.

57 Rasmussen rightly points out "that any court has to calculate its activism nicely because miscalculation is likely to provoke clashes with other organs of government". The same logic applies to clashes with States. H. Rasmussen, Between Self-restraint and Activism: a Judicial Policy for the European Court, *E.L. Rev.* 1988, 13(1), pp. 1–2.

58 *UPA v Council,* Judgment of the Court, para. 45; See also C. Harding who notes that the Court is not favourable to step into what it thinks to be the realm of member States'

Regarded as one of the most active Courts, the CJEU has been very reluctant to interpret expansively the provisions of the Treaty concerning the right of individual petition before the CJEU.[59] In the long list of cases dealt with by the CJEU the Court persistently refused to grant broader standing to applicants by more liberal interpretation of the words "direct and individual concern" stated in the Article 263(4) of the TFEU. As the above-quoted statement in the *UPS v Council* suggests the Court considered the question as one falling within the exclusive authority of States parties to the Treaty.

Although the CJEU did depart from the strict *Plauman* test in a certain limited number of cases in the areas such as anti-dumping[60] and state-aid,[61] etc. the standing rules in these cases were not relaxed so far as allow for *actio popularis*. The Court's restrictive interpretation of standing requirements is striking given the Court's established reputation of giving the law purposive/teleological interpretation.[62] However, the Court's unwillingness to take up the role of the legislator and depart from the wording of the Treaty text, and its perception of the Community mechanisms of judicial remedies as a complete system capable of redressing violations of the rights of the persons concerned served as bases to refuse to liberalize standing requirements under Article 263(4).[63] Some commentators in the field have, however, provided more nuanced analyses of the possible rationales underlying the court's restrictive

---

legislative power. The Private Interest in Challenging Community Action, 1980, 5 *Europe Law Review*, pp. 354–361.

59 J. Martinez, Towards an International Judicial System, *56 Stan. L. Rev* 429 (2003), p. 455. For similar view in the context of willingness by the ECJ to defer cases to political bodies of EC and impose self-restraint depending on the reactions of community institutions and member States to its decisions see Laurence R. Helfer & Anne-Marie Slaughter, Towards a Theory of Effective Supranational Adjudication, 107 *Yale L.J.* 273 1997–1998, at pp. 314–315.

60 Joined Cases 239 and 275/82 *Allied Corporation v Commission* [1984] E.C.R. 1005, para. 11; Case C-358/89 *Extramet v Council* [1991] E.C.R. I-2501, para. 14.

61 *Parti écologiste "Les Verts" v European Parliament*, Judgment of the Court of 23 April 1986, Case 294/83, (Grounds).

62 See Case 294/83 Parti écologiste "Les Verts" v European Parliament [1986] ECR 1339, para. 23. The Court notes that the Treaty established "a complete system of legal remedies and procedures designed to permit the Court to review the legality of measures adopted by the institutions". A. Albors-Llorens, The Standing of private parties to challenge Community measures: has the European Court Missed the Boat, *Cambridge Law Journal*, 2003, p. 90. L. Helfer, K. Alter, (2010), p. 482. J. Haynes, Revisiting the *Locus Standi* of Private Applicants in Judicial Review Proceedings under CARICOM and EU Law: A Comparative Perspective, *Commonwealth Law Bulletin*, 2015 Vol. 41, No. 1, p. 73.

63 M. Grange, Towards a Liberalization of Standing Conditions for Individuals Seeking Judicial Review of Community Acts: Jego-Quere et Cie SA v Commission and Union de Pequeños Agricultores v Council, *Modern Law Review*, Vol.66, January 2003. p. 128.

approach to construing the *locus standi* requirements, drawing on legal, historical as well as political considerations. For example, Eliantonio and Stratieva have argued that one way of interpreting the long-standing traditional interpretation of the standing requirements by the CJEU is through the theory of historical institutionalism. This theory holds that whereas the CJEU sought to engage in judicial activism in so far as the creation and development of the principles of State liability and direct effect, it has refused to do the same in respect of the *locus standi* requirements, arguably because the former advance the 'prominent status of the EU as a supranational structure', while the latter 'makes Community measures more vulnerable to external attacks'.[64] Other reasonable explanations advanced for the court's wholly restrictive approach are the idea that because the principal litigants before the EU Courts are usually corporate and commercial entities, any liberal construction of the standing requirements would in fact not bring an advantage to natural persons, but to corporate lobbying groups in relation to various EU policies.[65] Indubitably, the CJEU's concern about increase in its case load has also been one of the key factors in its refusal to open the door for *actio popularis*.[66]

In a very similar fashion the ECtHR has, since its inception, been very reluctant to interpret its standing requirements permissively. In fact the victim requirement under Article 34 of the ECHR and the Court's case law on standing prompts a conclusion regarding the ECtHR's unwillingness to allow for *actio popularis*.[67] However, unlike the CJEU and the ICJ, the ECtHR is less concerned about the possible reactions of States parties and of other organs' reactions.[68] The primary reason for the ECtHR's strict interpretation of the victim requirement lies in its caution against the opening the floodgate for individual applications. On the other hand, the ECtHR's case law suggests that in certain circumstances the Court is willing to relax the standing rules to allow for claims

64 M. Eliantonio and N. Stratieva, 'From Plaumann, through UPA and Jégo Quéré, to the Lisbon Treaty: The *Locus Standi* of Private Applicants under Article 230(4) EC Through a Political Lens'. Maastricht Faculty of Law Working Paper 2009/13, 2009, p. 10.

65 R. Dehousse, *The European Court of Justice: The Politics of Judicial Integration* (McMillan, London, 1998), p. 111.

66 D. Arts, K. Lenaerts, I. Maselis, R. Bray, *Procedural Law of the European Union,* (Sweet & Maxwell, London, 2nd ed., 2006), p. 163. P. Craig, *The Jurisdiction of the Community Courts Reconsidered,* 36 *Texas International Law Journal,* pp. 555–587, at p. 563.

67 *Klass and Others v Germany*, 6 September 1978, § 33, Series A no. 28; *The Georgian Labour Party v Georgia* (dec.), no. 9103/04, 22 May 2007; *Matija OČIĆ v Croatia,* Application no. 46306/99, 25 November 1999.

68 It is very unlikely that any of the parties to ECHR will denounce it simply because the ECtHR decided to liberalize the standing rules and allow for *actio popularis*. Political risks of denouncing the Convention are too high.

by persons which can hardly be considered as victims of the violation under Article 34. The Court's decisions in *Open Door Dublin Well, Karner v Austria* and *Câmpeanu v Romania* cases depict cloaked willingness to relax standing rules by providing a teleological interpretation of the Convention.[69] The Court took this approach for the purpose of "… raising the general standards of protection of human rights…" and ensuring their effective protection.[70]

The foregoing analysis prompts a conclusion that the admissibility of *actio popularis* before international courts and tribunals depends on judicial policy concerns. These policies vary from one international court to another. Courts, which adopt a deferential attitude towards States are more likely to impose self-restraint and interpret the rules of standing more restrictively. Conversely, activist courts engage in a more liberal construction of standing rules, which may result in opening the door for *actio popularis*. For instance, the analysis of the case law of CJEU revealed that the CJEU has been resisting numerous proposals to reverse the case law on standing and extend the scope of applicants beyond those, which are individually affected by the measures. Conversely, the ICJ exemplifies a case of gradual transition from refusal to recognize *actio popularis* to its eventual endorsement in cases where collective interests are involved.

---

69 Although the Court does not explicitly acknowledge that it allows for *actio popularis*, as discussed above the applicants do not always satisfy the victim requirement under the Court's established case law and act in protection of collective interests.

70 *Karner v Austria*, para. 26.

Conclusion

The present study began by identifying two main uses of *actio popularis*: non-judicial and judicial. The non-judicial references to *actio popularis* in the literature utilized the concept in the contexts of countermeasures, jurisdiction and third party institutionalized acts. The judicial references to *actio popularis* were rightly made in the context of the right to bring an action before various international courts and tribunals to protect interests extending beyond claimant's individual (special) interests. The book confined its scope to the study of *actio popularis* exclusively in the latter context. However, examination of *actio popularis* in the judicial context revealed a number of challenges. These challenges lie in the very nature of international adjudication with its numerous international courts and tribunals, a feature, which is most certainly not shared by municipal legal systems. This feature of international adjudication also naturally imposed the methodology for the study of the concept, which was to examine the concept independently as a right before every international court and tribunal. In fact, this methodological approach served as a basis to challenge the ICJ's 1966 *South West Africa* decision that the right of *actio popularis* although known to certain municipal legal systems was alien to international law. The central argument in the book and one of its conclusions is that the ICJ in this case, firstly, misrepresented the facts because there were at the time of the decision examples of treaty instruments which allowed for *actio popularis* and secondly, the ICJ pronounced on the question which can only be answered individually by each and every international court or tribunal based on its standing rules.

A careful examination of the ICJ's case law suggests that even after the ICJ's sweeping *obiter* in the *Barcelona Traction* case, which recognized the legal interest of all States in the protection of obligations *erga omnes,* it took the ICJ more than forty years to rule in favour of *actio popularis.*[1]

The book acknowledges that enforcement of collective interests which exist under customary international is permissible under optional clause declarations before the ICJ. However, such an enforcement action will be subject to satisfying standing requirements and persuasion by the ICJ that general international law authorizes invoking responsibility to enforce collective or community interests.

The examination of *actio popularis* in a comparative context of municipal and international legal systems revealed that such claims can be brought

1 In *Extradition Proceedings* case between Belgium and Congo and *Whaling in Antarctica case.*

DOI:10.1163/9789004380981_010

before domestic and international courts and tribunals in a centralized (via appointed representative) and decentralized manner (by states or persons individually). However, unlike municipal legal systems, with numerous examples of countries with all-purpose representatives appointed to protect collective interests, amongst the international courts and tribunals examined in the book such a right can be exercised before ITLOS only. This right is vested in the International Seabed Authority to protect interests in the Area. Otherwise, political differences at the international level serve as the main obstacle in appointing a *parens patriae* to represent interests of all States before a relevant international court or tribunal when protection of collective interests is involved.

The book departs from the premise that *actio popularis* and the notion of community and collective interests and obligations are closely linked. The former is a means of enforcing the latter. However, *actio popularis* is not invariably devised to enforce collective interests. For instance, *actio popularis* in WTO law by way of *lex specialis* allows invoking responsibility in the general interest (as defined in the book) under purely bilateralizable treaties, and the right of enforcement by all States only serves the purpose of protecting the system as a whole.

Nevertheless, the link between the nature of the primary norms (that they are established to protect collective interests) and the way the international courts and tribunals interpret their standing rules is undeniable. The link manifests itself in the willingness of some international courts and tribunals to interpret their standing rules liberally to allow for *actio popularis* when protection of collective interests is sought. Indeed, "bipolar" litigation is inadequate to enforce collective interests.

The interpretative powers of international courts and tribunals, especially of rules of procedure (standing rules), allows the introduction of *actio popularis* via judicial interpretation in cases where *actio popularis* is not expressly granted. In such a case international courts and tribunals fill the gaps in the law which are usually created as a result of the vagueness (or absence of a definition in the rules of procedure or standing rules) of some basic preconditions for standing e.g. "legal dispute", "victim requirement" and "direct and individual concern". In this case the right of *actio popularis* is inferred from the primary norm, which must be established to protect collective interests and the court's or tribunal's liberal interpretation of the preconditions of standing. The study suggests that this has become increasingly true about the ICJ and ITLOS, perhaps less so about ITLOS.

The ICJ's jurisprudence demonstrates that it has come to openly endorse *actio popularis* by making a long journey from construing the "legal dispute" very restrictively and thus explicitly rejecting *actio popularis* in the *South West Africa* cases to making a gradual transition in favour of openly recognizing *actio popularis* in the *Belgium v Senegal Extradition Proceedings* case and more implicitly in the *Whaling in Antarctica* case. Careful analysis of the ICJ's case law prompts a conclusion that the ICJ's interpretation of the concept of a "legal dispute" will invariably be based on its construction of the nature of primary obligations, i.e. whether the primary obligations are established to protect collective interests. This conclusion departs from the premise that although the question of interpretation of the standing rules (of the dispute) is one which falls within the ICJ's exclusive competence, the Court's willingness to construe the standing rules liberally will depend on its understanding that the States parties to the treaty instrument do not object to the invocation of responsibility to protect collective interests. The primary reason lies in the ICJ's policy of adopting a deferential attitude towards States in cases involving sensitive legal issues.

The book further concludes that the ICJ will not reject an *actio popularis* claim if the right to bring such a claim is expressly vested in States under a treaty instrument. It has to be noted that although the treaty instruments do not expressly use the *actio popularis* terminology the open-ended wording of jurisdictional clauses under some treaty instruments have allowed the ICJ/PCIJ to rule in favour of *actio popularis* claims. The *Polish Upper Silesia, Interpretation of the Statute of the Memel Territory,* and *Wimbledon* cases are conspicuous examples.

An interesting aspect of the adjudication before the ICJ is raised in the context of procedural rules, which preclude filing claims irrespective of the nature of the obligations involved. The indispensable third-party rule serves as a bar for bringing any applications involving the rights of States which have not consented to the ICJ's jurisdiction. The collective (*erga omnes or even jus cogens*) nature of obligations does not and cannot trump the indispensable third-party rule established in the *Monetary Gold* case. This view is plausible given that the nature of the rights should be separated from the question of consent to the Court's jurisdiction.

In the context of proceedings before the ITLOS the methodology of determining the legal basis for *actio popularis* is very similar to that of the ICJ. The reason lies in the similarity of the wording of jurisdictional clauses in the ICJ Statute and in UNCLOS. Both the ICJ and ITLOS decide on "disputes" submitted to them by the parties. Interpretation of the standing provisions in ITLOS is also influenced by the nature of the primary norms under UNCLOS, that is, whether the primary norms are established to protect collective interests. UNCLOS provisions relating to the freedom of the high seas, conservation of the living resources of the high seas and the Area can be mentioned as examples. The Area is considered as a common heritage of mankind and no State has a special interest in its protection. Although ITLOS has not expressly pronounced on the admissibility (legality) of *actio popularis* in any of the contentious proceedings, without effective means of enforcement of collective obligations such obligations will be devoid of any purpose. The Seabed Disputes Chamber's decision in the 'Responsibilities and Obligation of States Sponsoring Persons and Entities with Respect to Activities in the Area' advisory opinion recognizes *jus standi* for the Seabed Authority to act on behalf of mankind but also for all other users of the sea in cases involving environmental protection of the Area. This decision endorses both centralized (via Authority) and decentralized (via States) means of enforcement of collective interests. The Chapter concludes by questioning the cogency of the argument that interests in the Area can be perceived as an aggregate of the special interests of States. Though practical from the point of view of surmounting the hurdle of *actio popularis* it is difficult to theoretically substantiate. Broadly speaking all States have an interest in upholding the rules of international law and in this sense, they are specially interested. However, interests in the Area are not special to any particular State but are collectively shared by all States. The interests of one State do not prevail over the interests of others. Therefore a claim brought to protect interests in the Area is invariably (except if the claimant can claim a special injury) collective.

In contrast, the CJEU represents the other side of the spectrum. For many years the CJEU has refused to depart from the strictest standing test established in the *Plaumann* case even when collective interests were at stake. The CJEU's conservativeness in interpreting its standing requirements is informed by its perception of the completeness of the judicial protection system under the TFEU where potential gaps in the protection mechanisms may be filled by the preliminary reference procedure. The second reason underlying the CJEU's conservative interpretation of standing rules is its unwillingness to interfere with what it considers to be a question falling within the competence of the States parties to the TFEU. For the CJEU, relaxing standing requirements as far as to allow *actio popularis* falls beyond the scope of judicial powers and such a right must be 'legislatively' prescribed by amending Article 263(4) of the TFEU. This view most conspicuously reflects a policy of judicial deference towards States.

The context of the ECtHR is slightly different. The "victim requirement" under Article 34 of the ECHR was introduced as part of standing requirements with the sole purpose of precluding *actio popularis* claims. This view is affirmed in numerous ECtHR decisions. Nevertheless, recent case law suggests that in certain cases the Court is willing to interpret the standing rules more permissively and to open the door for *actio popularis* without openly stating so. The Court's relaxation of standing rules is informed by its willingness to live up to the main purpose of the European Convention, i.e. ensuring effective protection of human rights. In the line of decisions involving claims brought by persons other than the actual victim the Court has applied the victim requirement very liberally, thereby broadening the circle of potential applicants.

Actio popularis before the WTO DSB is distinct in the sense that WTO obligations are known as bilateralizable, rather than established to protect any collective interests. However, the bilateralist nature of WTO obligations does not preclude filing *actio popularis* claims before WTO DSB by virtue of *lex specialis*. Such *lex specialis* is envisioned in Article 4 of the Agreement on Subsidies and Countervailing Measures (SCM). Article 4 does not protect "collective interests" for such interests do not exist under bilateralizable treaties. The purpose of Article 4 is to ensure protection of the system as a whole, i.e. protection of the general interest in compliance with obligations under SCM. Entitlement to bring *actio popularis* claims is also expressly envisioned in GATT Article XXIII(1)(a) which allows WTO members to bring claims before DSB if "the attainment of any objective of the Agreement is being impeded ...".

However, outside the context of the above stated treaty norms, *actio popularis* in WTO law can only be instituted by inference from substantive WTO norms which are established to protect a particular collective interest. Preservation of the marine environment seems to be one of such norms. Although the law in this field is still in the process of development, the Shrimp/Turtle case can, subject to reservations stated above, be viewed as implicit recognition of *actio popularis*.

The final chapter explores the causes which underlie the international courts' willingness or unwillingness to allow for *actio popularis* claims. The book concludes that policy concerns of deference and increase in case-load are the key factors which affect the decision on *actio popularis*. Given the proliferation of international courts and tribunals such judicial policy concerns affect international courts differently. Each international court or tribunal prioritizes its own judicial policy concerns. This results in some international courts behaving more actively and interpreting the rules of standing liberally, while other courts exercising self-restraint and construing standing requirements restrictively to exclude *actio popularis*. For instance, the ICJ's years long conservative stance on the question of standing to enforce collective interests was informed by its caution about negative reactions from States and their refusal to accept the Court's jurisdiction, about an increase in case-load, as well as an unwillingness to interfere with the competence of other UN organs.

Conversely, the ECtHR has been least concerned about the reactions of States parties to the ECHR but rather its primary concern in dismissing *actio popularis* claims was to avoid increases in its case load. Therefore, *actio popularis* before international courts and tribunals becomes a mixed question of substantive and procedural law, as well as an important question of judicial policy.

Bibliography

Abi-Saab, G., 'The ICJ as a World Court' in V Lowe and M Fitzmaurice, Fifty Years of the International Court of Justice: Essays in Honour of Sir Robert Jennings (Grotius, Cambridge, 1996).

Abi-Saab, G., Whither the International Community? (1998), 9 *EJIL*.

Abtahi, H., & Webb Ph., *The Genocide Convention: The Travaux Préparatoires,* Vol. I, (Martinus Nijhoff Publishers, 2008).

Aceves, W., 'Actio Popularis? The Class Action in International Law', *The University of Chicago Legal Forum,* (2003).

Addis, A., Imagining the International Community: The Constitutive Dimension of Universal Jurisdiction, Human Rights Quarterly 31 (2009).

Ago, R., 'Pluralism and the Origins of the International Community' 3 Italian Yearbook of International Law (1977) 30.

Aland, D., 'Countermeasures of General Interest', (2002) 13(5) *EJIL* 2002.

Albors-Llorens, A., The Standing of private parties to challenge Community measures: has the European Court missed the boat, Cambridge Law Journal, 2003.

Alford, RP, 'The Proliferation of International Courts and Tribunals: International Adjudication in Ascendance' (2000) 94 *American Society of International Law: Proceedings of the Annual Meeting.*

Allot, P., Reconstituting Humanity-New International Law, 3 *EJIL* (1992).

Alter, K & R Helfer., Nature or Nurture? Judicial Law-Making in the European Court of Justice and the Andean Tribunal of Justice, 64 Int'l Org. (2010).

Antonious, T, C Tams., Leiden Journal of International Law, 2010.

Antonopoulos, C., Effectiveness v Rule of Law Following the East Timor Case, NYIL, Volume XXVII, 1996.

Arnull, A., 'The Action for Annulment: a Case of Double Standards?' in D. O'Keefe and A. Bavasso (eds.), *Judicial Review in European Union Law,* (Liber Amicorum in honour of Lord Slynn of Hadley, Volume I (The Hague, 2000).

Arnull, A., Challenging Community Acts – an Introduction, in Public Interest Litigation before European Courts, Hans – W. Micklitz/Norbert Reich (eds.), 1996.

Arnull, A., *Private Applicants and the Action for Annulment since Codorniu,* CMLR, 38, 2001.

Barav, A., *Admissibility of Individual Appeal to EEC Court* (1974) 11 CMLRev.

Barboza, J., 'Legal Injury: The Tip of the Iceberg in the Law of State Responsibility' in L Bartels., The Separation of Powers in the WTO: How to Avoid Judicial Activism, *I.C.L.Q.* 2004, 53(4).

Baslar, K., *The Concept of the Common Heritage of Mankind in International Law* (Dordrecht, the Netherlands: Martinus Nijhoff, 1998)

Bassiouni, C., "Universal Jurisdiction for International Crimes: Historical Perspectives and Contemporary Practice", (2001) 42 *Va. J. Int'l L.*

Bassiouni, C., International Crimes: *Jus Cogens* and Obligations *Erga Omnes, Law and Contemporary Problems,* Vol. 59, No. 4.

Bekker, P., 'Reflections on the ICJ's Oil Platform Decision: Protecting International Shipping Channels During Hostilities and the Oil Platforms Case: *Actio Popularis* Revisited?' (2004) 29 The Yale Journal of International Law.

Berg, G., Development of Judicial Control in the *European Communities*, The Hague, 1981.

Berger, A., *Encyclopedic Dictionary of Roman Law,* The American Philosophic Society, Philadelphia, 1953.

Berman, N, *"But the Alternative Is Despair": European Nationalism and the Modern Renewal of International Law*, 106 Harv. L.Rev. (1993).

Betlem, G., "Being Directly and Individually Concerned", the Schutznorm Doctrine and Frankovich liability in Environmental Matters Before European Courts, in European Public Interest Litigation (Miclitz eds, 1996).

Bogojević, S., Judicial Protection of Individual Applicants Revisited: Access to Justice through the Prism of Judicial Subsidiarity, Yearbook of European Law, 33 (2015).

Biernat, E., *The Locus Standi of Private Applicants under Article 230(4) EC and the Principle of Judicial Protection in the European Community,* Jean Monnet Working Paper, 12/03.

Bigwood, R., *Public Interest Litigation: Introduction and Overview in Public Interest Litigation: New Zealand Experience in International Perspective,* Lexis Nexis NZ Limited, 2006.

Birnie, P., A. Boyle, C. Redgwell, *International Law and the Environment,* (Oxford, OUP, 3rd ed., 2009).

Black's Law Dictionary 1114 (6th ed. 1990).

Bluntschli, J.C., *Das moderne Völkerrecht der civilizierten Staaten als Rechtsbuch dargestellt,* Nordlingen, Beck, 1872.

Bodansky, D., *What's in a Concept? Global Public Goods, International Law, and Legitimacy,* EJIL (2012), Vol. 23 No. 3.

Bogdandy, A., and I. Venzke, *Beyond Dispute: International Judicial Institutions as Lawmakers,* (2011) 12(5) *German Law Journal.*

Bonine, J., 'The Public's Right to Enforce Environmental Law', in Stephen Stec (ed.), *Handbook on Access to Justice under the Aarhus Convention,* (March, 2003).

Bork, R.H., Coercing Virtue: The Worldwide Rule of Judges, AIE Press, (2003a).

Bork, R., Coercing Virtue: The Worldwide Rule of Judges, Aei Press, (2003b).

Bothe, M., *Kosovo – So What? The Holding of the International Court of Justice is not the Last Word on Kosovo's Independence,* German Law Journal, Vol. 11, No. 08, 2010a.

Bothe, M., *Kosovo – So What? The Holding of the International Court of Justice is not the Last Word on Kosovo's Independence*, German Law Journal, Vol. 11, No. 08, 2010b.

Boyle, A., "Saving the World? Implementation and Enforcement of International Environmental Law Through International Institutions", Journal of Environmental Law 3 (1991).

Briggs, H., 'Barcelona Traction: The *Jus Standi* of Belgium', 65 *AJIL* 327 Issue 2, (1971).

Brilmayer, L., From 'Contract to Pledge': The Structure of International Human Rights Agreements, (2006) *BYIL*.

Brown, C., *The Inherent Powers of International Courts and Tribunals*, 2006, *BYIL*, 76(1).

Brownlie, I., *Principles of Public International Law,* (OUP, 1990).

Brüel, E., International Straits, (1947, Sweet and Maxwell, Ltd.), Vol. I.

Buckland, W., *A Manual of Roman Private Law,* second edition, (Cambridge, CUP, 1953).

Buergenthal, T., *Law Making by the ICJ and other International Courts,* Proceedings of the Annual Meeting (American Society of International Law), Vol. 103 (2009).

Buergenthal, T., Proliferation of International Courts and Tribunals: Is It Good or Bad? *Leiden Journal of International Law,* (2001) 14(2).

Byers, M., 'Conceptualizing the Relationship between *Jus Cogens* and *Erga Omnes* Rules' (1997) 66(2–3) *Nordic Journal of International Law.*

Cameron, J., J. Werksman & P. Roderick, *Improving Compliance with International Environmental Law,* (Routledge, 1990).

Cappelletti, "Vindicating the Public Interest through the Courts: A Comparativist's Contribution", in Access to Justice, Volume III, Emerging Issues and Perspectives (eds. Cappelletti and Garth), 1979, Milan/Alphen: Giuffré/Sijthoff.

Caranta, Roberto., Judicial Protection against Member States: The Indirect Effects of Art. 173, 175, and 177 in Micklitz, European Public Interest Litigation, eds., 1996.

Carmody, C., WTO Obligations as Collective, *EJIL* (2006), Vol. 17 No. 2.

Černý, Pavel, *Practical application of Article 9 of the Aarhus Convention,* in 10 EU Countries – Comparative Remarks, in Report on Access to Justice in Environmental Matters, 2010.

Chalmers, D., G. Davies, & G. Monti, *European Union Law: Cases and Materials,* 2nd edition, (Cambridge, CUP, 2010).

Charney, J., 'The Impact on the International Legal System of the Growth of the International Courts and Tribunals', (1998–1999), 31 *N.Y.U. J. Int'l L. & Pol.*

Charney J., *Compromissory Clauses and the Jurisdiction of the International Court of Justice, 81, AJIL, 1987.*

Charney, J., International Lawmaking – Article 38 of the ICJ Statute Revisited (p. 170), at p. 187 in Jost Delbruck, New Trends in International Law Making – International 'Legislation' in the Public Interest (Proceedings of an International Symposium of the Kiel Walther-Schucking-Institute of International Law, March 6 to 8, 1996).

Chayes, A., The Role of the Judge in Public Law Litigation, 1976(89) (7) *Harvard Law Review*.

Chen, M., H. Rassel, *Human Rights and the World Public Order,* (London, Yale University Press, 1980).

Chester, B., *A Common Law of International Adjudication*, (Oxford, OUP, 2007).

Chinkin, C., 'Symposium: The East Timor Case before the International Court of Justice', 1993 (4) *EJIL*.

Coffman, P., 'Obligations *Erga Omnes* and Absent Third-Party States', (1996) 38 *German Yearbook of International Law*.

Cojocariu, C., Handicapping Rules: The Overly Restrictive Application of Admissibility Criteria by the European Court of Human Rights to Complaints concerning Disabled People, Sweet and Maxwell, (Issue 6, 2011, Sweet and Maxwell).

Cojocariu, C., Hit and Miss: Procedural Accommodations Ensuring the Effective Access of People with Mental Disabilities to the European Court of Human Rights, in Peter Blanck & Eilionóir Flynn (eds.), *Routledge Handbook of Disability Law and Human Rights,* Routledge, London, 2017.

Coleman, A., *The ICJ and Highly Political Matters,* Melb. Journal of Int. Law, 29, 2003.

Conklin, W., The Peremptory Norms of the International Community, *EJIL* (2012), Vol. 23 No. 3.

Costelloe, D., *Legal Consequences of Peremptory Norms in International Law,* (CUP, Cambridge, 2017)

Craig, P., *Legality, Standing and Substantive Review in Community Law,* Oxford Journal of Legal Studies, vol. 14, No. 4, 1994.

Craig, P., *The Jurisdiction of the Community Courts Reconsidered,* 36 Texas International Law Journal, 2001.

Crawford, J., 'Responsibility to the International Community as a Whole', (2001), Spring, *Journal of Global Legal Studies*.

Crawford, J., 'The Standing of States: A Critique of Article 40 if the International Law Commission's Draft Articles on State Responsibility', in M Andenas & D Fairgrieve (eds.), *Judicial Review in International Perspective,* (The Hague, Kluwer Law International, 2000).

Crawford, J., The International Law Commission's Articles on State Responsibility: Introduction, Text and Commentaries, (CUP, 2002, Cambridge).

Cross, F.B. & A Lindquist Stefanie., The Scientific Study of Judicial Activism, *91 Min.L.Rev*. 2006–2007.

D'Aspremont, J., *The Recommendations Made by the International Court of Justice*, 56 Int'l & Comp. L.Q. 185 2007.

Daniel, Hare, Blue Jeans, 'Chewing Gum and Climate Change Litigation: American Exports to Europe', Utrecht Journal of International and European Law, 2013, Vol. 29/76.

Danilenko, G and W. Czaplinski, 'Conflict of Norms in International Law', (1990) 21 *Netherlands Yearbook of International Law*.

Dawidowicz, M., 'Public Law Enforcement Without Public Law Safeguards? An Analysis of State Practice on Third-Party Countermeasures and Their Relationship to the UN Security Council', BYIL, Vol. 77, Issue 1 (2007).

De Visscher, C., *Théories et réalités en droit international public*, 4th edn. (Paris, 1970).

Dehousse, R., The European Court of Justice: The Politics of Judicial Integration (McMillan 1998).

Dugard, J, The Revocation of the Mandate for South West Africa, 62 *AJIL* 78, 1968.

Dupuy, P., 'The Dangers of Fragmentation or Unification of the International Legal System and the International Court of Justice', (1999) 31 *New York University Journal of International Law and Politics*.

Dupuy, P., A General Stocktaking of the Connections between the Multilateral Dimension of Obligations and Codification of the Law of Responsibility, EJIL (2002), Vol. 13, No. 5.

Eagleton, C., The Responsibility of States in International Law (New York, New York University Press, 1928).

Eduardo, V., International Court of Justice and International Environmental Law, Asian Yearbook of International Law, 1992, Volume 2.

Edwin, V & R Davide., "Judicial Review of Anti-dumping Determinations in the EU" (2012) 7 *Global Trade and Customs Journal*, Issue 5.

Egede, E., The Common Heritage of Mankind and the Sub- Saharan African Native Land Tenure System: A "Clash of Cultures" in the Interpretation of Concepts in International Law? (2014) *Journal of African Law*.

Eliantonio, M & H Roer-Eide., Regional Courts and *locus standi* for Private Parties: Can the CJEU Learn Something from the Others? *The Law and Practice of International Courts and Tribunals* 13 (2014).

Eliantonio, M & N Stratieva., 'From Plaumann, through UPA and Jégo-Quéré, to the Lisbon Treaty: The Locus Standi of Private Applicants under Article 230(4) EC through a political lens' (Maastricht Faculty of Law Working Paper 2009/13, 2009.

Elias, T., 'Introduction to the Debate', in J Weiler, A Cassese, M Spinedi (eds.), *International Crime of States: A Critical Analysis of the ILC's Draft Article 19 on State Responsibility*, (Walter De Gruyter, Berlin, 1989).

Emerich De, V., "The Law of Nations; or Principles of the Law of Nature, Applied to The Conduct and Affairs of Nations and Sovereigns", translated by Joseph Chitty, (1834, A New Edition London, Sweet and Maxwell).

Ernest, B., *The State Immunity Controversy in International Law*, (Springer 2005).

Evensen, Jens., *The International Court of Justice: Main Characteristics and Its Contribution to the Development of the Modern Law of Nations*, 57 Nordic J. Int'l L. 10 1988.

Fabri, H., Is There a Case – Legally and Politically – for Direct Effect of WTO Obligations? *EJIL*, 2014, vol. 25, no. 1.

Faeh, A., Judicial activism, the Biotech Directive and its institutional implications: is the court acting as a legislator or a court when defining the "human embryo"? *E.L. Rev.* 2015, 40(4).

Falk, R., Realistic Horizons for International Adjudication, 11 Virginia Journal of International Law, 314, 1970–71.

Falk R., The South West Africa Cases: An Appraisal, *International Organization, Vol. 21, No. 1 (Winter, 1967)*.

Feinberg, N., *La jurisdiction de la Cour permanente de justice internationale dans le système des mandats,* Librairie Arthur Rousseau, (Paris, 1930).

Fitzmaurice, G., 'Hersch Lauterpacht—The Scholar as Judge' (1961) 37 *British Yearbook of International Law.*

Fitzmaurice, M & D Tamada., Introduction, in M Fitzmaurice & D Tamada (eds.), *Whaling in the Antarctic: Significance and Implications of the ICJ Judgment,* Brill Nijhoff, Leiden, 2016.

Fitzmaurice, M., 'Environmental Degradation', in D Moeckli, S Shah, S Sivakumaran, *International Human Rights Law,* (OUP, 2010).

Fitzmaurice, M., Contemporary Issues in International Environmental Law, (Edward Elgar (Cheltenham), 2009.

Fitzmaurice, M., Third Parties and the Law of Treaties, Max Planck UNYB 6, (2002).

Ford, C., *Judicial Discretion in International Jurisprudence: Article 38(1)(C) and "General Principles of Law".* (1994–1995), 5 *Duke J. Comp. & Int'l L.*

Francioni, F., Realism, Utopia and the Future of International Environmental Law, EU Working Papers, 2012/11.

Franck, T., *The "Powers of Appreciation": Who is the Ultimate Guardian of UN Legality,* AJIL, Vol. 86, No. 3 (Jul., 1992).

Franckx, E., The International Seabed Authority and the Common Heritage of Mankind: The Need for States to Establish the Outer Limits of their Continental Shelf, *The International Journal of Marine and Coastal Law* 25 (2010).

Freedman S., *Human Rights Transformed: Positive Rights and Positive Duties,* (Oxford, OUP, *2008*).

French, D., 'From the Depths: Rich Pickings of Principles of Sustainable Development and General International Law on the Ocean Floor—the Seabed Disputes Chamber's 2011 Advisory Opinion', (2011a) 26 *The International Journal of Marine and Coastal Law.*

French, D., *The International Journal of Coastal and Maritime Law, 26* (2011b).

Friedmann, W., *The Jurisprudential Implications of the South West Africa Case,* 6 Columbia Journal of Transnational Law, 1, 1967.

Fukunaga Y., *Securing Compliance Through the WTO Dispute Settlement: Implementation of the DSB Recommendations. Journal of International Economic Law*, 9(2) 2006.

Gaja, G., *Jus Cogens* Beyond the Vienna Convention, 172 RDC ADI 1981-III.

Gattini, A., 'A Return Ticket to "Communitarisme", Please', (2002), 13(5), *EJIL*.

Gazzini, T., 'The Legal Nature of WTO Obligations and The Consequences of Their Violation', (2006) (17(4) *European Journal of International Law*.

German, S., *Popular Actions and the Defense of the Environment in Colombia,* Third International Conference on Environmental Enforcement, President, Fundepublico, Calle 71-No. 5–83, Santafé de Bogotá, Colombia.

Ginsburg, T., 'Bounded Discretion in International Judicial Law-Making', (2004–2005) (45), Va. J. Int'l L.

Goldston, J.A., 'Public Interest Litigation in Central and Eastern Europe: Roots, Prospects, and Challenges', 28 (2006), *Human Rights Quarterly*.

Gordon, E., *Legal Disputes under Article 36(2) of the Statute* in Lori F. Damrosh "The International Court of Justice at a Crossroads", Transnational Publishers, Inc., New York, 1987.

Gordon, E., *Old Orthodoxies Amid New Experiences: The South West Africa (Namibia) Litigation and the Uncertain Jurisprudence of the International Court of Justice,* 1 Denver Journal of International Law and Policy, 65, 1971.

Gormley, L W., *Public Interest Litigation and State Subsidies* (European Public Interest Litigation, Miclitz eds., 1996.

Gould, H., *The Legacy of Punishment in International Law,* (Palgrave Macmillan, 2010).

Gowlland-Debbas, V., *Collective Responses to Illegal Acts in International Law: United Nations Action in the Question of Southern Rhodesia,* (Martinus Nijhoff Publishers, 1990).

Grange, M., Towards a Liberalization of Standing Conditions for Individuals Seeking Judicial Review of Community Acts: Jego-Quere et Cie SA v Commission and Union de Pequeños Agricultores v Council, Modern Law Review, Vol.66, January 2003.

Gray, C., *Judicial Remedies in International Law,* (Clarendon Press, Oxford, 1990).

Gray, C., 'The 2014 Judicial Activity of the International Court of Justice' (2015) 109 *AJIL*.

Green, C., *An Intellectual History of Judicial Activism,* Emory Law Journal, Vol. 58, No. 5.

Greenwood, C., 'The *Advisory Opinion on Nuclear Weapons* and the Contribution of the International Court to International Humanitarian Law' 316 *International Review of the Red Cross,* (1997).

Gross, L., Limitations upon the Judicial Function, (1964) 58(2) *AJIL*.

Gross, L., *The International Court of Justice: Consideration of Requirements for Enhancing its Role in the International Legal Order.* 65 Am. J. Int'l L. 253 1971.

Gross, L., *Underutilization of the International Court of Justice.* 27 Harv. Int'l. L. J. 582 1986.

Gruner, D., 'Accounting for the Public Interest in International Arbitration: The Need for Procedural and Structural Reform', (2003) 41 *Columbia Journal of Transnational Law.*

Hall, A., Treatise on International Law, (2nd ed., Oxford, 1909).

Hameed, A., Unravelling the Mystery of *Jus Cogens* in International Law, *BYIL*, (2014) 84 (1).

Harding, C., *The Private Interest in Challenging Community Action,* 1980, 5 European Law Review.

Harris, DJ., O'Boyle & Warbrick, Law of the European Convention on Human Rights, (2nd ed., 2009, OUP).

Hart, H., Concept of Law, (OUP, 1961).

Haynes, J., Revisiting the *locus standi* of private applicants in judicial review proceedings under CARICOM and EU law: a comparative perspective, Commonwealth Law Bulletin, 2015 Vol. 41, No.

Helfer, L.R., J. Karen, Legitimacy and Lawmaking: A Tale of Three International Courts, Theoretical Inquiries in Law, 2013(14).

Helfer, R., & Anne-Marie Slaughter, *Towards a Theory of Effective Supranational Adjudication,* 107 Yale L.J. 273 1997–1998.

Helfer, R., & A. Slaughter, *Why States Create International Tribunals: A Response to Professors Posner and Yoo,* (93 Cal. L. Rev., 2005).

Heredia, J.M., 'The Heritage Dimension of the Climate System and Its Protection for the Benefit of Mankind', in (eds.) M Fitzmaurice, S Meljean-Dubois and S Negri, *Environmental Protection and Sustainable Development from Rio to Rio +20,* (Brill, 2014).

Hernandez, G., A Reluctant Guardian: The International Court of Justice and The Concept of "International Community", *BYIL,* 2013.

Hershkoff, H., Public Law Litigation: Lessons and Questions, (2009) 10 *Human Rights Review.*

Hey, E., 'Global Environmental Law: Common Interests and the (Re)constitution of Public Space' (2009) 1 *Iustum Aequum Salutare.*

Hidalgo, P., Group Litigation in Spain, National Report, 2006 (available at http://globalclassactions.stanford.edu/sites/default/files/documents/spain_national_report.pdf.

Higgins, R., 'Aspects of the Case Concerning the Barcelona Traction, Light and Power Company Ltd.', (1970–1971), (11), Va.J.Int'l L.

Higgins, R., 'The International Court and South West Africa: The implications of the Judgment', (1966), 42(4) International Affairs.

Higgins R., *The United Nations: Still a Force for Peace, Mod. L.Rev. 1. 8 (1989).*

Higgins, Rosalyn, Policy Considerations and the International Judicial Process, ICLQ, January, Vol. 17, No. 1, Jan., 1968.

Hillbruger, C., 'The Right of Third States to Take Countermeasures', in C Tomuschat & J.M. Thouvenin (eds.), *The Fundamental Rules of the International Legal Order,* (Martinus Nijhoff Publishers, Leiden) 2006.

Hohfeld, N., *Fundamental Legal Conceptions,* (New Jersey, The Lawbook Exchange Ltd, 2000).

Hoogh, V., *Theoretical Inquiry into Obligations Erga Omnes,* (The Hague, Kluwer, 1996).

Hunter, W., A Systematic and Historical Exposition of Roman Law, 2nd ed., (London, William Maxwell & Son, 1885).

Hutchinson, D., Solidarity and Breaches of Multilateral Treaties, *BYIL,* 1988, 59(1).

Iwasawa, Y., WTO Dispute Settlement as a Judicial Supervision, *JIEL* (2002).

Jenks, C., 'The General Welfare as a Legal Interest', in G Wilner (eds.), *Jus et Societas,* Essays in Tribute to Wolfgang Friedman, (Martinus Nijhoff Publishers, The Hague, 1979.

Jenks, C., *The Prospects of International Adjudication* (Oceana Publications, 1964).

Jennings, R & A Watts., *Oppenheim's International Law,* 9th ed. Vol. I, (Longman, London, 1996).

Jennings, R., 'The Judiciary, International and National, and the Development of International Law', (1996) 45 Int'l & Comp. L.Q.

Jennings, R., *The United Nations at Fifty: The International Court of Justice After Fifty Years,* 89 Am. J. Int'l L. 493 1995.

Jennings, R., *The Role of the International Court of Justice,* BYIL, 1997.

Jessup, P., *A Modern Law of Nations: An Introduction* (New York, Macmillan, 1948).

Jia, B., The Regime of Straits in International Law, (Clarendon Press, Oxford, 1998).

Jodoin, S., Understanding the Behaviour of International Courts: An Examination of Decision-Making at the ad hoc International Criminal Tribunals, 6 *J. Int'l Law & Int'l Rel.* 1, (2010).

John, H, *Fragmentation or Unification Among International Institutions: The World Trade Organization,* 31 *N.Y.U. J. INT'L L. & POL.* 823 (1999).

Jolowitz, J.A., 'Protection of Diffuse, Fragmented and Collective Interests in Civil Litigation: English Law', (1983) 42(2) *Cambridge Law Journal.*

Joyner, C., "Legal Implications of the Concept of the Common Heritage of Mankind", 35 International and Comparative Law Quarterly (1986).

Kaczorowska, A., *European Union Law,* Third Edition, Routledge, London, 2013.

Kamminga, T.M., *Inter-State Accountability for Violations of Human Rights,* (University of Pennsylvania Press, Philadelphia, 1992).

Karagiannis, S., "Observations sur la Commission des Limites du Plateau Continental" (1994) 8 *Espaces et Ressources Maritimes* 163–194.

Kelly, P., *The Changing Process of International Law and the Role of the World Court,* 11 Mich. J.Int'l. L., 129, 1989–90.

Kelsen, H., *Principles of International Law,* The LawBook Exchange, Ltd. Clark, New Jersey, 2003a.

Kelsen, H., *Principles of International Law,* The LawBook Exchange, Ltd. Clark, New Jersey, 2003b.

Kingsbury, B., 'Foreword: Is Proliferation of International Courts and Tribunals A Systemic Problem?', (1999) 31 *New York University Journal of International Law and Politics.*

Kirgis, F., 'Standing to Challenge Human Endeavours that Could Change the Climate', (1990) 84(2), *AJIL.*

Kmiec, K., *The Origin and Current Meanings of "Judicial Activism",* California Law Review, 2004, Vol. 92.

Koch, Cornelia., *Locus Standi of Private Applicants under the EU Constitution: Preserving Gaps in the Protection of Individuals' Right to an Effective Remedy*, European Law Review, 2005.

Kolb, R., *Theory of International Law,* Hart Publishing, Oxford, 2016.

Kooijmans P., *The ICJ in the 21st Century: Judicial Restraint, Judicial Activism, or Proactive Judicial Policy* (*ICLQ, vol. 56, October 2007*).

Koskenniemi, M., Fragmentation of International Law: Postmodern Anxieties, *Leiden Journal of International Law,* (2002) 15(3).

Koskenniemi, M., Solidarity Measures: State Responsibility as a New International Order BYIL 2001, Vol: LXXII.

Kotzé, L., S Paterson, R Alexander., The Role of Judiciary in Environmental Governance: Comparative Perspectives, (Kluwer Law International, 2009), 314.

Kramer, L., Public Interest Litigation in Environmental Matters Before European Courts, in Miclitz, European Public Interest Litigation, Namos, 1996

Kritsiotis D., 'Imagining the International Community', *EJIL (2002)*, Vol. 13, No. 4.

Kuokkanen, T., *International Law and the Environment: Variations on the Theme.* Kluwer Law International, The Hague, 2002.

Kwakwa, E., The international community, international law, and the United States: three in one, two against one, or one and the same? in M. Byers & V.G. Nolte (eds.), *United States Hegemony and Foundations of International Law,* CUP, Cambridge, 2003.

Lachs, Manfred, The Development and General Trends of International Law in Our Times'(1980) 169, Recueil des Cours de l'Académie de Droit International.

Lamy, P., "The Place of WTO and its Law in the International Legal Order", *EJIL* (2006), Vol. 17 No. 5.

Lauterpacht, H., "Some Observations on the Prohibition of *Non Liquet* and the Completeness of the Legal Order", In Symbolae Verzijl: Présentées au Prof J.H.W. Verzijl, à l'occasion de son LXXième anniversaire. Edited by F. M. van Asbeck, 196–221. The Hague: Nijhoff, 1958.

Lauterpacht, H., The Development of International Law by the International Court of Justice, CUP, 1958b.

Lawrence, T., *Essays on Some Disputed Questions in Modern International Law* (Cambridge, 1885, Deighton, Bell and Co.).

Leckie, S., "Inter-State Complaint Procedure in International Human Rights Law: Hopeful Prospects or Wishful inking?", 10 *Human Rights Quarterly* (1988).

Lee, R., The Elements of Roman Law, (London, Sweet & Maxwell Ltd., 1956), fourth edition.

Lefeber, R., 'The exercise of Jurisdiction in the Antarctic Region and the Changing Structure of International Law: The International Community and Common Interests', (1990), (21) *NYIL*.

Lefeber, R., *Transboundary Environmental Interference and the Origin of State Liability*, (Martinus Nijhoff Publishers, 1996).

Leigh, K., Liability for Damage to Global Commons, (1993), 14 *Australian Yearbook of International Law*.

Lenaerts, K., D. Arts, I Maselis, *Procedural Law of the European Union*, (2nd ed., Thomson, 2006).

Letsas, G., The Truth in Autonomous Concepts: How To Interpret the ECHR, *EJIL* (2004), Vol. 15 No. 2.

Lietzau, W., Checks and Balances and Elements of Proof: Structural Pillars for the International Criminal Court. *Cornell International Law Journal*, (1999) 32.

Lowe, V., *International Law*, Clarendon Law Series, (OUP, 2007).

Lowe, V., *The Settlement of Disputes in International Law*, (Oxford, OUP, 1999).

Luard, E., *International Society* (New York, 1990).

MacDonald, R.St.J., *Changing Relations between the International Court of Justice and the Security Council of the United Nations*. 31 Can. Y.B. Int'l L. 3, 1993.

Magnusson, B., The Continental Shelf Beyond 200 Nautical Miles: Delineation, Delimitation, and Dispute Settlement, Brill, Nijhoff, 2015.

Marek, K., 'Criminalizing State Responsibility', (1978–1979) XIV, *Revue Belge de droit international*.

Martinez, Jenny S., Towards an International Judicial System, 56 STAN. L. REV 429 (2003).

Matsushita, M., T.J. Schoenbaum & Petros Mavroidis, *The World Trade Organization: Law, Practice, and Policy*, (OUP, 2nd ed., 2006).

Mavroidis, P., Remedies in WTO Legal Systems: Between a Rock and a Hard Place. *EJIL, 2000*, vol.11.

Mayer, L.H., NGO Standing and Influence in Regional Human Rights Courts and Commissions, 36 Brook. J. Int'l L. 911 2010–2011.

McCorquodale, R., International Community and State Sovereignty: An Uneasy Symbiotic Relationship, in Colin Warbrick and Stephen Tierney (eds.), *Towards an*

'International Legal Community'? The Sovereignty of States and the Sovereignty of International Law (British Institute of International and Comparative Law, 2006).

McDougal, M., H. Lasswell, and J. Miller, *The Interpretation of Agreements and World Public Order: Principles of Content and Procedure,* (Yale University Press, New Haven, 1967).

McHugh, PG., New Dawn to Cold Lights: Courts and Common Law Aboriginal Rights, in *Public Interest Litigation:* New Zealand Experience in International Perspective (by Rick Bigwood, Wellington, *Lexis Nexis NZ Limited,* 2006).

McNair, A., "Treaties Producing Effects 'Erga Omnes'", *in Scritti di Diritto Internazionale in Onore di T. Perassi,* vol. II, Milano, Giuffrè, 1957.

McNair, L., 'The Functions and Differing Legal Character of Treaties', (1930) 11 *BYIL*.

McWhinney, Edward., *The International Court of Justice and International Law-Making: The Judicial Activism/Self-Restraint Antinomy.* Chinese Journal of International Law (2006), Vol. 5, No. 1.

Meron, T., *The Humanization of International Law,* Martinus (Nijhoff Publishers, 2006).

Morgera, E., Bilateralism at the Service of Community Interests? Non-judicial Enforcement of Global Public Goods in the Context of Global Environmental Law, *EJIL* (2012), Vol. 23 No. 3.

Mosler, H., 'International Legal Community' in R.L. Bindschedler et al. (eds.), Encyclopaedia of Public International Law, (Max Planck Institute), (North-Holland, Amsterdam, 1995), Vol. 2.

Motoc, I. & C. Caufman, Romania and the European Convention on Human Rights: A Dialogue with Judges, in Iulia Motoc & Ineta Ziemele (eds.) *The Impact of the ECHR on Democratic Change in Central and Eastern Europe,* CUP, Cambridge, 2016.

Mowbrai, A., *The Creativity of the European Court of Human Rights,* Human Rights Law Review, 5:1, 2005.

Murphy, S., *The United States Practice in International Law: Volume I,* (CUP, Cambridge, 1999–2001).

Naumovič, B, 'Reflexions sur l'actio popularis en droit international, dans le cadre de la responsabilité internationale', in: Responsibility of States. Thesaurus Acroasium Vol. XX (1993); I Seidl-Hohenveldern, 'Actio Popularis im Völkerrecht?', 14 Communicazione e Studi (1975).

Nelson, L., The Settlement of Disputes Arising from Conflicting Outer Continental Shelf Claims, *The International Journal of Maritime and Coastal law,* 24 (2009).

Nettensheim, M, Article 173 of the EC Treaty and Regulations: Towards the Development of Uniform Standing Requirements in Public Interest Litigation before European Courts, Hans – W. Micklitz/Norbert Reich (eds.), 1996.

Neuhold, H., 'The United Nations System for the Peaceful Settlement of Disputes', in F Cede & L Sucharipa-Behrmann, *The United Nations Law and Practice, Kluwer Law International,* (The Hague, 1999).

Nollkaemper, A., International Adjudication of Global Public Goods: The Intersection of Substance and Procedure, *EJIL* (2012), Vol. 23 No. 3.

Noyes, J., 'The Common Heritage of Mankind: Past, Present, and Future', (2011–2012) 40 *Denv. J. Int'l L. & Pol'y.*

Noyes, J., *Judicial and Arbitral Proceedings and the Outer Limits of the Continental Shelf*, Vanderbilt Journal of Transnational Law, (42) 2009.

Noyes, J., 'The Common Heritage of Mankind: Past, Present, and Future', (2011–2012) 40 *Denv. J. Int'l L. & Pol'y.*

O'Keefe, R., "World Cultural Heritage: Obligations to the International Community as a Whole?", 53 *International and Comparative Law Quarterly* (2004).

Oellers-Frahm., 'Multiplication of International Courts and Tribunals and Conflicting Jurisdiction – Problems and Possible Solutions', (2001) 5 *Max Planck Yearbook of United Nations Law*, 67–104.

Okowa, P., 'Issues of Admissibility and The Law on International Responsibility', in M Evans (eds.), *International Law*, (3rd ed. Oxford, OUP).

Oppenheim, L & H Lauterpacht., International Law, Vol. 1, 8th ed., 1955a.

Oppenheim, L. and H Lauterpacht., International Law, Vol. 1, 8th ed., 1955b.

Orakhelashvili, A., *Peremptory Norms in International Law*, 2006, OUP, Oxford.

Orakhelashvili, A., *Peremptory Norms of the International Community: A Reply to William E. Conklin*, *EJIL* (2012), Vol. 23 No. 3.

Orlando, E., Public and Private in the International Law of Environmental Liability, in Federico Lenzerini & Ana Filipa Vrdoljak (eds.) International Law For Common Goods: Normative Perspectives on Human Rights, Culture and Nature, Hart Publishing, Oxford, 2014, p. 406.

Oxman, B., The Rule of Law and the United Nations Convention on the Law of the Sea, (1996), 7, Eur. J. Int'l L.

Pair, M., *Judicial Activism in the ICJ Charter Interpretation*, 8 ILSA J. Int'l & Comp. L. 181 2001–2002.

Palombino, FM, Judicial Economy and Limitation of the Scope of the Decision in International Adjudication, Leiden Journal of International Law, L.J.I.L. 2010, 23(4).

Partan, D., *Introduction: Increasing the Effectiveness of the International Court.* Harvard International Law Journal, Vol. 18, No. 3, 1977.

Pattaro, E., H. Rottleuthner, Roger A. Shiner, '*A Treatise of Legal Philosophy and General Jurisprudence*': *Vol. 1* (*The Law and the Right*), Springer, 2012.

Paulus, A., "Reciprocity Revisited", in U. Fastenrath/R. Geiger/D.E. Khan/A. Paulus/S. von Schorlemer/C. Vedder (eds.), *From Bilateralism to Community Interest: Essays in Honour of Judge Bruno Simma*, OUP 2011.

Pauwelyn, J., A Typology of Multilateral Treaty Obligations: Are WTO Obligations Bilateral or Collective in Nature? *EJIL*, 2003a, (14).

Pauwelyn, J., *Conflict of Norms in International Law: How WTO Law Relates to Other Rules of International Law,* (Cambridge, CUP, 2003).

Pellet, A., Commentary to Article 38 in A. Zimmermann, Ch. Tomuschat, Karin Oellers-Frahm, The Statute of the International Court of Justice: A Commentary. OUP, 2006.

Peters, A., Does Kosovo Lie in the *Lotus*-Land of Freedom?, *Leiden Journal of International Law,* 24(2011).

Petersmann, E., *The GATT/WTO System of Dispute Settlement,* (Kluwer Law International, Boston, 1996).

Pierre, K., 'Responsibility for Breaches of Obligations Deriving from Peremptory Norms of International Law', (2002), 13 *EJIL*.

Pinto, M., 'Fragmentation or Unification Among International Institutions: Human Rights Tribunals' (1998–1999), *31 N.Y.U. J. Int'l L. & Pol.*

Pirjatanniemi, E., Greening Human Rights Law: A Focus on the European Convention on Human Rights, in Gerhard Bos & Marcus Düwell (eds.) *Human Rights and Sustainability: Moral Responsibilities for the Future,* (Routledge, New York), 2016.

Polay, E., *Injuria Types in Roman Law*, (Akadémiai Kiadó, Budapest, 1986).

Politis, N., *Le Problème des limitations de la souverainté et de la théorie de l'abus des droits dans les rapports internationaux*, 6 R.C.A.D.I. 1, 6 (1925).

Popovic, D., 'Prevailing of Judicial Activism over Self-restraint in the Jurisprudence of the European Court of Human Rights', *Greighton Law Review,* vol. 42, 2009.

Posner, R., The Meaning of Judicial Self-Restraint, 59 Indiana Law Journal. 1, (1984).

Posnert, E & J Yoo., 'Judicial Independence in International Tribunals', (2005) 93, *California Law Review.*

Pozo Vera, E., An inventory of EU Member States' measures on access to justice on environmental matters. The Aarhus Convention: how are its access to justice provisions being implemented? (Belgium 2 June 2008), Available at http://ec.europa.eu/environment/aarhus/pdf/conf/milieu.pdf.

Proukaki, E., The Problem of Enforcement in International Law: Countermeasures, the non-injured state and the idea of international community (2010, Routledge, Taylor & Francis Group, London).

Ragazzi, M., *The Concept of International Obligations Erga Omnes,* (Oxford: Clarendon Press 1997).

Raggazi, M., *International Responsibility Today: Essays in Honour of Oscar Schacter* (Martinus Nijhoff Publishers, Boston 2005).

Ragolle F., *Access to Justice for Private Applicants in the Community Legal Order: Recent (r) evolutions, European Law Review, 2003.*

Rajeev, D., Whose Law? Whose Interest? in Public Interest Law 17, at 38 (Jeremy Cooper and Rajeev Dhavan eds.), Oxford. Basil Blackwell, 1986.

Rasmussen, H., Between self-restraint and activism: a judicial policy for the European Court, European Law Review, 1988.

Rayburn, C., Flexing the Judicial Muscle: An Empirical Study of Judicial Activism in the Federal Courts, *Northwestern University Law Review*, 2011, Vol. 105, No. 1.

Reich, N., *Public Interest Litigation before European Jurisdictions,* in *Public Interest Litigation before European Courts, Hans – W. Micklitz/Norbert Reich (eds.)* (1996, Nomos Verlagsgesellschaft, Baden-Baden).

Rodley, N., 'Corporate Nationality and the Diplomatic Protection of Multinational Enterprises: The Barcelona Traction Case', 47 No. 11 *Indiana Law Journal* 70 (Fall, 1971).

Rodley, N., 'Human Rights and Humanitarian Intervention: the Case Law of the World Court', 38 *I.C.L.Q* 321 (1989).

Root, E., 'The outlook for international law', (1916) *AJIL* 10(1).

Rosa, F, The 2014 Reform of Universal Jurisdiction in Spain: From All to Nothing, Zeitschrift für Internationale Strafrechtsdogmatik, 13/2014.

Rosenne, S., 'War Crimes and State Responsibility' in Y. Dinstein, M Tabory (eds.), War Crimes in International Law, (The Hague, 1996).

Rosenne, S., "Bilateralism and Community Interest in the Codified Law of Treaties", in Transnational Law in a Changing Society – Essays in Honour of P Jessup (eds. W. Friedmann, L. Henkin, and O. Lissitzyn), N.Y./London, Columbia University Press, 1972.

Rosenne, S., *The Law and Practice of the International Court, 1920–2005,* (Martinus Nijhoff Publishers, 2006), Volume II.

Rosenne, S., *The Law and Practice of the International Court:* 1920–1966, (Leyden, A.W. Nijhoff, 1997).

Rotkirch, H., *The Demilitarization and Neutralization of the Aaland Islands: A Regime 'in European Interests', Withstanding Changing Circumstances.* Journal of Peace Research, vol. 23, no. 4, 1986.

Roxburgh, R., International Conventions and Third States, (Longmans, Green and Co, London, 1917).

Rubin, A., '*Actio popularis, Jus Cogens* and Offences *Erga Omnes*?' (2001) 35 *New England Law Review.*

Ruda, J., *Some of the Contributions of the International Court of Justice to the Development of International Law.* 24 N.Y.U.J. Int'l L. & Pol. 35, 1991–1992.

Sachariew, K., 'State Responsibility for Multilateral Treaty Violations: Identifying the "Injured State" and its Legal Status' (1988) 35 *NYIL.*

Sakai, H., After the Whaling in the Antarctic Judgment: Its Lessons and Prospects from a Japanese Perspective, in M Fitzmaurice & D Tamada (eds.), *Whaling in the Antarctic: Significance and Implications of the ICJ Judgment,* Brill Nijhoff, Leiden, 2016.

Samuel G., 'The Notion of an Interest as a Formal Concept in English and in Comparative Law before the Court' (*Guy Canivet, Mads Andenas, and Duncan Fairgrieve, 2004,* the British Institute of International and Comparative Law).

Samuel, G., *Law of Obligations and Legal Remedies,* Cavendish (Publishing Limited, 2001, Second ed. London).

Sandars, T., *The Institutes of Justinian,* (The Lawbook Exchange Ltd., New Jersey, 2007).

Sands, P, P Jacqueline, F Adriana & M Ruth., *Principles of International Environmental Law,* CUP, New York, 2012.

Sands, P., Rethinking Environmental Rights – Climate Change, Conservation and the ECJ (2008) ELM, 17.

Sarooshi, D., 'Investment Treaty Arbitration and the World Trade Organization: What Role for Systemic Values in the Resolution of International Economic Disputes', *Texas International Law Journal,* Vol. 49, (2014).

Sarooshi, D., The Move from Institutions: The Case of the World Trade Organization, 100 *Am. Soc'y Int'l L. Proc.* 2006.

Schabas, A., Prosecutorial Discretion v Judicial Activism at the International Criminal Court, Journal of International Criminal Justice 6 (2008).

Schachter, O., *Disputes Involving the Use of Force, in* L. Damrosch, *The International Court of Justice at a Crossroads,* at p. 53 quoted in *Patrick Kelly, The Changing Process of Internat. Law...,* Michigan Journal of Int. Law, 1989–90.

Schall, C., 'Public Interest Litigation Concerning Environmental Matters before Human Rights Courts: A Promising Future Concept', (2008) 20 *Journal of Environmental Law,* 417–453.

Schwartz, B & H Wade., Legal Control of Government, Oxford, Clarendon Press, 1972.

Schweisfurth, T., 'Commentary on Article 35 of the UN Charter', in B. Simma, *The Charter of the United Nations: A Commentary,* 2nd ed., Vol. I, (OUP, Oxford, 2002).

Schwelb, E., 'The Actio Popularis and International Law' (1972) 2 *Israel Yearbook on Human Rights.*

Scobbie, I., *The Theorist as a Judge: Hersch Lauterpacht's Concept of International Judicial Function,* 8 EJIL, 1997.

Scott, L., *The Inter-State Complaint Procedure in International Human Rights Law: Hopeful Prospects or Wishful Thinking?* (1988), 10(2), Human Rights Quarterly.

Segall, J., Conceptualizing the Judicial Activism Debate as Judicial Responsibility: The Tales of Two Justice Kennedys, Arizona State Law Journal, Vol. 41, 2009.

Seidl-Hohenveldern, I., 'Actio Popularis im Völkerrecht?', 14 Communicazione e Studi (1975).

Selak, C., "Suez Canal Base Agreement of 1954 its Background and Implications", (1955) 49, AJIL.

Shabtai, R., *The Law and Practice of the International Court:* 1920–1966, (Leyden, A.W. Sijthoff, 1997)

Shaffer, G., International Law and Global Public Goods in Pluralist World, EJIL (2012), Vol. 23 No. 3.

Shany, Y., 'Assessing the Effectiveness of International Courts: A Goal-Based Approach' 106 Am. J. Int'l L.

Shany Y., *No Longer a Weak Department of Power? Reflections on the Emergence of a New International Judiciary. EJIL, Vol. 20, No. 1, 2009.*

Shaw, J., Citizen's Rights and Access to Law in European Public Interest Litigation (Miclitz eds, 1996).

Shelton, D., *Remedies in International Human Rights Law,* 3rd edition, OUP, 2015.

Sicilianos, L., 'The Classification of Obligations and the Multilateral Dimension of the Relations of International Responsibility', (2002) EJIL 13 (5).

Simma, B & A Paulus., "The 'International Community': Facing the Challenge of Globalization", (1998) 2, *EJIL* 9 (2).

Simma, B., 'Bilateralism and Community Interest in the Law of State Responsibility', in Y. Dinstein (eds.), *International Law at the Time of Perplexity, Essays in Honour of Shabtai Rosenne* (Martinus Nijhoff Publishers, Dordrecht, 1989).

Simma, B., 'Universality of International Law from a Perspective of a Practitioner' (2009), 20(2) *EJIL,* 265, 275.

Simma, B., The Antarctic Treaty as a Treaty Providing for an "Objective Regime", (1986), 19, *Cornell Int'l L.J.*

Simma, B., The ICJ and Common Goods: The Case of Human Rights, in Federico Lenzerini & Ana Filipa Vrdoljak (eds.), International Law For Common Goods: Normative Perspectives on Human Rights, Culture and Nature, Hart Publishing, Oxford, 2014.

Spinedi, M., "Les conséquences juridiques d'un fait internationalement illicite causant un dommage a l'environment", in F. Francioni and T. Scovazzi (eds.), *International Responsibility for Environmental Harm,* (London. Graham and Trotman, 1991).

Stein, E., & J. Vining, Citizen Access to Judicial Review of Administrative Action in Transnational and Federal Context, 70, AJIL, 1976.

Steinberg, R., Judicial Law-Making at the WTO: Discursive, Constitutional, and Political Constraints, 98 AJIL, 247 (2004).

Stone, J., Non-liquet and the Function of Law in the International Community, 35 BYIL, 124, (1959).

Suarez, S., *The Outer Limits of the Continental Shelf: Legal Aspects of their Establishment,* 2008, Springer.

Taggart, M., Rugby, the Anti-apartheid Movement, and Administrative Law in *Public Interest Litigation: New Zealand Experience in International Perspective,* by Rick Bigwood, Wellington, LexisNexis NZ Limited, 2006).

Tamanaha, B., Law as a Means to an End: Threat to the Rule of Law, (Cambridge University Press, New York, 2006).

Tams, C., 'Continued Relevance of Compromissory Clauses as a Source of ICJ Jurisdiction', in T. Giegerich (eds.), A Wiser Century? – Judicial Dispute Settlement,

Disarmament and the Laws of War 100 Years After the Second Peace Conference (Duncker & Humbolt, Berlin 2009).

Tams, C., 'Do Serious Breaches Give Rise to Any Specific Obligations of the Responsible State?' (2002) 13(5) *EJIL*.

Tams, C., 'Individual States as Guardians of Community Interests' in U. Fastenrath, R. Geiger, D.-E. Khan, A. Paulus, S. von Schorlemer and Vedder Ch. (eds.), *From Bilateralism to Community Interests, Essays in Honour of Judge Bruno Simma*, (Oxford University Press, 2011).

Tams, C., *Enforcing Obligations Erga Omnes in International law*, (CUP, 2005).

Tams, C., Roads Not Taken, Opportunities Missed: Procedural and Jurisdictional Questions Sidestepped in the Whaling Judgment, M Fitzmaurice & D Tamada, Introduction, in M Fitzmaurice & D Tamada (eds.), *Whaling in the Antarctic: Significance and Implications of the ICJ Judgment*, Brill Nijhoff, Leiden, 2016.

Tams, C., A Tzanakopoulos., *Leiden Journal of International Law*, (2010) 20(4).

Tanaka, Y., Protection of Community Interests in International Law: The Case of the Law of the Sea, *Max Planck UNYB* 15 (2011).

Tanzi, A., 'Is Damage a Distinct Condition for the Existence of an Internationally Wrongful Act?' in M Spinedi, B Simma (ed.), *United Nations Codification of State Responsibility*, (New York, Oceana Publications, Inc., 1987).

Tasiulas, J., 'In Defense of Relative Normativity: Communitarian Values and the *Nicaragua* case', 16 *Oxford Journal of Legal Studies*, (1996) 85.

Teclaff, L., 'International Law and the Protection of the Oceans from Pollution', (1971–1972), 40 *Fordham L. Rev.*

Teson, F R, 'Le Peuple, C'est Moi! The World Court and Human Rights', 81 *AJIL* 173 (1987). S Schwebel, 'Human Rights in the World Court', in R S Pathak & R P Dhokalia (ed.), *International Law in Transition*, (London, Martinus Nijhoff Publishers, 1992).

Thio, S., Locus Standi and Judicial Review, (Singapore, Singapore University Press, 1971).

Thirlway, H, 'The Law and Procedure of the International Court of Justice 1960–1988', *BYIL* 1 (1989).

Thirlway, H., 'Procedural Law and the International Court of Justice' in V Lowe and M Fitzmaurice (eds.), *Fifty Years of the International Court of Justice* (1996).

Tietje, C & A Lang., Community Interests in World Trade Law, Beiträge zum Transnationalen Wirtschaftsrecht, Issue 141, December 2016, p. 5, forthcoming in A Benvinisti & G Nolte (eds.), *Community Obligations in Contemporary International Law*.

Tomuschat, C., "Obligations Arising for States without or against Their Will", 241 *RCADI* (1993a).

Tomuschat, C., Collected Courses of the Hague Academy of International law (Recueil des Cours, 1993b, IV).

Tridimas, T, The Court of Justice and judicial activism, Eur. L. Rev, 1996.

Trindade, C., *International Law for Humankind: Towards a New Jus Gentium,* 2nd ed., The Hague Academy of International Law Monographs, Leiden, 2013, Vol. 8., p. 275.

Tsagourias, N., *International Community, Recognition of States and Political Cloning,* in Colin Warbrick & Stephen Tierney (n106), 211–240, in Colin Warbrick and Stephen Tierney (eds.), *Towards an 'International Legal Community'? The Sovereignty of States and the Sovereignty of International Law* (British Institute of International and Comparative Law, 2006).

Tzanakopoulos, A., The Permanent Court of International Justice and the 'International Community' in M Fitzmaurice, P Merkouris, P Okowa (eds.), Legacies of the Permanent Court of International Justice, Queen Mary Studies in International Law, Martinus Nijhoff Publishers, Leiden, 2013, Vol. 13.

Uitz, R., "May Less be More? Public Interest Standing and the Protection of Constitutional Rights. Lessons from Hungary's Actio Popularis" in *La Giustizia Costituzionale ed i suoi utenti: Atti del convegno internationale in onore del Prof. Valerio Onida, Milano, 15 aprile 2005,* Pasquale Pasquino and Barbara Randazzo (eds.), 2006.

Van Dijk, P., *Judicial Review of Governmental Action and the Requirement of an Interest to Sue, a Comparative Study on the Requirement of an Interest to Sue* (Alphen aan den Rijn, Sijthoff & Noordhoff, 1980).

Vermeer-Kunzli, A., 'A Matter of Interest: Diplomatic Protection and State Responsibility *Erga Omnes*', 56 Int'l & Comp. L.Q, (2007).

Vicufia, O., and C. Pinto, *The Peaceful Settlement of Disputes: Prospects for the Twenty-First Century, Preliminary Report Prepared for the 1999 Centennial of the First International Peace Conference,* C.E. Doc. CAHDI (1998).

Villalpando, S., 'The Legal Dimension of the International Community: How Community Interests Are Protected in International Law' (2010a) 21 *EJIL* 2.

Villalpando, S., "The Legal Dimension of the International Community: How Community Interests are Protected in International Law", *EJIL* 21 (2010b).

Villiger, M., *Commentary on the 1969 Vienna Convention on the Law of Treaties,* Commentary to the Article 36 of the VCLT, (Brill, 2009).

Voeffray, F., L'actio popularis, ou, *La défense de l'intérêt collectif devant les juridictions internationales,* (Institut universitaire de hautes études internationales, 2004).

Ward, A., Locus Standi under Article 230 (4) of the EC Treaty: Crafting a Coherent Test for a 'Wobbly Polity', Yearbook of European Law, 2003, Vol. 22, Issue 1.

Watson, J., 'The Limited Utility of International Law in the Protection of Human Rights', 74 *Proceedings of the ASIL* (1980).

Weatherill, S, Cases and Materials on EU Law (Oxford University Press 2014).

Weil, P., 'Towards Relative Normativity in International Law?' (1983), 77 *AJIL*.

Weller, M., Modesty Can be a Virtue: Judicial Economy in the ICJ Kosovo Opinion, Leiden Journal of International Law, 24 (2011).

Wenig, F., "Public Interest in Anti-Dumping Law" in Public Interest Litigation before European Courts, Hans – W. Micklitz/Norbert Reich, 1996.

Wolfrum, R., 'The Outer Continental Shelf: Some Considerations Concerning Applications and the Potential Role of the International Tribunal for the Law of the Sea', Statement by the President of ITLOS (2008) 73rd Biennial Conference of the International Law Association, Rio de Janeiro, Brazil.

Wyler, E., 'From "State Crime" to Responsibility for Serious breaches under Peremptory Norms of General International Law', (2002) 13 *EJIL*.

Zarbiyev, F., Judicial Activism in International Law – A Conceptual Framework for Analysis, Journal of International Dispute Settlement, Vol. 3, No. 2 (2012).

Zemanek, K., 'New Trends in the Enforcement of Erga Omnes Obligations', (2000) 4 *Max Plack Yearbook of International Law*.

Index

Printed in the United States
By Bookmasters